★ A ★
PROMOTER'S
TALE
ROCK
AT THE
SHARP END
BY GEOFF DOCHERTY

★ A ★ PROMOTER'S TALE ROCK AT THE SHARP END

BY GEOFF DOCHERTY

FOREWORD BY JOHN PEEL
PREFACE BY DAVE STEWART

FILLMORE NORTH 1969-91 ACCESS ALL AREAS

OMNIBUS PRESS

London / New York / Paris / Sydney / Copenhagen / Berlin / Madrid / Tokyo

Exclusive Distributors:
Music Sales Limited,
8/9 Frith Street,
London W1D 3JB, UK.

Music Sales Corporation,
257 Park Avenue South,
New York, NY 10010, USA.

Macmillan Distribution Services,
53 Park West Drive,
Derrimut, Vic 3030,
Australia.

To the Music Trade only:
Music Sales Limited,
8/9 Frith Street,
London W1D 3JB, UK.

Typeset by Galleon Typesetting, Ipswich.
Printed in Great Britain by Cox & Wyman Ltd, Reading, Berks.

A catalogue record for this book is available from the British Library.

www.omnibuspress.com

Foreword

In the summer of 1967, following the Marine Offences legislation that ended broadcasting from the pirate ship Radio London and prior to the launch of the BBC's Radio 1, I was compelled, in order to make ends meet, to take to the road as what eventually became The John Peel Roadshow. (The John Peel Roadshow was rarely anything other than a box of records that few people, other than myself, cared for. No games, no patter, no pop, no style. 'I strikkly roots.' There was a brief period during which the Roadshow featured a couple of go-go women from Luton, but they had joined the line-up in the hope that they would get to meet David 'Diddy' Hamilton and I had enlisted their supple skills in the hope of a shag. All three of us were doomed to disappointment.)

For a while, the only work I got was on the last nights at previously popular venues that had fallen on hard times. The word seemed to be that if you wanted your club closed properly, Peel was your man. I still recall the last night at Tiles in London's Oxford Street and even now can barely suppress a shudder. The crowd hated me and hated everything I stood for. They wanted Wilson Pickett and I was giving them Jefferson Airplane. No wonder they hated me.

With time, happily, and against the odds, I started getting better work at venues that planned to continue in business even after I had visited. One of the first of these was The Bay Hotel at Whitburn, Sunderland, where the promoter was Geoff Docherty. Not only was Geoff unusual in that he paid me – about one in three promoters of the time didn't – but realising that I wasn't making a fortune at the disc-jockeying, allowed me to sleep in his spare room. The alternative in those cruel and unusual times was to sleep in lay-bys in the Bedford Dormobile that transported me, at a top speed of 55 miles an hour, from engagement to engagement, so I was grateful to Geoff. He also thought to introduce me on these occasions to a succession of guileless young women but, despite what Geoff may tell you in these pages, nothing ever came of those introductions either.

In addition to being one of pathetically few promoters to engage The John Peel Roadshow and, despite everything, to re-engage it, Geoff was also responsible for promoting what I have no hesitation as describing as the best gig I ever attended. This was in Sunderland on the night the local team, then in the old Second Division, had defeated Arsenal at Hillsborough in the semi-final of the FA Cup in the year they went on to win it. Any band that could carry a tune and play roughly in time would have been guaranteed an hysterical response that night, but Geoff had booked The Faces – or, as they were eventually to become, Rod Stewart and The Faces.

The Faces were simply the perfect band in the perfect place at the perfect time. They came on an hour late but no one really cared. They kicked footballs into the audience. I helped them and was pleased to find that I could get my footballs further into the crowd than anyone other than Rod. There were – did I dream this? – artificial palm trees on the dance floor and I ended up dancing on stage and waving a bottle of Blue Nun above my head – and I'm a man who doesn't dance and who doesn't drink Blue Nun. For that magical night and for much else, including the wedding present you gave Sheila and myself – two porcelain figures that still stand by our bed 27 years later – thanks Geoff.

John Peel

Preface

This is a story of a world I am so familiar with. As I was reading the first transcript Geoff sent me, I could actually smell the Vaux beer and hear that eerie feedback from the WEM PA system as if it was just yesterday.

I remembered watching in wonder as an old Ford Transit van backed up and unloaded grimy, black, Vox AC30 guitar amps, a Ludwig drum kit and all the leads and cables that, once put together, could create more magic than any Disney spectacle could hope to achieve.

As I turned the pages I relived nights jamming on Seaburn beach, ears still ringing from The Who at The Bay Hotel, crushed velvet trousers covered in blood (from a run-in at Park Lane bus station after seeing T. Rex at the Mecca Ballroom and running down Newcastle Road to escape a beating, only to be caught and pummelled later by the Garth Lads).

I played a working men's club that was so rough I climbed out of the window in the break and managed to get to the Sunderland Empire in time to see Free take the stage and play an unbelievably brilliant 60 minute set in front of a horde of Free Disciples. When Free released 'The Hunter' I think half of the Sunderland male population thought it was written about them.

These were times when bands were meeting up at transport cafés up and down the M1 at one o'clock in the morning, comparing battle scars and tucking into egg, beans and chips with a mug of tea, in the middle of nowhere. Jimi Hendrix knew these times well and I'm sure he knew all about egg, beans and chips as well as 'Purple Haze'.

These were the times when you bought *NME* or *Melody Maker* and went straight to the gig section to see who was coming up north, to get another shot of magic. Helping us face the grim, grey truth of being out of work, out of luck and always, always, out of our heads.

I hope you enjoy reading this piece of rock'n'roll history. Some people like to escape reality and dream their life away. I think Geoff Docherty turned his dreams into reality and it's a reality I will never forget.

Read on . . .

Dave Stewart

Acknowledgements

I would like to acknowledge the help I received from the following in the writing of this book. Without their promptings, anecdotes or patience, it would have been impossible to write.

Nicky Stothard, teacher at Bede College, Sunderland (Word Processing for Beginners), Barry Walker, George Forster, Maureen Gamblin, David Lidster, Chas McIver, Ray Laidlaw, John Woods, Baz Ward, Bob Pridden, Nick Loyd, Rob Freeth, Dave Moss, David Clayton, Terry Wilson Slessor, Kenny Mountain, Monument Computers, Tony Maggiore, Stan & Marie Robinson, Mick & Val Brown, Kerry Newman, Rob Hutchinson, Paul McCartney, Dave Backhouse, Alan Tedder, Geoff Dickens, Joe Jopling, Nick Loyd, Bill Goldsmith, Mr & Mrs Ward and son Stephen. Chris Phipps, Ken Bolam, John & Sheila Peel, Peter Edge, Sheila Skellam, Dave Stewart, and all Newcastle Library Staff. Not forgetting Peter Watchman (PRINTCENTRE) who kindly reproduced many of the memorabilia items for the book free of charge after we'd reminisced over many of the gigs which he personally attended. If there is anybody else who has helped, and due to an oversight, is not mentioned, please forgive me. I also thank you.

I would also like to thank Elizabeth Weightman of the *Sunderland Echo* library section, for helping me trawl through past editions of the newspaper.

Thanks are also due to the *Sunderland Echo* assistant editor (Deric Walker) for allowing me to reprint relevant advertisements and articles from past copies.

Sunderland library staff are also to be commended for pointing me in the right direction to locate reference books, micro film of past editions of the *Sunderland Echo*, and other source material. Their patience with my sometimes tedious enquiries was brilliant.

Some of the material was also gleaned from the following publications: *Pete Frame's Rock Family Trees*, *The Guinness Book of Rock Stars*, *The N.M.E. Who's Who in Rock & Roll*, *David Bowie: The Pitt*

Report, *The Billboard Book of Top 40 Albums*, *The Guinness Book of British Hit Albums*, *The Guinness Book of British Hit Singles*, *Led Zeppelin Uncensored*, *Pink Floyd*, *Record Collector (1997/98 editions)*. *The Times* and *Daily Telegraph* obituary columns, *The Chronicle Of The Twentieth Century* (Longman).

Finally, special thanks are due to Karen Dawson who has helped me all the way through this book. Her unstinting efforts, tireless corrections, and unbounding enthusiasm have been absolutely invaluable. An ex-teacher, she came to many of the gigs at The Fillmore, and still travels hundreds of miles to see live bands. From the bottom of my heart, many thanks Karen.

Geoff Docherty
"Rock At The Sharp End", 2002

Chapter 1

The dressing room door opened. I looked up and, to my great relief, in walked Eric Clapton with his band. He was taller than I had imagined, with a statesmanlike, almost military posture. Quiet and unassuming, he seemed gentle and restrained for such a major star. He smiled, which put me at ease as I stood up to shake hands and introduce myself. His handshake seemed to linger, conveying the sincerity of his smile, but there was no need for that. I'd just shaken the hand, touched the fingers that had played a million notes and, although he wasn't God, right there and then he was damned close.

There was no big fuss. It was never my style to overdo welcomes. Besides, Eric was about to get one of the biggest he'd ever experienced. More than 3,000 fans were packed into The Mayfair Ballroom that night, every one of them eager to welcome God to Newcastle. Eric walked over to a chair where his newly tuned guitar, a brown Fender Stratocaster affectionately known as 'Brownie' was resting. He picked it up, strapped it over his shoulder, and began moving his fingers across the fretboard. The room fell quiet for a moment and all eyes turned towards him. He smiled, looking embarrassed. The electrifying opening bars of 'Layla', now instantly recognisable throughout the world but then new to these ears, reverberated around the dressing room. The hairs on the back of my neck stood on end at the unique thrill of being in the presence of such a renowned musician.

Baz Ward, Eric's roadie, came in and abruptly interrupted proceedings. "Right, we're on chaps," he beckoned as everyone stood up and began making their way towards the stage. For a moment I felt disappointed, but it was soon forgotten as I heard the tremendous roar of the audience as the band hit the stage. As I listened to the opening number, I once again felt amazed at the magnitude of what was happening. One of the biggest names in rock was up there on stage a few feet from where I stood and, unbelievably, I was promoting the show.

The music, loud and proud like the best rock always is, washed over me and, as each soaring note rang out across the hall, I was reminded of the huge, powerful breakers which lash the North East coastline. There was something about Eric's playing that cast my mind back to my childhood years; years that were all too often scarred by hardship and pain. Never in a million years would I have dreamt that rock music, the music of Eric Clapton and his peers, the music that rang in my ears that night, would prove to be my salvation.

"Don't cry, you're safe here with me," said the childminder as she placed me in another unfamiliar cot. I had arrived at St Anthony's Convent in Cambridge Road, Aldershot, after a long journey accompanied by Mr Sheldon, a kindly member of Sunderland NSPCC. My mother had died when I was a baby, and my father, a miner at Castletown Colliery in Sunderland, County Durham, had tried desperately to keep us together. Unfortunately, his unstinting efforts had proved to be in vain.

I was the youngest of four brothers, two of whom accompanied me, but I was too young to understand why at the time. We had first come to the notice of the authorities when our elder brother John, who was eleven, was kept off school to look after us in my father's absence. John often played football in the street outside and, not realising the danger, would leave the three of us on our own. At the time, I was a mere baby and my crying alerted a concerned neighbour who became anxious and reported our predicament to the social services. My father, who had pleaded without success for relatives to adopt me, was ordered to hand over the three youngest of us to the authorities. In carrying out my mother's dying wish for us to be kept together, he inadvertently ensured we were sent south to Aldershot, over three hundred miles away, which offered the only vacancy for three sibling boys. Thus we found ourselves in such austere and unfriendly surroundings.

I can remember little of the next two years. When I was five I was taken aside and told by a nun that I would have to leave the nursery and move into a block for older children. I remained fearfully silent, alarmed at what was in store for me. "Right off you go and remember to watch your manners," she warned as I nodded and went on my way. Inside the section for the five to seven year olds, I found a common room that was completely bare except for some brown polished lino on the floor, and a few sliding cupboards. No one seemed interested in me, and I felt lonely and unloved. Gradually it dawned on me that I was on my own from here on in, and life seemed daunting. Finally, after about two hours, a nun appeared and led me upstairs to a dormitory where I was shown the iron bedstead on which I was to sleep. Sheepishly, I looked around at my new roommates who were present. One of them eyed me up and down suspiciously before approaching me.

"You're new here, aren't you?" he asked in a superior tone.

"Yes," I replied nervously.

"My name's Peter Peplow and I'm in charge," he informed me.

I nodded in acknowledgement. His voice had a domineering tone to which I took an immediate dislike. After he'd gone, I spoke to a friendly, if rather shy and subdued boy named Ian.

"Who's this Peter Peplow, and why is he in charge?" I asked. "Is it because he's the eldest?"

"No," Ian replied. "It's because he's the best fighter and if you don't do what he says, he hits you."

"I see, thanks for the warning."

During the next few months I gradually became used to the harsh regime of my new surroundings. The strict discipline, lonely nights, poor food, and a failure to understand why I was there made it even more unsettling. One day Peplow, who had turned out to be a tyrannical bully, summoned me over.

"Listen Docherty, I've left my soap in the bathroom, go and fetch it for me," he ordered.

"Why don't you go yourself?" I indignantly replied. "After all, you're the one who forgot it."

Suddenly, without warning, he punched me. Instinctively I fought back, but he was too big, and I was soon overwhelmed. Unfortunately, Ian had proved to be right. I'd learnt a painful lesson.

Every morning, my eldest brother Donald came into the dormitory to help me make up my bed in the strict manner laid down by the nuns. It was great to see him and his friendly face was always a great tonic. One morning I told him about Peplow.

"He keeps hitting people for no reason, will you give him a good hiding for us?" I pleaded.

"You don't need me to do it, you can beat him yourself," he confidently asserted.

"I can't, he's too big."

"No he isn't, I'm telling you, you can beat him," he urged. "Next time he gets cheeky, don't be frightened, just get stuck into him."

"But won't you do it?" I pleaded again.

Donald patted the pillow and looked me squarely in the face.

"No, it has to be you, because if you beat him, he'll leave you alone after that."

After he'd gone, I found his words gave me courage and I worked out a plan of action. I decided the next time he picked on me, I was going to hit him first and see how he liked it. I didn't have long to wait. One day, as I was looking aimlessly out of the window, he purposely stood on my foot, smirked, and walked away. It was a deliberate act of intimidation and, inwardly, I was seething. Realising it was now or never, and remembering Donald's words, I took a deep breath and strode towards him.

"Peplow," I snarled with as much bravado as I could muster. Before I could finish, he turned and cut me off.

"My name's Peter, and if you don't call me that, you'll regret it."

His words sounded ominous and danger signals flashed through my brain as I prolonged the confrontation.

"Peplow," I repeated defiantly, as he closed in on me in a threatening manner.

"Look, I've warned you Docherty," he began. I was shaking with fear but I was committed, and it was too late to back off. In a split second, I sent a punch into his face and instinctively repeated the dose with the other fist. He jerked backwards in surprise as I followed through with more determined blows. Peplow doubled up in pain, and seemed unwilling to continue. I stepped back and stared menacingly at him.

"Had enough?" I said sarcastically. He remained silent and vanquished. In the time it took to administer half a dozen punches, his

4

bullying days were over and, in the manner that pecking orders are established, I had risen to a respected number one among the dormitory. Next morning I couldn't wait to tell Donald.

"You were right!" I eagerly told him.

"What about?" he asked bemusedly.

"Peter Peplow, I beat him," I trumpeted.

Donald grinned. "See, I knew you could."

At six years old, this was my first real fight, and it instilled within me a deep hatred of bullies which has never left me. Meanwhile, the orphanage regime was spartan and life was tough. Every morning, breakfast was porridge, and one day I wasn't allowed any because I had lost the buckle on my regulation issue sandals. The rules were very strict. I was regularly beaten by a sadistic nun who took pleasure in thrashing me across my bare buttocks until I was screaming in agony. She used a broad black leather belt which she wore around her waist and from which dangled a large silver crucifix; the irony of which was obviously lost on her. What was my crime? I had wet the bed despite my nightly cup of cocoa being withdrawn. It was a bewildering and cruel regime, yet it seemed normal to me.

The highlight of every year was when my father, who had saved his every penny, visited us for two weeks and spared no expense in his attempts to make the three of us happy. After Dad left, it seemed like an eternity before he reappeared. He was wonderful to us, and we loved him dearly.

During our stay at the orphanage he sent us food parcels which proved an immense morale booster, especially those delicious chocolate scones. Whenever he visited, we pleaded with him to take us home, but we were too young to understand the reasons why he was unable to do so.

School was St Anthony's in Aldershot, and walking the half-mile there could be a harrowing experience. In the winter, as we huddled together in a regimented line along the kerb, a youth who lived opposite the convent in Cambridge Road would jeer and throw snowballs with rocks inside. It was unnerving as well as dangerous, and at 14 he was far too big to be challenged by any of us. One year, my father arrived with our elder brother John who had been allowed to stay at home. When we told Dad about this insufferable bully, and pointed out where he lived, Dad was so incensed, he went over to the house, hid behind the privet hedge, and waited. Before long, this youth appeared and my father took him by the arm.

"Listen, son," Dad said, "I'm getting reports that you're throwing snowballs with rocks in them and calling the lads from the home horrible names. You're making their lives a misery and I bet you think you're clever. Well, let's see what you're like against someone your own size."

With that, John stepped forward and thrashed the living daylights out of him. When Dad finally thought the cringing coward had had enough, he issued a warning. "Listen bonny lad, if I ever get another report that you have upset anyone from the home, I'll bring my son back down and you'll get the same again."

My brothers and I watched with a mixture of awe and jubilation. We had endured this bully's incessant taunts for so long, it was wonderful to see him get his comeuppance. From now on, we could walk to school unhindered.

When I was eight, father remarried and brought us out of the home and back to Castletown, a small mining village on the outskirts of Sunderland. Once again I found myself thrust into a new and strange environment.

One day, soon after we came back, there was a knock at the door. Father opened it to find himself confronted by an irate parent.

"Your son has just given my lad a good hiding and split his lip. What are you going to do about it?" he asked angrily.

"Which one was it?" my father enquired.

"His name's Donald," came the bitter reply.

"I'll go and fetch him."

When they reappeared, my father turned towards my brother and spoke sternly to him.

"Did you give this man's lad a good hiding?"

"Yes Dad," came the reply.

"Why, what did he do to you?"

"He kept taking the mickey out of our cockney accents. It's

been going on for days and I warned him, but he took no notice."

My father's attitude immediately changed. "I see," he said before turning to the aggrieved man. "Listen, my boys have just come out of a home and don't have a mother. You tell your son to leave them alone and let them settle in. If he does, I promise you there won't be any more trouble. But I must warn you, if he continues to taunt my lads, I'll come looking for him myself."

Suitably chastened, the accuser promptly turned and left. Back inside we gathered around the kitchen table. Tears welled in my eyes at the pride I felt for my beloved dad. Once again, we had witnessed him sticking up for us against adversity.

Every year Dad took us to the Durham Miners Gala and one of the highlights for him was to watch the fights in the boxing booth. Young, fit, well-muscled pit lads, egged on by their friends, would enter the gladiatorial arena aiming to prove they were superior to the well-oiled and bandaged booth fighters. One of Dad's heroes was the great Welshman, Tommy Farr, who had majestically failed to wrench the world heavyweight title from the immortal Joe Louis on a split-points decision after fifteen gruelling rounds. He often reminded us of Tommy's attributes and would enthuse about them.

When Dad was in these moods, we listened because we knew he loved us and it was important to him that we learnt how to look after ourselves. In his earlier days, Tommy Farr had been a booth fighter, and was obliged to take on all comers. Dad told us how skilful he was, how he never wasted a punch and, just as important, knew how to take one. He could punch his weight with either hand, was fast and courageous. As the drama of the booth fights unfolded, he would point out certain things. "See how he covers up when he's in trouble, son. You've got to be able to do that when things go wrong, and notice how he hits on the break."

"Isn't that a foul, Dad?" I asked during one savage bout.

"Not when you're in a street fight son. In fact, it can come in more than useful," he replied.

Dad himself was a good scrapper. One night when he was drinking in a local bar called The Tramcar Inn, at Southwick, just outside Sunderland, he and John went to the toilet. When they came out, someone had stolen their drinks. Dad looked around and spotted some local layabouts laughing at him. His suspicions were aroused when he noticed two of their beer glasses were nearly full compared to the others. A hardened coal worker, Dad was fit and never drank more than two pints. His body was lean and muscular, and used to taking hard knocks down the pit. John, my eldest brother, had just come back from a three-year stint in the Malayan jungle where he had been mentioned in dispatches for bravery after being ambushed. He was also the regimental boxing champion and, in situations like this, didn't back down.

Their opponents were renowned hard cases from Southwick who ruled the roost in that area. No one dared challenge their authority under pain of being taught a severe lesson. Eventually, they made some sarcastic comment to my father and a fight ensued. Two were on the deck in seconds, while a third tried to pick up a hot poker from the coal fire. Unfortunately for him, my brother beat him to it and, in a sudden role reversal, John threatened his four cronies with it. They backed off, frozen in fear, whereupon Dad and John calmly walked out and made their way home.

Next day, still incensed, my father went back to The Green, a piece of common land where these no-hopers all congregated, and offered any two out. They declined his invitation and the myth of their invincibility was finally dispelled. After this incident, no one took these layabouts seriously any more, excepting the police. After all, if they'd steal your pint, what else would they steal, given half a chance?

Dad was a real stickler for physical fitness, and was forever impressing upon us the importance of it. "Remember, son, if you get into a fight and you're not fit, the chances are you'll get beat," he would say. Another piece of advice he often gave was "Don't forget, your body is like a car, if you look after it, it will look after you. You only get one, so look after it." This was usually followed by his daily swig of cod liver oil to combat the inexorable ravages of coal dust slowly accumulating in his lungs.

At home in the backyard, Dad would have me simultaneously box against him and my elder brother Leo and, after a while, he would switch us around. With two sets of fists coming at you, you had to be ultra sharp to avoid them, and it certainly honed the reflexes. If nothing was happening in the house, he would beckon us outside and say, "C'mon son, let's see your style." Within minutes we were at it hammer and tongs in the backyard until exhaustion set in. There were no breaks or stoppages, you just had to keep going.

Rightly or wrongly, Dad wasn't too keen on punch bags. "They don't hit you back son," he would warn. "In a real fight, the other fella has two fists as well." He also bought us a punchball and rigged it up with two nails hammered into the entrance of the wash house door in the backyard. "Make sure you get your timing right, if you bring him onto the punch, it lands so much harder." Perhaps the most important piece of advice he passed down was, "Don't go looking for trouble son, because if you do, you'll always find it. Remember, where there's one, there's always one better."

Although we were a complete family once more, our stepmother failed to show us any real affection. When I was picked for the school football team and harboured genuine dreams of becoming a professional footballer, she had other ideas and forbade me from playing. Instead, I was forced to do the shopping every day until I left school at fifteen. It seemed I had left one unfriendly environment for another, and once again I was very unhappy.

I wasn't to know it at the time but these setbacks were slowly but surely instilling within me a desire to escape the constraints inherent in my working-class environment. I began to realise that a whole world was waiting out there; never more apparent than when travelling into town on the upper deck of the bus. Sitting there, we often passed the colliery manager's house, the sight of which represented a symbol of wealth and power.

Dad had no desire that we should follow in his footsteps and become miners. He warned us of the perils of working down the pit, where there were often fatalities, serious injuries and as yet undiagnosed respiratory diseases.

"Listen son, you want to be breathing God's fresh air," he advised. "Don't be a mug like me and work down the pit, it's no life for anyone. Learn all you can and get a better job."

Our small upstairs house was owned by the colliery. If Dad stopped working down the mine he would have to leave it, and in those days no miner could afford to risk losing his family home, thus tying them to the job for all their working life. Realising he was trapped on a never-ending treadmill, Dad tried desperately to ensure that we avoided the same fate. His concern and love for us was always endearing.

The colliery manager's house had high walls surrounding a huge garden. There was a tennis court and magnificent lawns which in the summer were bordered with beautiful flowers. Looking towards the house, it was difficult to see inside because the many windows were covered with heavily embossed curtains to keep out prying eyes. For some strange reason, I never saw anyone leave or enter through its tall wooden gate. There was a mystery about the house which was both fascinating and, in some strange way, ghostly. "See what a bit of education gets you," Dad would remind us as the bus drove past. "What's more, he doesn't even have to get his hands dirty. But if you want money, you have to be prepared to work for it."

Dad was forever educating us about life. I feel now that he was trying hard to make up for the lost years when we hadn't been together. Whenever there was a disagreement with our stepmother, he was there to console us, to remind us of what might have been. "When you lost your mother, son, you lost the best friend you'll ever have," were words we heard often. In his own way he manfully sought to fill the void she left. His strength of character was an inspiration to us, and even though he didn't learn to read or write until he went into the army, he commanded our eternal respect. His lack of education drove him to instil in us a passion for knowledge, and the will to attain something in life.

Within a year of arriving back in Sunderland, Donald took a short cut home across a farmer's field after competing in the school sports day. Unfortunately, the farmer spotted him and gave chase. Tragically, in his desperation not to be caught, Donald ran straight out onto the road near Sunderland Greyhound Stadium, and was hit by a van. Forty-eight hours later he died in hospital. He was twelve. Father was distraught, and never forgave himself for bringing us out of the home. The sadness in his eyes never left him, and every week until he died in 1977, he placed flowers on his grave.

Chapter 1

At the funeral, as I watched my brother's coffin being lowered into the ground, I remembered how in the children's home he had helped make my bed up every morning, and taught me how to stand up for myself. Now he was gone forever. I was only eight years old, but was already learning about the frailties of life.

Chapter 2

My next school was St Hilda's in the Southwick area of Sunderland where five of us were singled out for special tuition in order to pass the 11 plus exam. Unfortunately, whenever the teacher called out our names to leave the class, I was too shy to stand up. The other four all passed for St Aidan's Grammar School while I failed, much to the disappointment of my father. The academic standards at St Hilda's may not have been the highest in the land, but the teachers imbued in us a sense of honesty and integrity that was second to none, and I remain grateful for that.

The first job I had after I left school was a van boy at Binns department store. One day, Dad passed by and saw me loading parcels. The same look of disappointment appeared on his face again, even though he tried to hide it. I went to West Park night school to get some qualifications and passed for the A stream. The second week there, the instructor told us we would have to buy a T-square, drawing board and protractors. Unfortunately, the wages as a 15-year-old van boy were so minimal, I had to ask Dad to lend me the money, but he couldn't afford to. His health was deteriorating and he'd been forced to move to lighter work because he could no longer manage the heavy shifts at the coalface. This meant he received a much lower wage, and I was too embarrassed to tell the instructor, so I left. When I did, Dad was heartbroken. Despite this, he constantly urged me to make something of my life.

Later, I enrolled at RAF Cosford in Shropshire as an instrument and electrical engineer. After about a year, I was discharged and shortly afterwards joined the Army as a technical storekeeper in The Royal Corps of Signals at Catterick Camp in North Yorkshire. I was 17, five foot one inches tall and weighed only six stone two pounds. My father and the military doctors were extremely

12

concerned at my lack of physical development and on the parade ground I looked and felt ridiculous. A fixed bayonet was taller than me, while my groundsheet trailed along the ground, causing me to trip over during training on the Yorkshire moors. After seven weeks of hard square-bashing, they discharged me for being too small, and on the bleak day I left the barracks, it seemed that no one wanted me. I was beginning to wonder if I would ever find a niche in which I felt comfortable.

Back in civilian life, I became apprenticed to a motor cycle mechanic at Cowie's, where I worked with Malcolm Hobbs from Gosforth, near Newcastle, who went on to become British motor cycling sidecar champion. Unfortunately he was tragically killed in the Isle of Man Tourist Trophy Races and I can't let this pass without saying he was one of the nicest and most unassuming people you could ever wish to meet. Many years later I had the sad experience of visiting the site where he crashed.

After about a year, I became restless to see the world and decided to join the Fleet Air Arm as an aircraft engineer. I was now 18, and had been in all three services, completing three sets of square-bashing which certainly broadened my horizons at an early age. During my service in the Fleet Air Arm I volunteered to spend two years on loan to the Army Air Corps in Hildesheim, Germany, as an aircraft mechanic. After returning to the Navy, I spent two and a half years aboard the *Ark Royal* aircraft carrier. This proved to be a fantastic experience and was to leave me with many great memories, including a ten-day visit to Manila where I was twice picked to play football for the Far East Fleet against the Philippine Olympic Eleven. Four days later, I played against a Philippine Select Eleven in the National Stadium where The Beatles later performed in 1966. It was a great honour and sailors from every ship were there to cheer us on to victory in both games.

After buying myself out and being discharged at Portsmouth, I returned to Sunderland and took lodgings in a local housing estate since my stepmother refused to let me stay at home, claiming there was no room for me. I then applied to the Government Training Centre at Felling to be enrolled as an agricultural mechanic which seemed a healthy environment in which to fix broken machinery.

"Come in, Docherty," said the interviewing officer while perusing my aptitude tests. "I notice you're very good at maths, so we intend to train you as a precision miller."

"But I was hoping to become an agriculture mechanic," I protested.

"There aren't any vacancies, and besides, I think this will suit you better," he replied.

My heart sank. He seemed so uncaring and I realised that, to him, I was just another statistic who could be pigeonholed into any vacancy which suited him. Nevertheless, I completed the six month course and started work at Cole's Cranes in Pallion which turned out to be one of the most boring jobs I have ever undertaken. As soon as I finished machining one piece of metal, I had to do likewise to hundreds more. When this was completed, another skip-full arrived. The chap on my left had stood at his machine for eleven years and the one on my right for seventeen. They both looked like death warmed up, and I half expected them to expire at any moment. It was mind numbing, and after four months I left to find something more challenging and worthwhile.

In the evenings, I often visited the local dance hall at Park Lane, known locally as The Rink. I prided myself on my appearance and always wore smart suits with a matching tie and handkerchief, which were fashionable at the time. Unfortunately, it seemed that dressing smartly and drinking in certain pubs in the town presented its own dangers. A few undesirable elements, seeing me on my own, assumed I was an easy target and sometimes chose to pick on me. Fresh out of the navy, I was at a difficult stage in life, and in trying to re-establish myself I found this aggression very unsettling.

I had already encountered bullies in the home and my dislike of them hadn't diminished. If they decided to invade my privacy, I was determined to stand up for myself, and this was how I came to experience my first serious altercation in Sunderland town centre.

That night a couple of guys in a bar had been passing sarcastic comments about my dress sense. As I went to leave, one of them moved forward and blocked my path.

"What's wrong?" I asked.

Chapter 2

"We don't like the look of you, and I bet you think you're great, don't you?" he said in a threatening tone.

"No I don't," I replied politely.

"Give him it," the other one urged. "Don't mess about Frankie, give him it now."

The stakes had risen. I took a rapid appraisal of the situation. My only escape was to turn and run, but I had no intention of doing so. Just then, one of them came forward and I could see the evil intent in his eyes. Dad's words came to mind. "Don't forget son, if you look for trouble, you'll find it, and where there's one, there's one better." I hadn't looked for trouble, so that was the first part of the equation out of the way.

What these chaps didn't know was that I felt supremely fit. Apart from football and boxing, I'd also spent two years as a member of the gymnastic display team at the Royal Naval Air Station in Yeovilton. We had trained over a high box every day and in the summer gave displays around Somerset and Devon, as well as at Portland Navy Days. Fitness provides real confidence, but beer gives an exaggerated impression of it. I was in no doubt that I possessed the former, and him the latter.

Just then, one of them threw the first punch. Sidestepping it, I immediately closed in and sent a quick and powerful right and left hook into his jaw. He looked surprised, if not visibly shaken. Without hesitating I unleashed another right and left onto the side of his chin, causing his face to rock from side to side, and down he went. I spun to face his alarmed colleague who came running towards me to avenge his friend. As the adrenalin surged, I prepared to meet this new challenge but, inexplicably, he stopped, eyed his fallen colleague, and dragged him away to safety.

The confrontation over, I made my way to The Club Eleven, a newly opened nightclub. Inside, some onlookers who had been watching from the other side of the road approached me.

"Do you know who you've just beaten?" they asked.

"No," I replied.

"That was Frankie Jacobs, he's got form for GBH."

I smiled and turned away. It must have been a schoolgirl he'd hit because he wasn't very good. Not on that showing anyway.

Returning to Sunderland after my stints in the services, both at home and abroad, was a strange experience. It was a thriving ship-building and mining town with barrow boys, billiard halls, two-way streets, no yellow parking lines, and a famous Town Hall in Fawcett Street, named after Colonel Fawcett. As I walked around, I could sense unrest and lack of opportunities for younger people. Those with ambition seemed to rise to a certain level, and then get stuck in a frustrating log jam.

Once anyone reached the status of foreman, it seemed years before he progressed on to management, if at all. There appeared to be a slow moving, two-tier system in operation which wasn't readily apparent until you looked beyond the façade. Solicitors, doctors, police inspectors, successful businessmen, or anyone in high authority, never seemed to frequent the bars working people did. The main commercial business centre was John Street, a prestigious office address which signified a step up in the underlying class system.

Of course, this lack of opportunity didn't apply to everyone, and union stewards, or councillors with true altruistic concerns, steadfastly fought to improve our lot. Strangely, there was a perverse irony in this, because the very things they railed against were actually the things they most wanted, both for their members and themselves. Sadly, for most of them, winning the pools was the only hope of ever achieving this and it seemed the rest were destined to remain on a hopeless, never-ending treadmill. Such was the lot of being born working class.

At the bottom of the heap were the undesirables who had neither the finances nor the inclination to better themselves, other than to try to acquire status with their fists, especially after a few drinks. If someone could fight, people invariably listened to their viewpoint with greater attentiveness, but I came to realise that whatever audience they managed to attract was listening through fear, rather than genuine interest. It all contributed to an aggressive atmosphere, especially in certain pubs at the weekends when newly paid wages kept the beer flowing.

I was to have first-hand experience of this a few weeks later in Terry's, a small restaurant in Olive Street, just off Park Lane in the town centre, where I had taken a girl for a meal. As we were eating, the guy at the next table began swearing in a loud and over-bearing manner. I turned and politely asked him to mind his language as there was a lady present. As time went on, his loutish behaviour became more objectionable, and after my request was ignored a second time, I decided to invite him to step outside to resolve the situation, one way or another. Suddenly, he brandished a steak knife at me in a threatening manner. Without hesitation, I sent a right hook flush onto his jaw. As he reeled back in shock, I picked up a spare knife from another table and pointed it at him.

"You're not the only one with one of these," I challenged. "Are you coming outside or not?"

He remained motionless, staring at me with hate-filled eyes, fearful of what the outcome would be. He got up, paid his bill and left. Later, Terry, the restaurant owner, called me over and told me he wasn't charging me for the meal. "I've had trouble with him before," he explained. "When he gets a few drinks inside him, he's murder. That's why I was delighted when you hit him."

Refusing to be intimidated, I continued to dress smartly and drank on my own. A couple of months went by without any further incidents and I began to think that maybe I'd just been unlucky. Unfortunately, I was proved wrong when leaving a pub in Norfolk Street. A middle-aged man wearing a trilby gave me a filthy look and, for absolutely no reason, called me scum.

Seeking retaliation, I remained composed before sending a left into his ribs, followed by a right hook onto his jaw. To his credit, he stayed on his feet. Unfortunately the guy had three sons, the hardest of whom happened to be with him. I'd hit his father, and now he wanted revenge. As we rained punches on each other in a mad frenzy, I sensed I had the upper hand and he was tiring. As I moved in to deliver the final kill, he broke away, shouting "Police!" – an old trick to fool you into lowering your guard – but I was wise to it and ignored him. Realising his ploy had failed, he stepped back and offered no further resistance. The fight was over and I'd won on a technical stoppage. I was happy to leave it at that, and walked away.

I was now at the stage where girls were increasingly in my thoughts, and I was keen to meet the right one. When the *Ark*

Royal had visited Perth in Australia, thousands of people queued to visit the ship, including hundreds of girls. After an exciting, action packed ten-day visit, including a football match against Western Australia which we lost, we eventually prepared to sail for Singapore. Such was the intensity of our welcome, over forty sailors went missing, opting to stay with Australian girls they'd become acquainted with.

On the night before sailing, my girl and I stood on the dockside at Fremantle. She asked if I had anything she could remember me by. "Yes, I think I have," I replied. I ran on board to 3Q2 mess, found two small silk Chinese dolls I had bought in Hong Kong, rushed back and handed them to her. As we kissed and hugged our teary-eyed farewells, an overwhelming feeling of despair hit me. Deep down, I didn't want to leave her, or Perth where we had been treated so well. I'll always remember that trip and to this day, whenever Perth or Fremantle is mentioned in the news, I think of the girl with my Chinese dolls. Yet, here I was back in my hometown, and it seemed I couldn't meet anyone who quite captured the magic I'd experienced in Australia.

Coming out of the forces was unsettling. I had a succession of jobs, including a porter at Sunderland railway station and on the production line of Vauxhall cars in Luton. I had spells on the dole and, under interrogation by suspicious staff, I began to feel like a misfit. Life left me feeling unfulfilled and disillusioned, and I yearned for some real excitement.

Nevertheless, Sunderland offered some compensations. There were beautiful twin beaches just a mile from the town centre, and the Empire Theatre with an interior that always took my breath away. The Empire had played host to stars such as Margot Fonteyn, the *Folies-Bergère*, Marlene Dietrich, and rock and pop acts like The Everly Brothers, Chuck Berry, Little Eva, The Beatles and dozens of others. At that time, Sunderland was the largest shipbuilding town in the world and the launch of a ship was always a day of immense pride as everyone lined the river to watch it glide smoothly into the water.

The city was also a world-renowned glass blowing centre, while Washington Hall, the ancestral home of the First American President, George Washington, was only five miles away. As I walked around, there was still much to be proud of and one could sense that the young people aspired to achieve something meaningful with their lives. I was no different but I wondered if an opening would ever present itself and, if so, how and where. I was sure of one thing: it wouldn't be machining lumps of metal all day, or working at Sunderland railway station.

It's funny how fate can dramatically intervene in life, and my next confrontation was to result in an unforeseen consequence. The skirmish occurred at The Beach Club in South Shields, a small coastal town, not far from Sunderland. With licensing laws becoming more liberal, nightclubs were opening everywhere with roulette, black jack and other types of gambling becoming accessible. Beautiful women were employed as croupiers, while attractive cigarette ladies in fishnet tights smiled at anybody looking their way. Inevitably, gambling and pretty girls often attract an unsavoury element, and The Beach Club was no exception.

One night, a regular, who happened to be a notorious villain, pushed some notes into my top pocket and ordered me to fetch his cigarettes. Not wishing to be treated like a messenger boy, I took exception and a heated argument ensued, which culminated in him offering me outside. I took a quick appraisal of my prospective opponent. He was about five foot ten, stocky, with a barrel chest, and was obviously a lot heavier than me. As we made our way out of the club, he pulled me swiftly towards him, and tried to head butt me. In the nick of time I saw it coming and moved my head away. His head caught me a glancing blow on the cheekbone, inflicting a slight graze, but I was unhurt and ready for the ensuing battle. His friends followed us out, keen to witness what they assumed would be my ritual slaughter.

I took a quick mental note of the area. The first thing I noticed was that there was a big expanse of car parking space, which would enable me to utilise what I hoped would be my superior speed. The great Muhammad Ali didn't stipulate the maximum ring size of 22 feet for nothing. It was dancing space, and while I wasn't there to dance, it would afford me vital room to manoeuvre should things go wrong. As we squared up to each other, he charged towards me like an enraged bull and began throwing a series of wild punches. There was predictability about his tactics which lacked any sort of guile or finesse, and I was confident that provided I kept out of trouble, I could pull off a shock. He did catch me with a swinging right to the ribs but, fortunately, I was moving away and this lessened its impact. By now, the Queensberry Rules were thrown out of the window, with head butts, savage kicks and harsh punches being thrown with great ferocity.

I knew he had a lot riding on this fight, especially as his friends and the doormen were watching, and should he lose to a smaller person, his reputation would be in tatters. Having already assessed his style, it soon became clear that he was simply a bruiser with a dangerous right hand. After weathering the initial storm, it was time to take the initiative. Seizing my chance, I closed in and feinted with a left to the body, before quickly letting loose a solid right hook to his jaw which struck home with all the sweetness of a Valentine card from a loved one. At this, he went crashing down into a pitiful heap and lay spread-eagled against a wall. I stopped and looked at his limp body as his friends stood in stunned silence before making my way back into the club. Inside, people were staring at me and I felt self-conscious as someone came over, threw a congratulatory arm around me, and offered to buy me a drink.

I glanced over at Elsa, the cigarette girl. She was tall with blonde hair and a gorgeous figure with long Hollywood-type legs enmeshed in sexy fishnet stockings. She smiled, seemingly pleased for me, even though she had to appear impartial. The funny thing was, if this guy had asked me nicely, I would have willingly gone to get his cigarettes for him so I would have had an excuse to talk to her.

Next day, the chap I'd fought was telling people that he'd tripped over a kerb, and I'd been lucky. One thing was certain: there was no kerb there, and was a figment of his imagination. Later, I found out he'd had three stitches in his lip as a souvenir, and I knew his hurt pride ensured we would clash again. Because of this I continued to maintain my fitness levels, training over the winding country roads of Warden Law, on the outskirts of Sunderland. Two months later, the waiting was over.

I was standing against a back wall in The Beach Club, adjacent to the roulette table when he came over and started issuing menacing threats about the harm he was about to inflict on my person. Without warning, I stepped forward and head-butted him, following it up with a fusillade of blows. He hadn't expected an attack inside the club and down he went. As he did so one of his friends jumped on my back which unbalanced me, sending us sprawling to the floor. I reacted quickest and was back on my feet, ready for the next confrontation. I then challenged him to come outside so we could finish it off, sarcastically pointing out that there would be no kerb this time. He stared at me, shocked and confused, then backed down. Mercifully, the return fight hadn't lasted more than fifteen seconds.

After this second confrontation, strangers began to greet me, and I felt quite happy with my new found popularity. One day, two tough-looking locals approached me, but this time they weren't looking for trouble. Their names were Jimmy and Dicky Laws and they worked as strong arm men for Vince Landa, a wealthy, somewhat notorious, one-arm bandit king.

Despite their fearsome reputations, Jimmy and Dicky were actually quite reasonable provided you played it straight down the line.

"We've heard what happened at The Beach Club and we've been getting some good reports about you around town," Jimmy began. "There's a vacancy over at The Bay Hotel for a doorman. Ronnie Pranelle books the acts there and has asked us to find someone for the manager. It's two pounds a night and a couple of free drinks. Why don't you go over?"

"No thanks," I replied. "I don't like sorting out other people's troubles. Besides, I seem to get plenty of my own."

Over the next two weeks, I turned the offer over in my mind. It was a depressing time and I didn't know where my life was heading. Things had become desperate; no money, on the dole and the rent was always due. With circumstances getting bleaker by the day, Dicky and Jimmy approached me in Park Lane again. "That job at The Bay is still there if you want it. It's only one night a week and there are some nice girls who go over there."

My pockets were empty and I felt unwanted and unloved. It was time to make a positive move. "Okay," I smiled resignedly, "I'll give it a go."

Chapter 3

The following Friday, I caught a single-decker Economic bus from Park Lane Station to The Bay Hotel where I was introduced to the manager, Mr Forrest. He was an imposing figure, about six feet four and around 18 stone. He greeted me with a firm handshake and a warm smile. I sensed my five feet eight and ten stone ten stature failed to impress him. After some small talk he gave me my instructions. "Just keep an eye on things and if there's any trouble-makers, throw them out." I felt a lump in my throat but nodded in agreement. The reality was I didn't have the slightest clue what to do should trouble occur.

I hadn't expected to see such a towering figure of a manager and couldn't help wondering why someone of his size would need assistance to eject people from the premises. I was nervous and apprehensive. After all, sorting out your own trouble is different from sorting out other people's. At school, Sister Elfrida had constantly reminded us of a quote from the Bible, "Blessed are the peacemakers for they shall see God," but I had no desire to meet him just yet. Within a few minutes the reassuring sight of Mr Forrest had gone and I was on my own.

As the ballroom filled up for the night, I looked around and resolved to use diplomacy rather than violence wherever possible. Bouncer – how I hated that word. It was almost laughable, if not ridiculous, when you thought about it. Somebody employed to hit people in an otherwise civilised environment. That's what a bouncer is supposed to do, but at what point do you hit somebody, and who gives the signal? Still, if things got too bad, maybe Mr Forrest would come to the rescue. They'll soon run when they see the size of him. At least I hope they do.

By now, there were about four hundred people in the ballroom, who, for the most part, seemed well-behaved, although there were one or two that you certainly wouldn't want your sister going out with. After talking to a few people, I quickly learned there was a fairground just a few hundred yards down the road which could sometimes attract the wrong element. I hadn't been warned of this and it dawned on me that at some stage, I might have to earn my two pounds.

On my first night, a girl singer was on stage singing cover versions. She was an attractive long-haired brunette, dressed in skin-tight blue trousers which left nothing to the imagination. On the up-tempo songs, she energetically gyrated her hips while accompanying herself on guitar. Every male eye, including mine, cast an approving look. She certainly kept the boys happy, and at the end of the night they dutifully trooped out in an orderly manner. It served to demonstrate how the powers of such a pleasant female diversion could calm down a potentially threatening situation. However, I was under no illusions that my presence would have the same calming effect.

At the end of that first trouble-free night, I collected my two pounds and made my way outside to join the bus queue. On the way home, I rustled the notes in my pocket as if to reassure myself they were still there. It was the easiest two pounds I'd ever earned in my life. As the teenagers on the bus chatted away, I wondered about the future, would I fit in and was the girl guitarist being re-booked? I certainly hoped so.

A week later, I had formulated a few ideas on how to improve things. My first rule was to make everyone feel welcome. I'd learned the importance of this from my aunt Anne in Washington, who, whenever we visited, was a fantastic host. Nothing was too much trouble, and after each visit, my brother Leo and I couldn't wait to go back, such was the warmth of her welcome.

Secondly, no matter what strata of society anyone came from, be they a millionaire's daughter, a hotel porter, or unemployed, if they knew and used six simple words, namely "please", "thank you", "excuse me", and "sorry", they would be treated like royalty. Those six words had taken me all around the world without the slightest trouble, and I'd found that on hearing them, people were invariably prepared to forgive a multitude of sins. It seemed this was not too much to ask. However it could be – especially on a Friday night.

The Bay Hotel was situated on the seafront in Whitburn, just outside Sunderland town centre. Across the road was a fabulous sandy beach that stretched for nearly a mile. The hotel itself consisted of a detached white building surrounded by a car park, and was fairly close to some residential houses. The main entrance was through revolving doors which led to a large ballroom, which came complete with a polished sprung wooden dance floor. In the centre, hanging from the ceiling, was a revolving mirror ball which reflected light throughout the interior. At the far end was a small stage about two feet in height with a grand piano. Down the length of either side were a series of large windows reaching from floor to ceiling, with heavy satin curtains hanging by their side. It was an impressive room, full of regal splendour. Every Saturday night a dinner dance was held with the men dressed in dinner suits, and their partners in gorgeous evening gowns or cocktail dresses. Everyone was impeccably behaved as they danced to Ray Chester & His Band and it was heart-warming to see people dressing up and enjoying themselves in such relaxed surroundings.

Those Saturday nights were a real eye opener. Immaculately dressed waitresses in starched uniforms delivered exotically named cocktails and drinks to dinner tables around the outer edge of the ballroom. As couples danced together, each graceful movement made the ladies dresses swish against their partner as they looked lovingly into each other's eyes. Having been raised in a children's home, this seemed like another world. As people left at the end of the evening, they would smile and bid me goodnight. Yes, I was beginning to like The Bay more and more.

In complete contrast to the Saturday dinner dance, the manager usually put on local groups on Fridays, or some form of entertainment to attract the younger people. As the weeks passed, I set about trying to implement my ideas to encourage good behaviour, firstly by endeavouring to be diplomatic and polite. I soon realised I was being far too optimistic, as no matter how carefully I vetted people, there always seemed to be a minority who wanted to ride roughshod over others out to enjoy themselves.

As I mentioned earlier, being a bouncer was a strange experience. Mecca halls throughout the country called bouncers 'supervisors'. On reflection, this was a clever name. If ever court proceedings were involved, no matter how brutal the conflict, the term appeared more gentle and refined. "He was only supervising your honour," the defending solicitor would say to a nodding magistrate. Inevitably, the fine would be minimal. But how do you supervise a fight when you're in danger of being battered? Sad to say, I never did master this art.

In 1968, The Bay ballroom and the upstairs room, The Lighthouse Bar, were converted into a new and innovative space known as a discotheque. I became employed full time to re-stock the bars each morning which took up to a couple of hours. Weekly dray day and continually lifting those heavy kegs and beer crates up the steep steps to the Lighthouse Bar helped keep me fit, and afterwards I was given a sumptuous free dinner by the chef. During the week The Lighthouse Bar successfully opened every night but it wasn't long before I was forced into my first real confrontation with two unruly youths.

I was standing in the foyer when a waiter came rushing towards me and asked me to hurry upstairs where two men were swearing and threatening Annie, our dear old barmaid. Reaching the scene I asked the pair to cool it and tried everything to placate them, to no avail. Suddenly, one of them pushed me away, squared up menacingly and told me to "f★★k off". He wasn't particularly big, except in the tonsorial department, and smelled strongly of drink. There was no further point in arguing, so I 'nutted' him and then spun towards his friend, unleashing a succession of speedy and rapid blows. Seizing the initiative, I turned towards the first guy lying prostrate on the floor, grabbed his legs, and began dragging him down the stairs.

As I did so his spine mercilessly thudded against each step. When we reached the bottom, he collapsed in a pitiful heap. I thought of Dad's words. "Don't forget son, ten minutes talk is better than five minutes fight," and a notice in my doctor's waiting room, "Prevention Is Better Than Cure." Well, I'd talked and tried preventing, but ended up giving a practical lesson against bullying. I'd survived my first, but not last, fight at The Bay.

After watching my new colleague Tommy Donnelly unceremoniously throw the other one out, I was summoned to see Mr Forrest. As I made my way, I feared the worst, thinking he was going to sack me for viciously overreacting. "If that's the case, he can stuff his job," I decided. After all, I was only defending Annie. As I entered his office, I was surprised to see him smiling. "I've heard what happened," he began. "Annie's told me everything and I'd like you to come in every night. What do you say to that?"

I looked at him in astonishment. "Yes of course," I stammered.

"From now on I'm putting you in charge. Whenever you think the discotheque is full, close it, and don't let anyone else in till somebody comes out. The decision is entirely up to you."

I could hardly believe what I'd just heard. In the space of a few minutes my rent problems were over, and far from being sacked, my methods had been vindicated.

Mr Forrest turned out to be a fantastic boss, although that's the wrong word because he never acted bossy. One day I happened to mention that I'd just moved into a bedsit and had no plates or cutlery. "Come with me," he beckoned as he led me into the kitchen. There he filled a huge cardboard box full of plates, cutlery, jugs, cups, saucers and condiments. I was overwhelmed by his kindness and became even more determined not to let him down. Hopefully, I never did. One of those large dinner plates has survived to this very day, and whenever I eat from it, I often think of his remarkable generosity.

After about a year, Mr Forrest and his wonderful wife left, but not before assuring the incoming manager, Mr Dixon, of my unstinting support. This unsolicited recommendation speaks volumes for how much I owe him. Mr Dixon was smaller in stature than Mr Forrest, with a thick bushy moustache covering most of his upper lip. He also wore a pair of large horn-rimmed glasses which he constantly adjusted. If awaiting an impending decision, this habit used to make me nervous as it implied I was about to receive bad news. An unhurried type of person, no matter how heated a situation might be, Mr Dixon remained cool and detached. Tommy and I took an immediate liking to him and it was to be an enduring partnership, which survived many difficult situations. On the rare occasions I saw him agitated, his face would redden as he spluttered out his words. To his credit, this was never in public, as he was the perfect host when dealing with customers.

Downstairs, the ballroom was still holding Saturday night dances, and because of the popularity of the upstairs disco, this was extended to downstairs on a Friday. The rest of the week the ballroom remained empty, excepting Saturday mornings when it was usually hired out for wedding receptions or the occasional function.

The ballroom had a jukebox with four huge speakers, but it became clear that people wanted to experience groups live. Noticing my interest in music, Mr Dixon asked me to book some local bands for the Friday nights. Booking and becoming involved with groups rekindled my love of music which had lain dormant for a short while.

My earliest recollection of rock'n'roll was at RNAS (Royal Naval Air Station) Bramcote, now an army base just outside Nuneaton in Shropshire. One of the other trainees brought a Dansette record player back with him from leave and possessed only one LP, a Buddy Holly & The Crickets record which included 'That'll Be The Day', 'Peggy Sue' and 'Oh Boy'. At the end of each day, as soon as we entered the mess, he would play it over and over again, and our tired limbs would instinctively jerk into life. It was a great grounding for everything that followed and I'm indebted to that chap who introduced rock 'n' roll into my life.

In the Sixties, numerous clubs opened throughout England to accommodate the era of new sounds. Never a city to be left out, Newcastle had its own pioneering club scene with The Downbeat and The Club-A-Go-Go, opened and run by Mike Jeffrey. Many illustrious names graced the upstairs stage of the Club-A-Go-Go, including The Rolling Stones, The Yardbirds, John Mayall's Bluesbreakers, Jerry Lee Lewis, Spencer Davis Group,

Steampacket, John Lee Hooker with Savoy Brown, Julie Driscoll and The Brian Auger Trinity, Zoot Money's Big Roll Band and, of course, Newcastle's own heroes, The Animals, and The Junco Partners. Keith Gibbon, now a well-known club owner in the North East who used to work there, was once confronted by the visiting Kray Twins who pulled a gun on him in the Club-A-Go-Go toilets. Fortunately, it was all a misunderstanding, and Keith is still with us.

Each year, hundreds of hopefuls tried to make it but, sadly, the North East seemed unable to find a group able to follow in The Animals' footsteps. In 1964, they had achieved a worldwide number one with 'The House Of The Rising Sun'. This was followed by a string of hits which made the band internationally famous.

Between 1966 and 1969, Skip Bifferty, a Newcastle band who had moved down to London, came close. They gained an excellent reputation and, after skirting around the fringes of success, they later evolved into Bell & Arc. Unfortunately, the group eventually ran out of steam, despite Graham Bell being one of the finest vocalists of his era. Meanwhile the search for new heroes continued.

Two of our local Sunderland musicians ended up in major bands. Mickey Grabham, who was an excellent guitarist, and drummer Nigel Olsson had previously been in a group called Enterprise. Mick and I shared a cottage in Eglinton Street, Monkwearmouth. In January 1968, I was approached at the La Strada night club by a keyboard player named Paul Raymond (later with Chicken Shack, and UFO), who was backing that night's cabaret artist. Having spotted my Jimi Hendrix haircut, he introduced himself and asked if I knew any good guitarists in the area as his group's first single was selling so well that they were due to appear on *Top Of The Pops* the following week, and it had become urgent that they find someone.

I recommended Mick and immediately took Paul back to the cottage to meet him. I couldn't believe my eyes as I watched Mick and Nigel on *Top Of The Pops* a few days later. They moved to London permanently, where everything took off from there. Mick joined Procol Harum after their guitarist Dave Ball left, while Nigel was staying at music publisher Lionel Conway's house, who eventually recommended him to Elton John. (Incidentally, Lionel is now head of Madonna's Maverick Record label's song publishing division in Los Angeles.)

In the centre of Sunderland at this time was The Bis-Bar, a stylish coffee bar and restaurant in Park Lane, where all the city's switched on teenagers met up during the day. It had a relaxed and friendly atmosphere, and its large glass windows afforded a clear view of all that was taking place outside. One day, while sitting there, I couldn't help overhearing the conversation of two attractive girls nearby.

"Never seems to be anything much happening in Sunderland," said one, whose name turned out to be Debbie. "Why is it we always have to go to London to see any decent bands?"

"I know," replied her friend Sarah. "All anyone talks about here are the shipyards, or the football team."

"If it wasn't for Rob, life would be extremely boring."

"Are you still seeing him then?" asked Sarah.

"Yes, of course I am," Debbie replied indignantly. "We have a smoke, and then get it together . . . what else is there to do?" she said resignedly.

"Well you could try the new discotheque that's opened at The Bay."

"No thanks. I went there last week and it was nothing special," Debbie replied.

"What's wrong with it then?" asked Sarah.

"We saw a couple of fights when we were there, and Rob hates violence of any kind. Besides, they're just playing the same music as everywhere else. Rob and I can't wait to go back to London to see some decent bands and get some new gear."

"What sort of gear?" Sarah queried. "Do you mean cannabis?"

"Of course not, haven't you heard? There's a new shop which has just opened in Kensington High Street by someone called Barbara Hulanucki. It's called Biba's, and everyone in London is wearing their stuff. Kensington Market's just down the road and that's class too. Last time we were in London we saw an underground group called Pink Floyd at Middle Earth. They were excellent, but I don't think they'll ever come here. We're thinking of moving to London. There's more jobs there."

The conversation was depressing to hear, and not just because it looked like another attractive girl was set on leaving town. If it carried on like this, I thought to myself, there'd be no decent ones left for the local boys to marry. They finished their coffee, and I watched them head towards Maurice Velody's, a high-class furriers on the opposite corner. They stopped to gaze in the window at the expensive furs that seemed out of place in this working-class town. However, a gleaming Mark 10 Jaguar parked outside was clear testimony that somebody in Sunderland had money. Debbie lifted her chin, flicked her woollen scarf over her shoulder like an expensive fox stole, and turned to walk to Park Lane bus station. I liked that. You don't have to be from class to recognise class, and somehow I sensed that no matter what it took, she wouldn't be getting the bus for much longer.

Park Lane was a seething mass of people at night. It was the unofficial bus station where everyone congregated to catch the last bus home. The Northern buses travelled to outlying districts, while the council owned Corporation buses took people to within the borough boundaries. It was a fascinating sight of couples petting in doorways, while unaccompanied girls were chatted up by 'last chancers' making one last desperate effort to find romance, if only for one night.

Then there were the gangs of youths from different areas who often clashed and, inevitably, fighting erupted. Fortunately, the barking of excited police dogs inside the van, usually calmed things down if things got nasty. Inevitably, there was always a heroine who would run in to try and stop things. If she was too persistent, more often than not, one of the combatants would strike her. On being hit, no matter how lightly, the girl would collapse onto the ground as if mortally wounded, her skirt hitched up her legs. This was the cue for the lads to crane forward in mock concern, their real aim to catch a glimpse of knickers. Eventually, she would be helped to her feet, sobbing her heart out while playing to the gallery, as everyone gathered round to comfort her. Now was the moment for her to bask in their admiration while other, more fearful, types remained in the background. There was no admission charge for this sort of entertainment. All you needed was the price of your bus fare.

As Debbie and Sarah disappeared into the distance, in walked Alan Hogg. 'Hoggy' was a snappy dresser and was about to open a select shoe shop in Derwent Street. Straight talking, good-looking, and diplomatic, he'd previously been an engineer on the *Queen Elizabeth* Cunard liner and New York had become his second home. His tales of lonely women summoning him to their cabins on the slightest pretext were legion, and his dashing naval officer's uniform was evidently more appreciated off than on. Popular music was important to him and he communicated his enthusiasm for it all the time.

"I love The Who," he enthused, "but I still haven't seen them. They were playing in America when I was there, but I couldn't go because the ship was sailing."

"How's New York?" I asked.

His face lit up. "It's great there, Geoff. When you sail up the Hudson River and dock at Pier 55, it all hits you. There's a DJ there called Murray The 'K' who plays some great sounds. One of the last times I was there, I spotted about a hundred girls screaming and looking up at a window."

"What were they looking at?" I asked.

"The Rolling Stones. They were doing a radio broadcast and were standing by the window."

"So did you force your way to the front?" I joked.

"Listen, Geoff," he warned, "if you've got any sense you don't cause street disturbances in America. There's no second chance there, a lot of people carry guns and you'd quickly end up in the morgue."

"Have you been to The Bay yet?" I asked him.

"Yes I have, but I like to go down to London with a friend of mine, John Harker, to see groups. He works for The Tremeloes and the Spencer Davis Group."

These conversations got me thinking. There was a consistent pattern of dissatisfaction emerging. Like anywhere else, young people in Sunderland craved excitement. But what sort? And who was going to give it to them? Someone had to do something, so why not me?

When I'd served as an aircraft mechanic on the *Ark Royal*, I'd seen officers holding private cocktail parties with stewards from the lower deck serving drinks. The officers had their own private gangplank and whenever we berthed, beautiful girls arrived in taxis and limousines to be escorted to the officers' quarters on board the ship. It was out of bounds to us but it left a deep impression on me. These were privileges denied to us which I thought was manifestly unfair. The officers were always given the best of everything and received the finest seats at any function. It wasn't jealousy or inverted snobbery that made me think this way. It was simply the idea of trying to make the very best available to everyone, and not just the few. Now I was working at The Bay, I realised it might be possible to implement some of these ideas, while at the same time eliminating the petty restrictions and outdated rules which were prevalent at other venues.

In my determined attempts to improve relations at The Bay, I'd been forced to visit the casualty unit at the local Royal Infirmary on three occasions. These visits included twice having head wounds stitched, and once being detained overnight after swallowing broken glass when the revolving door entrance was savagely kicked in against my face during a fight. After each altercation, the perpetrators were barred and, as a result, the friendly atmosphere improved in leaps and bounds.

To the uninitiated, my injuries might seem a high price to pay, but in actual fact 90% of the disputes were resolved with tact and diplomacy. It was when a fight had already started that I was occasionally attacked. When fists are flying and kicks are being delivered, it comes down to survival of the fittest. In Hollywood, heroes seem capable of soaking up inordinate amounts of punishment, and have an insatiable appetite to keep coming back for more. Take it from me, real life's not like that, not in Sunderland anyway.

After managing to weed out most of the undesirables at The Bay, a camaraderie built up among those who attended regularly. I realised they wanted more, especially in the way of music, but unfortunately there remained what seemed to be an insurmountable obstacle. Although allowing me to book bands, Mr Dixon had placed a limit of £50 on what I could spend. No matter how hard I tried to persuade him, he was adamant that under no circumstances was this amount to be exceeded. It was frustrating and I knew that if The Bay was to move forward and be at the cutting edge, things had to change.

Bass Breweries, who owned The Bay, had a contract with a jukebox company who sent a rep to change the records once a month. Apart from The Beatles and The Rolling Stones, it was stocked with pop records from the Top 10 like Cilla Black and Engelbert Humperdinck that didn't appeal to the crowd I was attracting to The Bay. When the rep left the building, I would borrow the keys from Mr Dixon and change the selection to more progressive bands like Pink Floyd, Family, Tyrannosaurus Rex, The Who and Steppenwolf. Interspersed with these were soul records by Arthur Conley, James Brown, Aretha Franklin and Sam & Dave, that people could dance to. Two local favourites were 'Mony Mony' by Tommy James & The Shondells, and 'Hot Smoke And Sassafras' by Mooch. It was obvious that young people loved this music, and the merits of a particular band were often intensely argued at The Bay.

During these discussions, a name kept cropping up. John Peel was a breath of fresh air, playing new and innovative music from both Britain and America. His broadcasts featured a multitude of groups like Jefferson Airplane, Quicksilver Messenger Service, Captain Beefheart, Frank Zappa, The Byrds, Buffalo Springfield, Pink Floyd, Family, Tyrannosaurus Rex, The Pretty Things, Soft Machine, and dozens of others. He seemed totally insulated from the normal commercial pressures which afflicted mainstream DJs, and his programmes *The Perfumed Garden* and *Top Gear*, had a spark and vibrancy about them which was both challenging and invigorating. Radical changes were taking place and Peel was fearlessly championing them. It's difficult to describe what it was like at the time, but it was all incredibly exciting. Matching this new music were a maze of 'underground' clubs which sprang up all around Britain in support of it. These were to become important breeding grounds for new groups, and without them, many major names of today might never have developed.

All these musical changes were accompanied by a major social upheaval which was sweeping the world. Young people's outlooks had changed. They now felt freer to express their individuality and assert their own viewpoints. There was an air of expectancy and excitement as the whole movement gathered pace, and I desperately wanted The Bay to be part of it.

Individuality in the way young people dressed was also becoming more prevalent as they railed against restrictions on what they could wear. Thus, one of the first tasks I achieved at The Bay was to get rid of the ridiculously outmoded dress restrictions. Those with long hair and jeans found it was no longer necessary to conform and were readily admitted.

Another liberating factor, which caught on immediately at The Bay, was somewhat daringly started by a guy named Ritchie Wooler. Whenever the right music came on, he would unashamedly leap onto the dance floor and begin dancing by himself. It was a remarkably brave step for those days as it was accepted protocol to dance only with a female partner, and to do otherwise at any other establishment would have meant instant removal from the dance floor, or even being asked to leave the building. Once other lads found it was permissible, it gave them the courage to do likewise, and soon the floor was heaving with both sexes, accompanied or not. While Emmeline Pankhurst and her ilk had fought bravely for female emancipation, in Ritchie Wooler, Sunderland had found its own dancing male equivalent.

As the music improved and a friendlier attitude prevailed, word about The Bay gained momentum and queues began to form nightly. In the main, these were sensible, intelligent people who were to become a vital part of the club's burgeoning success, and in their youthful days, future musicians, writers, actors, businessmen and lawyers were to attend regularly.

Despite all the changes taking place, Mr Dixon steadfastly maintained the £50 spending ceiling he had placed upon me. One day, I plucked up the courage and approached him with a proposal. "Why don't you let me hire the ballroom and I'll take the risk of putting the bands on?" I asked, half expecting to be refused or laughed at for my cheek.

He stared at me with a pained look on his face, adjusted his glasses, and thought for a few nerve-wracking moments. "If you're prepared to take the risk," he said, "then that's fine."

His response was to change my life forever.

Chapter 4

The following day, Mr Dixon called me into his office, and even before he spoke, I knew something was wrong.

"I'm very sorry, but there's a problem with this new arrangement," he began. "I've just found out that employees of Bass Breweries aren't allowed to hire the premises, so we'll have to call the whole thing off." I felt devastated. I was back to being a bouncer, before I'd even got started.

As I turned to walk away I got a flash of inspiration. What if two brothers who were old school friends of mine, joined me in a partnership? They could officially hire the venue while I remained in the background. Surely the brewery couldn't object to that. On putting this to Mr Dixon, he paused for thought, adjusting his glasses as I nervously awaited his answer. "I suppose that would be all right, providing they're trustworthy," he replied.

"They are, and I'll contact them immediately," I replied, heaving a huge sigh of relief. My hopes for achieving something positive at The Bay were revived and I was desperate to make it work. If there was even one dissenter or disgruntled customer, I was determined to address the problem, and put it right.

The brothers I had in mind were Dave and Billy Rogers, who, once I put it to them, eagerly took up my offer. We started by showcasing the best groups from the North East: Junco Partners (one of Newcastle's top bands), The Sect, This Year's Girl, and The Gas Board (featuring a young Bryan Ferry) being some of them. As our confidence grew, we began bringing groups up from Manchester and other areas, all the while steadily building up funds to spend on bigger names in the future.

During this era, differing youth factions often clashed, and at The Bay, we had our own occasional skirmishes. The bikers usually congregated in a separate side bar known as The Anchorage. One night, a bunch of mods, hell bent on revenge from an earlier incident, stealthily removed one of their machines parked outside, and wheeled it across the road, down onto the beach. After laying it at the water's edge, they watched with immense glee as the tide completely engulfed it. At the end of the night, the biker was aghast to find it missing, and after a lengthy and fruitless search, reported its absence to the police. Next morning they were able to reunite him with his sand encrusted machine. Later, some of the Bay's rockers were to appear as extras in The Who film *Tommy*, although I bet one of them never had salt on his chips for years!

As word of our successful promotions spread, it reached more dangerous ears, leading to an unwelcome confrontation. It started when a local villain, whose usual tools of trade were a long-handled toffee hammer and a cut-throat razor, approached me in a town centre bar. I recognised him immediately. Such was his reputation that whenever he entered local pubs, people, fearful for their own safety, usually drank up and left.

"Oh, it's the dance promoter. I hear you're doing really well over there," he sneered sarcastically. "I'll be over this Friday for my cut and make sure you have it ready."

"Don't bother, there'll be nothing for you," I replied.

"There'd better be, otherwise there'll be the sort of trouble you won't be able to handle," he said with more than a hint of menace.

"I'll be waiting, but it won't just be with my fists," I warned with as much conviction as I could muster.

He laughed, finished his drink, and turned towards me before leaving. "I'll see you on Friday, and don't forget to have the money ready."

After he'd gone, I reflected on his threats, knowing this could seriously undermine, and even ruin, everything we had worked towards. I drove over to see my two partners and informed them of this development. They were appalled and seemed unable to grasp that it was happening.

"This is all getting too serious for my liking," said one. "He carries a razor and is crazy enough to use it. We're not prepared to risk getting cut up. It's too dangerous so we're pulling out."

"Look, I'll handle him if he comes over," I reassured them.

"No thanks, what about if he sees us in town when you're not there? It'll be too late for you to do anything then."

Their reaction was a huge disappointment and all that I'd worked for seemed to be crumbling before my eyes. In a last act of defiance, I spoke out. "All right, if you don't want to carry on, I'll go it alone."

The partnership was over and again I faced an uncertain future. Meanwhile, Friday was looming and the problem of dealing with the local thug would soon be upon me. I'd heard of the Mafia and the Krays, as well as protection rackets run by gangsters, but here in Sunderland, it seemed inconceivable. I was determined to ensure he received nothing, unless it was over my dead body. Weighing up my options, I realised that going to the police would hold its own danger. At the time, The Bay was policed by the Jarrow Division which was over six miles away, and could take up to twenty minutes to arrive. By then, I knew it could be too late.

Nevertheless, I was young, fit, and determined not to be intimidated, especially by a wretched villain who earned his living from fear. Besides, The Bay was far too precious to give up. With the odd exception, the people coming to The Bay were wonderful, and the kindness shown to me by the management and staff made working there all the more enjoyable.

The fateful Friday finally arrived and while I must confess I've never been under any great illusions about my looks, a scar certainly wouldn't compliment them, especially the manner in which it was likely to be inflicted. Mindful of the Boy Scouts motto 'Be Prepared', I hid a small iron bar in my front hip pocket, obscured from view by my buttoned-up jacket. As the evening wore on, the staff seemed to sense my nervousness as I paced up and down in the foyer throughout the night, but to my amazement, the villain failed to show. After everyone left for the night I drove home with a certain degree of trepidation. Arriving home, and knowing he probably knew where I lived, I drove warily with the car headlights blazing, but there was no sign of him. With the iron bar resting on a chair beside the bed, I spent a restless night, tossing and turning at the slightest sound.

Chapter 4

Three days later, I bumped into the brute in the town centre. He shot me a menacing stare, before sidling over. Immaculately dressed, tall, sun-tanned, with a leathery looking face, he gave out an aura of affluence that somehow seemed to imply he was smarter than the rest of us. On other occasions, he wore a long black overcoat with a velvet collar, which led people to call him 'the undertaker'. Ironically, this added to people's fear of him, and he seemed to revel in his notoriety.

"I couldn't make it last week, but I heard you were very busy," he sneered. "I'll definitely be over this week so have the money ready."

"You're getting nothing," I said, throwing him a contemptuous look. "If you do come over, I have a nasty surprise waiting for you, and it's one that you won't like."

"What sort of surprise?" he asked, the confidence visibly draining from his face.

"You'll find out when you come over," I warned.

"Just be a good boy and have the money ready if you don't want to get badly hurt," he threatened as his trademark sneer reappeared.

With that, he climbed into his flash American car, tooted the horn, and stuck two fingers up at me. I was furious. This confrontation succeeded only in making make me even more determined that he received his comeuppance. After his show of bravado, one thing was certain. I couldn't have him walking around the town threatening me whenever it suited him. One way or another I wanted matters brought to a head, and the sooner the better.

Over the next few days, I sent out warnings of severe retribution should he decide to make an unexpected appearance. Now, as I waited, everything depended on him. Was he prepared to do battle, or was it all bluff? Either way, I was ready.

The following Friday duly came and with the iron bar safely nestling in its by now familiar position, I awaited his arrival. Once again, he failed to show. Nevertheless, I resolved to stay on my guard. To do anything else would have been symptomatic of complacency, and this was something Dad had always warned me against.

With the traumas of the previous few weeks behind me, and the threats of the thug having come to nothing, I booked Family for my first ever solo promotion on January 6, 1969. It was a nerve-wracking prospect. I earned just £2 a night, and their fee of £150, plus the hire of the hall, posters, and other costs, weighed heavily on my shoulders. As the days ticked by, everything, including my future at The Bay, depended on it.

As the pressure started to mount, I jogged along the beach each morning, or alternatively, little Tommy Clark would call for me and we'd kick a ball about. Tommy was a character in his own right with an ambition to become a professional footballer. He was small in stature and came from a large family. They were tough, and people knew not to mess with them. If you did, you invariably got hurt, and if you reappeared on their patch, the chances were you would receive a second dose. One morning Tommy sensed I wasn't my usual self and asked what was wrong. How could I burden him about my own private thoughts and troubles? There seemed so many as I began thinking about them.

What if not many people came, or that thug returned to spring a surprise? What if I lost all my savings in one night, or the group didn't turn up. Suddenly, the ball soared over my head into the water. "Geoff!" shouted Tommy. What did a plastic ball matter to me now, we could soon buy another one. "Geoff!" shouted Tommy again. I snapped out of my thoughts and ran for it. The tide was coming in and it swept the ball towards me as I came to a halt at the water's edge. Life seemed full of contradictions. I was worried about getting my feet wet, yet I might get my fingers burnt the following Friday.

"Get the ball Geoff," Tommy urged. The worries continued to pile up. Will these people like Family? Will they like me? Will Mr Dixon be pleased? Will I be unharmed come Saturday morning? I waded into the water and kicked the ball back to Tommy. He took it on his chest and allowed it to drop onto his knee before volleying it back towards me. I smiled as I realised the simple things are best. A beach, a ball, a good friend, and God's fresh air.

As I looked up at the sky again, a new surge of confidence flowed through me, suppressing all my self-doubts. Just before she died, Mother had told Dad that she'd be watching over us and if anyone harmed her babies she would see that they came to no good. Suddenly the thug no longer held any fears for me. It was as if divine intervention had taken over, and in an inkling everything had changed. Now I began looking forward to Friday and, somehow, I sensed hundreds of other people were too.

The night finally came, and after an anxious wait, I glanced out of a side window to see a long queue had formed, making it look as though the night was going to be a huge success. I thought of those nurses at the local hospital who had urged me to pack the job in. "You're crazy to stay there," they had berated me in their caring manner. If only I'd remembered to give them some complimentary passes, then they could have seen for themselves what I meant about working at The Bay. It wasn't just a job, but a way of life, which for me had rewards far in excess of anything I'd previously encountered.

I glanced outside again and noticed the queue had lengthened as the doors were opened to accommodate them. Soon, Family took to the stage where they received a rapturous reception from a packed audience. The band had recently released their first album, *Music In A Doll's House*, and they attacked their set with verve and confidence. Roger Chapman's unique voice, with its wonderful falsetto vibrato, was powerful, controlled and sustained. Looking around, The Bay was a hotbed of musical enthusiasts who sensed that something special was happening, and I wondered why I'd done all that needless worrying.

Family left the stage to wild applause, and people were coming up to thank me for bringing the group to Sunderland. What could I say? Really, it was me who should have been thanking them for coming. I'd never experienced this sort of gratitude before, and it was both rewarding and humbling. To this day, when younger people ask me to describe Family, it's rather difficult, but the people of the North East and myself owe them a huge debt of gratitude, because they were undoubtedly the catalysts who started everything that was to follow at The Bay.

That night, one audience member had especially good reason to thank me for booking Family. Debbie – tall, attractive, sexy, with her gorgeous figure and endless legs – preferred her men to be in a well-known group, and wasted no time in making this unashamedly obvious to Roger who was drinking at the bar upstairs. Young, slim and energetic, he was quiet and rather shy, but like any red-blooded male appreciated an attractive girl and off they went together. That fox stole from Maurice Velody's wasn't quite around Debbie's neck yet, but neither was her scarf.

Over the next few days, as I walked around town, people stopped me and eagerly asked who was coming next. The answer: Pink Floyd. Buoyed by the success of Family at The Bay, I went to London to meet Pink Floyd's management at their offices at 3 Hill Street, Mayfair, which made me think of all the games of Monopoly I'd played. The excitement I felt whenever anyone landed on my property was tiny compared to what I was feeling now.

As I walked up the richly carpeted stairs, there was a huge picture of John, Paul, George and Ringo on the landing. Since the death of Brian Epstein the previous August, his company NEMS had operated from the same building. Only a short while ago I was in lodgings, watching The Beatles on the telly. Now, as I continued up the stairs, the aura of their success seemed to permeate from every nook and cranny, and I began wondering if I might bump into them

Within thirty minutes I was on my way out of the building. The meeting had left me in a daze. Pink Floyd, the premier underground group in England, and one that John Peel had so assiduously championed, were coming to The Bay on February 17. Their fee was a huge increase on Family's but, more importantly, anyone who harboured doubts about the seriousness of my intentions would now surely be convinced. I sensed we were entering into a bigger and better league, and could no longer be ignored. I thought of my two friends back at Steel's factory operating their milling machines. They had done so much to help me settle in. If I went along and told them what was happening, they would surely have had me certified.

After arriving back in Sunderland I told everyone the news. Yes, I assured their ecstatic faces, Pink Floyd really are coming, and it will only be 7*s* 6*d* (37½p) to see them. I walked into The Bis-Bar to put up a poster and people stared incredulously. Sunderland was no longer a musical wilderness. This was one gig Debbie and her friend Sarah wouldn't have to go to London for.

Chapter 4

Meantime, as the Floyd's appearance was five weeks away, I needed a group to fill one of the spare dates. I was still in touch with Mick Grabham and one day I asked him if he'd seen any good bands lately. "There's one called Free," he told me. "They're pretty good, you should get them." Acting on his tip, I decided to take a chance and booked them for £35, never realising the repercussions it would have for me personally, or the music lovers of the North East.

Unfortunately, on January 13 – the night of their first appearance – the attendance was dismal, mainly because no one had heard of them, but as Mick had promised, Free turned out to be excellent and for a group so young, seemed to have everything; an electrifying stage presence, unique musicianship, and some great songs. Having seen their potential, I decided to book them again at the first opportunity with a group who could pull a crowd.

Chapter 5

"How did you get Pink Floyd?" Eddie Fenwick asked one day in The Bis-Bar. Eddie was a law unto himself and didn't live by any conventional rules. He had his own values and friends, but come to think of it, everyone was his friend. Eddie played guitar and composed songs which he sang to anyone prepared to listen. He was also first on anyone's party invitation list; his easy-going manner and love of music saw to that. There was a mystique about him which made it hard to rationalise how he managed to live. He seemed carefree, unhurried and laid-back. Never a smart dresser, fashion seemed to pass Eddie by, but he and another chum named Dave Stewart were determined to make it. They went to see emerging bands at every opportunity, and in many cases wondered how some of them had got as far as they had.

With Eddie, night merged into day and back into night. He didn't like clocks or schedules. They inhibited creativity he explained. His mind was constantly searching for a route into the upper echelons of the music business, having realised that from Sunderland, it wasn't easy. "Geoff, will you listen to a demo tape I've made?" he asked. You didn't say no to Eddie, he was too nice a guy to offend and, besides, his stuff was always interesting. Soon we were listening to his compositions which though promising, suffered from the poor sound quality. It was impossible not to admire Eddie's tenacity and determination. Yes, he was a character all right.

Dave was different. He'd been educated at The Bede, a local grammar school which had a long list of luminaries who'd become prominent in other spheres. Dave, in his wisdom, had decided that if he wanted to make it, London was the only place to be. Determined to find stardom, and an outlet for his talent, he made his way there. For him, entering into this friendless world was tough, and without money it could be a lonely place. He soon found it wasn't just a question of talent, it was knowing the right people. Important contacts never seemed to be in, or were always in a meeting when he called. It was soul destroying and as the rejection letters piled up, his frustration grew but he steadfastly soldiered on.

As the days neared to Pink Floyd's appearance I found myself in a state of quiet disbelief. Events had been moving at such a pace that I found it hard to come to terms with. I wandered into the empty ballroom and found myself daydreaming about the gig. I imagined the group playing to a packed ecstatic audience, transfixed by the sight of their heroes.

It's no apparition, Pink Floyd are really up there playing 'Interstellar Overdrive'. A hush falls over the crowd as they crane their necks; ears attuned to every note. The wonder of what is actually happening begins to sink in as I spot Debbie positioned stage-right so the group can't miss her. If they do, she won't miss them. A waiter comes running up with an anxious look on his face. "Geoff, there's still a massive queue outside, can we let any more in?" "Let me check," I answer. Within seconds I'm in the foyer which is jammed with pleading faces who are offering double the admission fee. A beautiful girl hugs and kisses me, pleading to be admitted. "Please let me in, I'll do anything if you do."

As I look down, her mini skirt is riding high, and is having the desired effect. It's a tempting dilemma. Should I weaken and tell her to go round to the side door and meet me there? I begin to wonder what's happening to me. England's biggest underground group is on stage, and I'm thinking about something else. I come to my senses, and compromise by letting another forty people in. The group are due on stage so I arrange to meet up with her afterwards, and hopefully, experience some 'free love'.

Suddenly, Mr Dixon's voice interrupted my daydreaming and jolted me back to reality. "Geoff, can you go into town and get some cloakroom tickets?"

I turn to look at him with a vacant expression and ask him to repeat what he has just said.

"Are you all right?" he asked worriedly.

"Yes, everything's fine," I assure him.

Arriving in the town centre, I enter the shop to find the girl assistant is wearing a pink jumper. The ten rolls of tickets I buy have some pink ones among them. Her lipstick is pink, and her fingernails are pink. I've heard of colour co-ordination, but this is ridiculous. I'm beginning to wish the group were named Blue Floyd, or Black Floyd. But hang on a minute, that would be silly, people might think they're a soul group. I leave and wander into Atkinson's record shop to check out the new releases, when suddenly, Eddie Floyd's 'Knock On Wood' comes on the turntable. Just then, I begin to wonder if there is to be no escape from this name, it seems to be everywhere. Pink Floyd, it's a clever name. No one ever forgets it because it sticks in the mind. Maybe I should be grateful they're called that, everyone else seems to be. On the drive back, I pull up at the lights. Red, red & amber, green. There's no pink and I'm disappointed. I must ring the council and tell them Pink Floyd are coming. They're a big enough name to change the lights for. Don't they know I nearly met The Beatles when I booked them? 'See Emily Play'. We had it on the jukebox and people used to dance really weird to it. Now, they'll be able to hear the song live.

The phone rang yet again. "Is it true Pink Floyd are playing there?" a voice asks.

"Yes," I reply enthusiastically.

"How much is it?"

"It's 7s 6d"(37½p).

"Only 7s 6d, are you sure?!"

"Positive."

"But how come it's so cheap?" they would ask in disbelieving tones.

It must be explained that what the people didn't realise was that I had a huge advantage over other clubs because I was a one-man operation with negligible overheads. There was no secretary to pay, no phone bills (the manager allowed me to use The Bay's phone), no ticket percentages to box offices, no DJ (only a jukebox), and I was one of the doormen as well as the promoter. The other important factor was that it was my own money and, being single, I could freely risk losing it without any recriminations if things went badly wrong.

On February 17, 1969, the weather was atrocious, with snow and blizzards raging with such fierce intensity, people were being warned to keep off the roads. Inside, The Bay was warm and comforting, shielded from the merciless savagery of the North East winds whose icy blasts were biting into everything with unrelenting harshness.

"Weather's not very good, is it?" Mr Dixon amiably reminded me as we bumped into each other.

"No, it isn't," I replied.

"I don't think you can expect many people tonight when it's like this," he continued.

"I know, it's typical isn't it? Just when everything seems to be going really well, weather like this happens."

"Well, that's the risk you take," he replied knowingly.

I retreated into the bar. Did he have to tell me something which was patently obvious? Still the weather wasn't Mr Dixon's fault, and I decided to seek him out and redress any touchy impression I might have created.

"Anything you need doing?" I cheerily asked.

"Actually there is," he replied. "Can you clear the snow away from the front and sides of the hotel? I don't want people slipping when they come in." My heart sank as I wished I'd kept my big mouth shut. Snow clearing in this weather wasn't something I'd envisaged on such an important day. Nevertheless, promoting Pink Floyd and still being given this unenviable task was one way of keeping my feet on the ground.

After an anxious few hours, evening finally came. Word had reached me that Pink Floyd had safely arrived and were booked into a local hotel, relieving me of one major worry. Just then I spotted an Economic single-decker bus pulling up and, to my astonishment, out stepped hordes of people. Cars were continually skidding into the car park, while local Corporation double-decker buses were regularly disgorging people at the nearby Seaburn

Camp terminus. On arriving, people were stamping their feet in the foyer to shake off the snow with a half-apologetic look on their faces as it scattered beneath their feet. I gave them a warm and welcoming smile, having realised it was the very least they deserved for making the effort in such atrocious conditions.

Over the next hour, the crowd continued to build up, and The Bay was packed to capacity when the Floyd finally stepped on stage to a wonderful reception. Dave Gilmour, Rick Wright, Roger Waters and Nick Mason then began their musical journey and tracks like 'Set The Controls For The Heart Of The Sun', 'Careful With That Axe Eugene', 'Astronomy Domine' and 'Interstellar Overdrive' magically unfolded before us. When it was finally over, everyone seemed becalmed and reflective before suddenly breaking into ceaseless applause. For those who were present, Pink Floyd were a musical and spiritually uplifting experience, while consolidating their position as the premier underground group.

Years later, I heard a touching story about that night. Four of the regulars who came to The Bay – Val Clark, her sister Norma, Sandra Brown and Hilary Watson, who we nicknamed the four 'freakers' – were outside in the car park waiting for their parents to pick them up, when they heard music coming from a van. To their astonishment, they discovered it was Pink Floyd playing acoustic woodwind instruments, accompanied by a guitar. As they edged nearer, they were greeted warmly and allowed to listen. A small tape deck was recording everything, and the group later played it back for the benefit of this small bunch of devoted followers.

Earlier that evening, I spotted Debbie and drummer Nick Mason heading towards the dressing room. She never did waste any time and, on seeing me, smiled.

"You don't mind me being here, do you, Geoff?" she asked politely.

"Of course not," I replied.

Her friend Sarah was at the bar and looked a little bewildered. The rest of the group were in the dressing room and I knew she wanted to be with them. I considered inviting her in but thought better of it. Debbie and Nick Mason were together and I left them to enjoy a passionate farewell. Sarah jumped into my car, and later into my bed.

Pink Floyd told me how much they had enjoyed the gig, and promised to come back and play again. Eight months later, they were to be as good as their word.

"What were Pink Floyd like?" somebody asked me the next day. I kept myself in check realising that, being the promoter, it would be imprudent to say "great", because they may have thought I wasn't being impartial. However, my enthusiasm overrode all sense of diplomacy, casting it wantonly aside in a mad rush of excitement.

"Great," I unhesitatingly replied as I spotted a passing stranger with a dole card protruding from his pocket. It was yellow, the same colour as the one I had previously possessed.

"Floyd were excellent last night," he enthused.

"Thanks," I answered quietly, wanting to hug him.

How the hell can anybody call this work? I wondered. If somebody asked me what I did for a living, how would I answer them? Stocking bars, changing light bulbs and records, booking groups, shovelling snow, and fighting, none of it a recognised trade. Whatever it was, I didn't want it to stop. It felt too exciting.

Although peace and love were the bywords of the era, it seemed there were still some individuals who were ignorant of its ideals. Around this time, I had been receiving reports about an individual who was continually causing trouble at The Bay, and attacking people for no apparent reason. Unfortunately, whenever I arrived to investigate, the assailant had always mysteriously disappeared into the crowd. The one factor which always remained constant was his description. It was frustrating because whenever I confronted him, he vehemently protested his innocence. On each occasion this occurred, he had a shifty look about him and I was convinced he was lying, but I needed definite proof. Sooner or later, I knew we would inevitably clash and I didn't have long to wait.

One night a girl came running towards me at the top of the ballroom, screaming hysterically and in floods of tears. "Someone has just attacked my boyfriend," she sobbed.

"Will you point him out to me?" I asked urgently.

"Yes, but be careful," she answered, "he's dangerous." After dispatching a waiter to attend to her boyfriend, I followed her down through the ballroom. "That's him," she screamed, pointing at my prime suspect. Previously, I'd always given him the benefit of the doubt, but this time it was different.

"You've just hit someone," I asserted.

"It wasn't me," he protested strongly.

"Yes, it was," I angrily replied. "I have a witness who saw you and I want you out of here now."

He glared at me with a hint of menace, before turning and walking towards the exit. While slowly threading our way out through the crowded ballroom, he appeared calm and I was relieved he was leaving quietly and without fuss. Then, as we reached the top of the ballroom exit, without the slightest warning, he spun round, pushed himself off the door stanchion, and struck me with a vicious, full-blooded head butt.

I'd been caught napping and I immediately went down from the severity of its impact. The last occasion I'd hit the deck quite so hard had been during a football match in the local football league. A team from Chester-le-Street had a huge centre-half who was notorious for kicking anything above grass. During one match, he caught me with a bruising tackle. Fortunately, mud is soft and yields to the contours of the body, as well as helping to absorb the shock. Nevertheless, while lying there in agony, you begin to wonder if you'll ever walk again as the referee blows his whistle for a foul. Unfortunately, in the ballroom that night, there was no sign of a referee.

The crowd, fearful for their own safety, surged back. Luckily, by the time I hit the floor, my head had cleared. I instinctively locked an arm tightly around his legs to prevent him from kicking me and, in an instant, I was up on my feet, sending out retaliatory blows in a savage backlash of fury. Surprisingly for someone of his reputation, he began back-pedalling, and I could tell the speed and ferocity of my attack was becoming a telling factor. I continued to rain blow after blow upon him, driving him trapped and defenceless into a corner. Ever since he'd struck that first blow, it had been mostly one-way traffic. Momentarily, he dropped his guard in the mistaken belief that the fight was over and cautiously peeped out. It was an error of judgement that was to cost him dear.

His pain stricken and tormented face now looked as big as a white dinner plate. It was the clear-cut opening I'd been waiting for. In a split second I sent a crushing right into his face. Blood came gushing out of his nose as his head rocked back and thudded against the wall. Suddenly, he doubled up and made a mad dash for the door, before running out into the car park like a scared animal. He was barred for life, while The Bay was all the better for his absence. Justice had prevailed and I felt vindicated. Unfortunately, this brute continued to create further havoc around town, and was subsequently convicted twice in the courts for GBH.

Thinking about this fight, reminded me of when Dad used to take us to the boxing booths. If it had been a hard fought contest, people would toss coins into the ring as a sign of their appreciation. Occasionally, there would be a jingling noise as one coin hit another, and the boxers subconsciously knew they would be sharing in the spoils later.

This flashed back to me seconds after the fight as I heard a jingle and momentarily glanced at the floor. Realising there was nothing there, I turned to see it was Mr Dixon with the hotel keys in his hand.

"C'mon Geoff, I'll take you into the office so you can get cleaned up."

Later, when he'd paid me, I stared at the two pound notes before pocketing them.

"Anything wrong?" he asked.

"No, nothing at all, but next time I'm in trouble, don't jingle your keys, it makes me think I'm getting more money!" I replied half-jokingly.

Next morning, I looked into the mirror and saw it had been a hard won victory. My two front teeth were loose, my top lip was badly swollen, and there was bruising to the side of my face. It wasn't a pretty sight and the whole town seemed to be talking about the confrontation. I'd never realised the depth of feeling against this miscreant, and how delighted people were that he'd been taught a salutary lesson. Later, I had to relive the fight with Dad who was extremely disappointed that I'd been caught napping. "I told you not to trust anybody," he reminded me. He was right, and I wouldn't in future. A week went by, the teeth re-tightened, the swelling went down, and girls were beginning to smile at me again. Life was back to normal.

The Bay was now open seven nights a week, and I strove to make it even better. As a schoolboy, I often went to a local cinema where an advert for local butcher, Austin E Brown, always caught my eye. Its closing words were, 'Service, Civility and Satisfaction Always Guaranteed', and I never forgot them. We had a great team, including waiters Frankie Donaldson, Billy Stevens, Tommy Trotter and little Harry, not forgetting Davy Moss the trainee chef, and all were on hand if ever I got into any physical danger.

Despite the availability of late transport home, the unique situation of The Bay meant that in the summer, many people just strolled out onto the darkened beach to hold parties. Fires were usually lit to keep warm but, unfortunately, the authoritarian stance of the local police, who often came along and extinguished them before ordering everyone home, remained a bitter source of consternation to the young.

These weren't the only fires being lit. It seemed that couples everywhere were basking in the sexual revolution sweeping the world. Just to illustrate this point, some years earlier a club named The Blue Note had opened in Sunderland, and the owner Ray Grehan had installed a condom machine in the toilets. Inevitably, there was a huge public outcry as parents instigated a campaign to have it removed. "It's immoral and encouraging our children to be promiscuous," they protested. Letters started appearing in the local press and eventually, it was forced to close. On the last night, DJ John Harker freely distributed the remaining condoms, causing an even bigger uproar. Nowadays, you could argue Ray was a visionary who was way ahead of his time, as society now actively encourages their use. Sadly, he's no longer with us, but his pioneering contribution to safe sex is still remembered.

Then of course there was Debbie. There were other groupies

but they didn't have her class. Whenever she climbed into a group's van, her deportment and style were obvious. The local lads looked on enviously but they weren't stars, not in Debbie's eyes anyway. Then there were the girls who I classed as BTOs (been there occasionally). They often tagged along with the groups and it was all part of the scene. I occasionally spoke to the night porter at the nearby Roker Hotel. He knew the regulars and sometimes saw them sneaking out in the early morning. Inwardly, this made me smile. So that sweet little girl who innocently parades around town as though butter wouldn't melt in her mouth is just as vulnerable as the rest of us. Still, who cares as long as she's enjoying herself? My lips were sealed and the music continued, even if it was in someone else's bedroom.

Chapter 6

Like others around the world, Sunderland's youth were searching for a more fulfilling and adventurous way of life. Two prime examples were Dicky Robson, who lived on a council estate with his parents, and Chas McIver. To describe Dicky as a music fanatic would be an understatement. Bob Dylan was his hero and I remember him eagerly making plans to see Dylan at the 1969 Isle of Wight festival. Like Dylan, Dicky had an impeccable way with words and was never afraid to use them. Conversations were always stimulating and, for one so young, he was very aware. 'Bourgeois', 'egalitarian', and 'proletariat' were just three of the words he often threw into conversations. I respected his views and eagerly looked forward to our chats, especially about music.

Chas was perceptive and had an almost encyclopaedic knowledge of blues, soul and jazz. He often travelled down to London, and ended up working in Dobell's, the specialist jazz record shop in Charing Cross Road, for a number of years. To his great delight, he was able to meet many of the world's foremost blues and jazz greats, who often popped in to the store. An added bonus was being made an honorary member of Ronnie Scott's Jazz Club in Soho, which was to become his second home. Speaking to him on the subject of music was always an educational experience because of his natural enthusiasm for the subject. Amos Milburn, Otis Spann and Meade Lux Lewis were just three of the incredible keyboard players he enthused about, while Otis Rush, B.B. King, Freddie King, Buddy Guy, Albert King, Muddy Waters, and dozens of others peppered his conversations.

The Bis-Bar and The Bay were Sunderland's equivalent of New York's Greenwich Village. Wander in on your own and you were bound to meet someone interesting. Among those was a young teacher from Ryhope Richardson School named Malcolm Gerrie.

He first made his mark locally by producing a school production of *Tommy* in 1974. Later, he became a producer at Tyne Tees Television and, in 1982, Malcolm launched the national rock programme *The Tube*. Malcolm gave one of his ex-pupils Chris Cowey a break at Tyne Tees and Chris has now gone on to become a success in television in his own right, and is currently executive producer of *Top Of The Pops*.

Things were going extremely well as I continued to promote gigs on a weekly basis. I decided it would be a great idea to bring John Peel to The Bay, and after booking him to appear on March 3, I drove to Newcastle Central railway station to pick him up. I found he was very friendly and I was pleasantly surprised at how ordinary he was. At The Bay that night, people were delighted to meet him, and it was wonderful to have him mingle among us. The two bands playing that night he visited were Van Der Graaf Generator and Black Sabbath who, as far as I can recall, gave no real indication of just how big they were to eventually become. John took a liking to The Bay and mentioned it on his *Top Gear* programme on a number of occasions. I was thrilled as it was another important step in establishing us nationally.

Time and again, people ask me what was my all-time favourite Bay gig. Choosing from a whole array of excellence is difficult, but it was undoubtedly the night of March 24, 1969, when American West Coast group Country Joe & The Fish appeared. It was their only appearance north of Manchester, and this made it all the more special. As an added bonus, a receptive audience were rewarded with a gig that can only be described as superb. Country Joe McDonald, Barry Melton, David Cohen, Bruce Barthol and Gary 'Chicken' Hirsh incorporated between them all that was good about music at the time, and how lucky we were to have seen them in such an excellent setting.

Just before they were due on stage, a waiter came running towards me with a panic-stricken look on his face.

"Geoff, one of the band is smoking a joint in the bar. Isn't he aware that you can be arrested in England for being in possession of even the smallest amount of cannabis?"

"Thanks," I replied before hurrying off to investigate.

There was Country Joe in the bar, nonchalantly smoking a fat joint, seemingly oblivious to the pungent smell filling the room. I looked around and could see the older locals were bewildered, while others were downright shocked.

"Excuse me," I began, not knowing which name to address him by. "Do you mind going to the dressing room to smoke that?" He leaned back and without replying, looked at me rather scornfully.

"I'm sorry but smoking cannabis isn't allowed in England," I continued in a conciliatory tone.

"Who are you?" he asked bemusedly.

"I'm the promoter," I confirmed.

He paused and held the joint up for inspection as if checking whether it was worth throwing away. It wasn't. A puzzled look crossed his face and he smiled while people watched in amazement.

"Are you serious, man?" he asked disbelievingly.

"Yes, I really mean it," I replied nervously.

To my great relief, he slid off the barstool and began making his way back to the dressing room, while I followed close behind.

Once inside, he told the rest of the group what had just happened.

"Hey, this guy says we can't smoke." The others in the band stared at me in amazement as I stood there feeling sheepish.

"I didn't say you couldn't," I meekly replied in an effort to justify myself. "It's just that I'm asking you not to smoke it outside the dressing room because it's against the law."

A look of relief crossed their faces as they realised I was "with it".

"Hey man, are you going to join us?" one of them asked.

"No thanks," I replied. "I just get high on the music."

A short while later, they left to begin their set in an induced state of euphoria. I quickly flushed away the roaches, before hurrying into the gig. As I looked out, people at the front and centre of the ballroom were sitting on the floor, while others stood on the outside and at the back of the hall. It was an amazing sight, which gave a bowl effect, and with no obtrusive or ungainly pillars, supporting beams, or mixing desks to block the view, everyone was able to see in absolute comfort. 'Colours For Susan', ' Thought Dream', 'Here I Go Again', 'Doctor Of Electricity', 'Superbird', 'Eastern Jam',

'Section 43' and, of course, the Fish's classic anti-Vietnam War anthem, 'I Feel Like I'm Fixing To Die Rag', were all delivered.

Overwhelmed by his warm reception, Joe urged the crowd on. "Give me an F, give me a U, give me a C give me a K. What's that spell? What's that spell? What's that spell?" Everyone knew the answer, of course, but were rather reluctant to respond because in 1969, obscenities in public were frowned upon. A silence fell over the crowd as Country Joe berated them.

"What's the matter, don't you f**k in England?" he asked. Someone in the crowd screamed out "Yes," to which, everyone immediately followed. Without question, that night was magical. As they listened, the crowd responded to the warmth and camaraderie that was hitting them like a shock tidal wave, visibly washing away the last remnants of retarded pop. Later, everyone agreed that Country Joe and his band had been a revelation, both in their attitude and playing ability. No single member had tried to outplay the other, and it was a lesson for all the local groups present on how to play in complete empathy with each other. It was undoubtedly the best gig I promoted. Afterwards in the bar, Country Joe was drinking a bottle of Newcastle Brown Ale, and commented to Joe Jopling, a friend of mine, "Man, this is better than acid!" Surely there's no compliment higher for the local brew, and what's more, it's legal.

Now we'd seen one of America's premier West Coast bands, I began to realise that anything was possible. People from all over the North East of England were coming on a regular basis, and I felt a great responsibility towards them, while they in turn helped contribute by recommending groups they'd seen or heard. Behind the scenes, everyone was working hard, and it was after the Country Joe gig, that I sensed that The Bay staff, or should I say friends, suddenly realised how enjoyable the whole enterprise had become.

On Saturdays, I usually visited a small health food shop in Moran Street, Fulwell, run by a Mrs Walker who was about sixty. One day, as I walked in, she greeted me enthusiastically with a huge smile. "Geoff, John Peel's just mentioned your name on the radio." I smiled as I'd already heard his *Top Gear* show on my car radio and felt sure he would have been highly delighted to know that his music was reaching older and more discerning ears.

As each week passed, I was determined to make The Bay better in every way. In my school days, we occasionally went on cultural trips in luxury coaches with deep sumptuous seats, lumbar supports and headrests. In the winter, the buses were warm, had large panoramic windows for a perfect view, and were faster and quieter than the noisy Corporation buses we usually travelled in.

While doing an excellent job in getting people home, the Corporation buses I had originally hired for late transport were cold and draughty, and were no match for those luxury coaches. I realised it would be more comfortable if people could travel home in warmth and comfort. After weighing up the cost, I decided to switch to them and make it free to travel on them. The following week, I asked a girl what she thought about the new transport.

"Well Geoff, they're very nice, but when we got in, they were freezing," she replied.

The following week I arranged to pay each driver an extra ten shillings if they would go out twenty minutes earlier, start their engines, and warm the buses up. This proved instantly successful as people could now come out of a warm ballroom, step straight into a warm coach, and travel home in style, absolutely free. A pleasant side effect to this was that worried parents were now prepared to let their daughters stay out late, knowing they were safe, and had reliable transport home.

Another irritating task at the end of a night is a long and tedious cloakroom queue. To eliminate this often overlooked problem, I asked Mr Dixon to put on extra cloakroom staff in order to reduce waiting time, to which he readily agreed. I'm sure it helped many couples to start some lasting liaisons. It was also instrumental in helping the buses to get away quicker; after all, a boy's wilting ardour can only be sustained for so long.

Chapter 7

The next band I set my sights on was Led Zeppelin who were booked to appear on April 17, 1969 for £75. Having received a signed contract from their manager Peter Grant, everything seemed fine and I settled back to await their appearance.

However, in between booking them and the date they were due to play, some amazing things happened. Their first album rocketed into the American charts at number 10, while it also entered the British chart at number six, and stayed in the Top 20 for 79 weeks. All their gigs were selling out with the crowds outside London's Marquee bringing traffic to a virtual standstill.

At The Bay, everybody was incredibly excited about their impending visit, and I could hardly believe my good fortune at booking a group for only £75 that was rapidly becoming world famous. As the day of their appearance grew closer, my mind was in a whirl. Surely, it couldn't get any better than this and, in all honesty, I was absolutely delighted at having had the foresight to book them.

In The Bis-Bar, I bumped into Chas McIver.

"How do you feel about getting Led Zeppelin? Jimmy Page is a great guitarist, you know."

When Chas said something like this, you had to listen, because he knew his stuff.

"I just hope they live up to people's expectations because I've never known anything like it," I replied.

"Don't worry Geoff," Chas said reassuringly. "They haven't built up this reputation for nothing, I bet they're superb."

I relaxed a little at this vote of confidence and decided to tell him about my new appointment. "I've just started a new lad who helped me out in a scrap on the stairs at The Bay. I was in a bit of trouble with three guys while trying to get them out, and he stepped straight in. There wasn't an ounce of fear in him, and I was very impressed. He hit one lad and that was it. They didn't want to know after that, and went out like lambs. I offered him a job on the spot, even though he's only nineteen. He's coming in for Zeppelin because goodness knows how many people will turn up," I added.

"What's his name?" asked Chas.

"John Tansey. I've heard he can fight for fun."

A worried frown crossed Chas's face.

"But is he diplomatic, Geoff? I know you've had your fair share of bother in the past but you don't want to go to the other extreme and put someone on who can't think for himself," he added cautiously.

"Oh no, I've met him a few times since then. He's rather quiet actually till he's roused, but God help anyone who does upset him."

"Well, I'll be there Geoff, a good guitar player always makes me get off my butt. Anyway, I must go, I'll see you at the gig."

Just a few days before Led Zeppelin were due to appear, I received a phone call, and in a flash everything changed.

"It's Peter Grant, the manager of Led Zeppelin here. I'm just ringing to let you know they won't be coming," he coolly informed me.

"Why not?" I asked in shocked disbelief.

"Because they're going to the States the day after your gig," he answered.

"But I have a signed contract from you for them to play here next week," I reminded him.

"Well, I'm just letting you know they won't be there," he said, without the slightest sign of remorse or sympathy.

"In that case I'll sue you for breach of contract," I replied angrily.

I'll always remember his exact words.

"Well that's your prerogative, but I'm just telling you they won't be there."

Before I could speak again, the phone went dead.

I was in a daze, but was determined that come what may, I

wasn't going to be treated as shabbily as this and decided to pursue the matter with all the energy and single-mindedness that I could muster. I'd heard Peter Grant was big with a frightening reputation, but he was about to experience the resolve of someone determined to seek justice. He owed us a date, and that was all that mattered.

The news of the cancellation rapidly spread around town and I felt inadequate. Everywhere I went, people seemed disappointed. Even the waiters, who were normally my staunchest allies, seemed to have lost faith in me. There was no escape, Led Zeppelin were everywhere, and I felt like tearing up every magazine that mentioned them.

As soon as anyone started a sentence with "Never mind, Geoff," I knew what was coming. Sympathy and solace were useless, as I felt both helpless and powerless at the same time. "Did you have a signed contract on them Geoff?" became another much dreaded question which made me wince at the sheer ineptitude of the enquirer. If anyone asks me that again, I thought, I'll scream until the police or social workers take me away.

A few mornings later, I took a walk along the cliff-tops which stretched along the North East coast, breathing in the invigorating sea air. Once again, I thought of my dad. He'd always been there in the past when my brothers and I were in trouble, but this was trouble of a different sort. "You're a man for yourself now son, you've got to stand on your own two feet," was his advice to a question I once asked. He was right. I'd have to see this through on my own, despite the problem being 300 miles away.

Suddenly, I realised I needed The Bay more than ever. We'd come a long way together and still had a long way to go. As I turned and started walking back, the clouds parted and the sky became clearer. I looked towards the horizon and my mind was made up. The enthusiasm was back, the adrenalin was flowing, and the spark was re-ignited.

Standing in the foyer one night I was distracted by a pair of shapely legs making their way down the stairs. I swivelled to take in the rest and held my breath in anticipation of what might follow. I didn't have long to wait. Their owner was wearing a white woollen crocheted mini dress that left little to the imagination, had long shoulder length dark hair and a friendly smile. Her name was Dot Fisher, and she lived locally. As her visits became regular, I got to know her better, and found that although she was quiet and rather shy, she had an endearing personality to which people took an instant liking. Music seemed to be her only love, but I quickly set out to alter that.

Within a few weeks, I offered her the cashier's job in reception and soon, we were working together. By nature, I'm shy around women, so in my efforts to become better acquainted, I began by cautiously giving her a lift home. Before long, I was taking her to other gigs, which she seemed to enjoy tremendously; John Mayall's Bluesbreakers at Newcastle's Club-A-Go-Go was the first.

On other occasions Dot, who was the epitome of peace and love, would wear long hippie dresses, and regulars soon looked for her joyous face upon entering The Bay. With her softly spoken voice and patient manner, the effect she had can only be described as magnetic. Just by having her there, The Bay had gone up another notch and she soon became an important part of our extended family.

Apart from Led Zeppelin, there was still one group everyone wanted to see. "What about The Who, Geoff?" It was a question I was to hear many times. Unfortunately, our capacity was 800, or maybe 1,000 people at a real push, and the group had by now become massive. I mean, The Who in a small seafront hotel in Sunderland. Were these people aware that the group already had a dozen hit singles and three charting albums in Britain alone, and were about to undertake another successful tour of America?!

"They'll never come here now, they're too big," chided a good-natured friend of mine. I sensed that just talking about The Who made people's faces light up. "Why?" a younger reader may ask? I can only answer by saying The Who combined imagination, rock theatre, and excellent songs, together with a stage presence which was positively riveting.

By now, people from London were constantly ringing up and offering me bands. While gratifying, it was frustrating not being offered the group everyone was desperate to see. The name kept cropping up, and it was driving me crazy. Finally, I decided to risk being ridiculed, and started to make discreet enquiries about their availability.

Having set my course, I pursued them with unrelenting vigour, but seemed to be constantly led up blind alleys. Dad's words echoed around in my head. "Remember son, if you really want something, never give up." For The Who I was prepared to mortgage my whole future and get a loan from the bank, if only they would come.

After weeks of intensive phone calls, I had a tip-off that the group were playing in Scotland and had a free date the following day on April 28. It was a heaven sent opportunity and one The Bay couldn't afford to miss. I walked into the office and looked nervously at the phone. This was the big one and, if they said no, in all probability it could be the last chance The Bay would have of getting them.

With mixed emotions, I picked up the phone to contact their manager. As I dialled, my mind shuddered at the thought of what his reaction might be.

"You've got a real nerve, haven't you? How many did you say it holds? 800? For heaven's sake, we've nearly got that many road-crew. Anyway, how did you get my number? Look, I'll send you their new album, *Tommy*, just play that instead, and don't ever bother ringing me again."

"We've already had Pink Floyd."

"Pink Floyd, they're not a rock group. Are you sure you know what you're doing? It seems to me you're out of your depth."

My desperate thoughts were interrupted when someone picked up the receiver. I paused momentarily before speaking. "Hello, is that Pete Rudge, the manager of The Who?" (Kit Lambert and Chris Stamp were the actual managers of the group, but during this time, Pete Rudge, who now manages Pulp, Madness, and James, worked at Track Records and co-ordinated The Who's dates.)

"Yes, it is. What can I do for you?"

I took a deep breath. "I'm Geoff Docherty from Sunderland, and I'd like to book The Who."

"Where at?" he asked pointedly.

"At The Bay Hotel in Sunderland. I've heard they are playing in Scotland and are free the next day."

"Yes, they are," he replied.

"Couldn't they call in on their way back to London and play for us? After all, we're just a few miles down the road from the A1, and they'll get a fantastic welcome," I promised.

"As it happens, I've heard about The Bay Hotel. They say it's a good place to play," he enthused.

My heart was pounding as I continued to press the point home.

"We'd all love them to come and play for us here at The Bay, do you think that's possible?"

"How many does it hold?" he asked.

"About a thousand," I replied, realising I had to get the capacity up as much as I dared. There was silence for a few agonising moments while he considered his answer.

"I don't see why not," he replied. At that moment I looked around and spotted the office safe. Would it hold enough to pay for The Who? But what did I care. I was ecstatic and could have kissed him. Within minutes we had tied up the details and The Who were finally coming. It's impossible to describe the exhilaration I felt at that moment. It seemed like passing my driving test, running a four-minute mile, being given a degree, and having Brigitte Bardot say she fancied me, all at the same time.

I put the phone down and walked out of the office into the empty ballroom, still reeling with shock. All I wanted to do was run into The Bis-Bar in some demented manner and shout "The Who are coming! The Who are coming!" over and over again. Two days after the advert in *The Sunderland Echo* appeared, the phone never stopped ringing and I knew The Bay had finally made it nationally. Pink Floyd, Country Joe, and now The Who, all within a few short months.

We'd played The Who's singles on the jukebox, and their latest, 'Pinball Wizard', was steadily climbing the charts. It seemed the whole country wanted The Who and they were coming to our little ballroom. Dad had said, "If you try and do what's right, right will come your way." He'd never spoken a truer word, but he never said it would be this exciting.

Chapter 7

Soon the great night – April 28, 1969 – arrived just as 'Pinball Wizard' reached number four. The days leading up to it had been mayhem with the telephones red hot with incessant calls pleading for tickets. One fan even travelled down from Edinburgh while a local police inspector rang and asked if I could make sure his daughter got in.

The whole town was excited and I could sense it. People in cars were hooting their horns and waving at me. As I walked around, my father's words were ringing in my ears. "Never get big-headed, son." But there was nothing to be big-headed about. I knew I was only the same as the people who were coming because I'd been brought up to realise that everyone is equal. Some may be more talented than others, but with The Who maybe I'd make an exception and concede that they were more equal than the rest of us mere mortals.

Finally, the waiting was over. As I was stocking the bars, a car load of girl students arrived and approached me.

"Are you Geoff Docherty?" asked one.

"Yes," I answered.

"We're from Newcastle University and want to make sure we get in tonight. Are there any tickets on sale?"

"No, there isn't. It's pay at the door," I answered. When their faces immediately clouded over, I assured them that if they came to the door later, I'd make sure they got in.

It was early afternoon and in an effort to relieve the nerves I was feeling, I moved upstairs to The Lighthouse Bar and began staring out of the window for any sign of the group arriving. As the clock ticked away, I cursed every passing vehicle and prayed that one of them would stop and turn into the car park. Where the hell are they? I wondered. The phone continued to ring non-stop, and every call had to be answered. After all, it could be The Who saying they couldn't make it. If they didn't, what would I do? This was no ordinary gig, it was rock royalty coming to town, and their non-appearance would be a major catastrophe.

I wandered over to the jukebox and fed in some money as 'Pinball Wizard' blared out of the speakers and reverberated around the empty room. "That deaf, dumb and blind boy, sure plays a mean pinball." Suddenly, a van swung into the car park and came to a halt. I jumped up and with my heart beating excitedly, raced down the stairs. and out into the car park. A small chap jumped out and approached me.

"Where do we put the gear?" he enquired.

"I'll show you," I answered eagerly. "What about the group, when are they coming?"

"They're on the way, they shouldn't be too long," he assured me. His name I subsequently learnt was Bob Pridden, The Who's roadie and trusted confidant who had been with them since 1966. He was as good as his word and a few hours later the group members arrived and were encamped in the dressing room while the packed ballroom was buzzing with expectation. Hoggy arrived breathlessly in the foyer.

"Are they here?" he asked excitedly, as if half expecting to be told they weren't coming.

"They're here, all right," I replied with a sigh of relief. "Come on, I'll take you into the dressing room to meet them."

His face lit up. Free admission, going to the dressing room to meet his favourite group, and then seeing them play. What more could he wish for? As we entered the dressing room, Pete Townshend was busy tuning his guitar, and looked up as I introduced my friend. He shook hands and smiled before turning his attention back to his instrument. Keith Moon, John Entwistle and Roger Daltrey seemed more relaxed and friendly, while Hoggy and I continued staring at them through disbelieving eyes. Not wishing to intrude, we made our excuses and rejoined the packed and expectant crowd. The Who were about to hit the stage and everyone's excitement had by now reached fever pitch.

Finally, the group ran on stage to a tumultuous welcome, and what a night it turned out to be. 'Substitute', 'Pinball Wizard', 'Magic Bus', 'My Generation'. The songs were driven along at a mind-blowing and unrelenting pace that was awe-inspiring. At the front, there were no barriers or 'heavies', which was to become all too prevalent in later years. That night, people were so close, they could reach out and touch the group without fear of being rebuked. At the side of the stage, Bob Pridden stood calm and alert should anything break down. He needn't have worried because it didn't, not until the group's self-inflicted finale. Eddie

Cochran's 'Summertime Blues' was the chosen song and its finale was followed by Pete Townshend smashing his guitar to smithereens like some deranged maniac who had just escaped from the local asylum.

His adrenalin seemed to be gushing in spurts of unrestricted ferocity, which was exhilarating and even a little frightening to witness. None of us had ever expected anything as spectacular as this. Never one to be outdone, Keith Moon contemptuously pushed and kicked his drums, scattering them everywhere with carefree abandon before stepping forward to receive the crowd's adulation. During all this, Daltrey swung his mike in a frenzied whirlpool of motion, as if it was a huge propeller, while Entwistle coolly and steadfastly played through it all as if an earthquake wouldn't unsettle him. Now we had seen for ourselves the reason why the whole world wanted to see The Who, and without question they were majestic. In just a few short months they played at Woodstock where they were to cement their lasting worldwide reputation. In Sunderland that night, they had already achieved immortality.

Afterwards I went into the dressing room to find the group smiling, saying they'd really enjoyed the gig. They must have done because I was to promote them on a further three occasions. It was The Who at their finest, a night never to be forgotten and one of my top three gigs. A few weeks earlier, Country Joe had posed the question, "What are we fighting for?" I could now answer him: it was for nights like this.

Afterwards, I went to a local nightclub called Annabel's with Keith Moon in his Rolls. It was a new experience for me because I'd never been in one before. Dad had sometimes talked about Rolls-Royces and how only rich people could afford them. "If I win the pools, son, we'll get one," he often reminded us. As we pulled away, people were staring and among the crowd at the bus stop I noticed a young Dave Stewart carrying a guitar, waiting for the bus to arrive. Inside, I was immensely proud. The Who and a drive in a Roller in one night; it all seemed like a dream.

Keith was endlessly cracking jokes. His wit and repartee were as sharp as a craftsman's chisel, and I couldn't stop laughing. He was in a great mood and repeatedly said how much The Who had enjoyed the gig. It was certainly an eye opener witnessing the pulling power of a successful rock star at first hand. Girls drooled over him, and he soon had them in stitches. He didn't need a PR, his own warmth and natural friendliness were wonderful to behold, and nobody who approached him, regardless of who they were, was ignored. An hour later he left with none other than Debbie and I had to admire her skill. She didn't miss chances as gift-wrapped as this, and Keith was about to experience his second gig of the night. If it was half as good as the first, he was in for a real treat. Debbie would see to that.

I still have two autographed photos of the group from that night. Keith has written "Cool gig man", which I think says everything. Incidentally, he wrote these words before leaving The Bay. Maybe Debbie has one describing the second gig!

After my failed attempt to bring Led Zeppelin to The Bay, the callous disregard in which I'd been treated rankled. About three weeks after that brusque phone call with their manager Peter Grant, on a trip to London, I walked up the office stairs of Rak Music in Oxford Street, and asked to see him.

"Why do you want to see Mr Grant?" asked his secretary.

"I've come to get a replacement date on Led Zeppelin," I replied.

"Where at?" she said bluntly.

"The Bay Hotel in Sunderland."

"How many does it hold?"

"Eight hundred," I confidently answered.

She looked at me incredulously.

"Are you being serious? Do you know that Led Zeppelin are filling stadiums all over America? I'm afraid you've got no chance."

Undeterred, I again asked if Peter Grant was in.

"I'm afraid not," she stubbornly replied. "He's in America with the group."

"In that case, will you give him a message from me. My name is Geoff Docherty, and will you please remind him he owes me a date on the group. I'd also be grateful if you would ask him to ring me."

"Okay, I'll pass the message on," she replied unconvincingly.

She wasn't to know it then, but it was the beginning of a long campaign to get Led Zeppelin to Sunderland. The group owed us a gig, and I didn't care how many American dollars they were being paid to play elsewhere. If their office thought I was crazy, so be it. It had become a matter of honour for me and I was determined not to give up, no matter how big the group became.

On my next visit to London, I again called into Peter Grant's office.

"Oh! It's you again. Don't tell me, you want Led Zeppelin," said the secretary with a resigned look.

"That's right, I do," I emphatically replied.

She called to her colleague seated further away. "It's that chap from Sunderland who wants to book Led Zeppelin." She looked up, while staring long and hard at me and seemed lost for words. "Can I get you a coffee?" she asked, as if it was the only thing she could think of to break the awkward atmosphere.

"I'd rather have tea if you don't mind," I said politely.

With Peter Grant's secretaries providing me with tea and biscuits I began to feel more relaxed. In an effort to break the silence, I attempted to explain the warm and friendly community spirit we all enjoyed up in Sunderland. After listening, one of the girls administered a veiled sort of warning, as if to frighten me. After all, it was well known that you didn't mess with Peter Grant. He was a legendary figure with a dangerous reputation. Cross him, and you could be nailed to the floor.

"I hope Peter doesn't get upset with you keeping coming in," she gently chided.

"Why should he?" I replied. "We're not going to harm the group, we just want them to play."

"You do realise how big Led Zeppelin are?" she said sarcastically.

"Of course, that's all the more reason why I want them."

She frowned, and I could sense her frustration at my uncompromising stance. As I stood up to leave, the relief on their faces was evident. On impulse, I turned as I headed for the door.

"See you next time I'm in London, and don't forget to tell Peter I called in," I cheekily reminded them. They nodded in acknowledgement and, in some strange way, I felt a bond was being forged which might lead to a successful conclusion.

By now, word had got round in the business that I was trying to book Led Zeppelin for Sunderland.

"Why don't you give up, they're far too big now," said one of my friends.

"Listen, if my dad can go down the pit and work on his knees in water for six hours, I can go into their office and have tea and biscuits for twenty minutes," I replied.

"That's a stupid answer," he sneered dismissively. "We're talking rock 'n'roll here."

"It might be a stupid answer to you, but if you came from where I do, then you'd understand," I countered. "Can't you see, Led Zeppelin owe me a date? I could sue them for thousands."

"Well, why don't you?" he asked.

"Because I'm not that sort of guy, and anyway, I'd never get the group if I did."

"By the looks of it you're not going to get them anyway," he added, before turning and walking resignedly away.

Chapter 8

During the late Sixties, attitudes were changing so rapidly, it was becoming difficult for world authorities to suppress unhappy factions. In the North East of England, as in many other troubled black spots, the fight was for jobs, and a better way of life.

Students from all over the world came to study at Sunderland's Naval Architectural College where they were taught vital skills on how to build ships. Unfortunately, orders for ships became harder to obtain as other countries capitalised on our generosity and began building their own, using the very knowledge which we'd unwittingly taught them. This was to have devastating consequences. Mining and many other skills were also passed on, as our teaching schools welcomed all nationalities with open arms. These decisions were of course political, and beyond the scope of the working man, but ran throughout most of Britain's industrial base. It was to eventually lead to the closure of all the North East's main industries, accompanied by massive unemployment problems. To those losing their livelihood, it seemed our own wilful disclosure of hard-earned expertise had cut off our very lifeblood, from which we have never recovered. Because of this, young people began looking for a way out.

If you had a predilection for the arts, the limited university opportunities offered hope to those fortunate enough to gain a place. Music was another way out which, however tenuous and potentially soul destroying, offered a lifeline that many chose to take. Bands from all over the country were forming and ploughing endlessly up and down the country's motorways. In many cases, their tenacity had to be admired although, when disillusionment set in, most gave up, and younger inexperienced stalwarts would step forward to replace them. Of course, being in a band presented its

71

own unforeseen dangers; excessive consumption of drugs and alcohol inevitably taking its toll. Sadly, some weren't to make it, and inevitably succumbed to its perils.

In the late Sixties, people were continually being apprehended for possession of even the smallest amount of cannabis. In an effort to combat this, the authorities set up drug squads, and The Bay did not escape their attention. One particular officer, who was supposed to be undercover, was known to every teenager in Sunderland, and the joke was, he couldn't spot a cannabis plant if it was growing on his mother's grave.

The issue of drugs is an emotive one and can bring out the best, or worst in anyone, depending on their viewpoint. The question centres around 'hard' or 'soft' drugs. At The Bay, all drugs were strictly forbidden although I realised that some people were smoking dope before being admitted. I often mused on what the politicians or authorities would say if they could see for themselves the horrendous consequences of someone who'd been glassed, or viciously assaulted. In my experience, 99% of the assailants had been drinking, or were drunk, and when asked to leave, invariably became aggressive, whereas someone who was high, just smiled or giggled, and left peaceably. The difference in attitudes was immense, and certainly made one wonder if the law had got it wrong. As for me, I've never smoked or taken drugs, but I do like a sensible drink.

The local constabulary was to grace us with a most unwelcome visit when a chief inspector, followed by about twenty police officers, burst into the foyer.

"This is a police raid," he announced. "Switch the music off and nobody leaves unless I say so."

"What are you raiding us for?" I asked.

"Under-age drinking and drugs," he replied in a stern and superior manner. No sooner had they arrived than the posse of police officers returned into the foyer, looking red-faced. Unfortunately, the door through which they had hoped to gain entry to the ballroom was locked, and they had collided with each other as the ones at the front turned back in exasperation, only to meet their onrushing colleagues. It was a true Brian Rix farce as the police inspector looked sheepishly at me, having realised his carefully planned raid hadn't got off to a very good start.

"How do we get in?" he asked in exasperation.

"I'll show you," I obliged. So it was that I found myself leading the raid and felt like asking them if I could borrow a helmet and truncheon as I was improperly dressed.

"Put the main lights on," the inspector ordered as we entered the ballroom. I was tempted to ask, "Why, can't you see?" but thought better of it.

After questioning anyone who didn't look 18, from about 400 people present 16 were taken away for further questioning. Personally, I thought the whole thing was ridiculous because I just couldn't fathom out what we were supposed to have done wrong. While this was happening, the inspector looked smug and immensely pleased with himself. He usually called into The Bay three or four times a week for a free drink and sandwiches, but now he had betrayed our hospitality. I looked him straight in the eye and, as I did so, I sensed his treachery was sitting uncomfortably on his shoulders.

A few weeks later, the 16 appeared in court for under-age drinking, while not one person was found in possession of drugs. As I sat in the public gallery, each in turn was asked by the clerk of the court, how they pleaded. "Guilty, your worship," they meekly replied as their parents anxiously watched from the public bench. After a stern warning about the perils of under-age drinking, they were each fined and warned as to their future conduct, before being allowed to leave.

Finally, the last girl was brought in and led to the old oak stained witness box. It was higher than the public gallery, and with an array of judicial faces staring at her, it seemed as though she was being tried for murder. "How do you plead?" the court clerk asked. "Not guilty, your worship." There was a deathly hush in the court as a look of utter amazement appeared on the prosecuting lawyer's face.

"How old are you?" he asked, his harsh and unforgiving voice reverberating around the courtroom. She hesitated for a moment before replying, "Seventeen."

A triumphant look immediately crossed the prosecutor's face as he thrust out his chest in anticipation of an easy kill.

"Were you drinking at The Bay Hotel on the night in question?" he asked.

"Yes," she answered.

In true courtroom drama, he glanced knowingly at the public gallery.

"You are only 17, and yet you say you were drinking. Surely this is an admission of guilt," he reminded her.

As her voice echoed around the hushed courtroom, it seemed as if her words had doomed her to a heavier sentence for having the audacity to plead not guilty. "But it wasn't alcohol I was drinking, sir."

"What was it then?" he asked, with a bemused and disapproving look across his learned face.

"It was a bottle of Pino," she replied.

"But that's a strong alcoholic drink."

"I didn't know that, did I?" she protested. "It has a picture of a pineapple on the front, and I thought it was pineapple juice I was drinking."

"A pineapple on the front," jeered the prosecutor, determined to secure a conviction. "Do you expect us to believe you were unaware of its alcoholic content?"

"Yes," she stubbornly replied. "How was I to know it was anything else?" Unable to afford a solicitor, she looked a forlorn figure and I couldn't help admiring her spirit and bravery in the face of such an intimidating atmosphere. Silence descended over the courtroom as the magistrate deliberated on his verdict. He leant forward and motioned to the clerk of the court.

"Does it have a picture of a pineapple on the front?" he queried. The clerk was unsure and turned to ask the police inspector. For a few moments the court remained hushed as the judiciary and police conferred with each other. After a lengthy consultation, they reluctantly agreed it had.

On hearing this, the magistrate thought carefully. I glanced at the girl in the witness box and thought what a guilty verdict could mean for her. It seemed an unrealistically high and unjust price to pay for a small bottle of Pino. Moments later, the judge spoke.

Chapter 8

"I find you not guilty," he announced. The hushed courtroom gasped in astonishment while the police prosecutor shook his head in disbelief. "You are free to go," the magistrate said reassuringly to the acquitted girl. Smiling in appreciation and relief, she turned and waved to a friend before walking out of the courtroom.

In actual fact, Pino was a strong alcoholic drink, and was commonly known among the local lads as a 'knicker dropper'. Girls usually drank it because it was cheaper than 'shorts', and most were well aware of its potency.

On the way out of court, a policewoman wryly commented to me, "I wouldn't care, but she was the worst one of the lot. On the way to the police station, she was sick all over the inside of the van." I chuckled. The proverb, "The wheel that squeaks gets the grease," had in this case proved to be correct.

The raid caused Mr Dixon to issue firm instructions that we were to be stricter on not admitting anyone who didn't look 18. This proved quite difficult at night so the only answer was to insist on birth certificates. Nevertheless, the young teenagers' ingenuity often used to amaze me. Amended dates, their big sisters' or friends' birth certificates, and a convenient change of identity were all used to try to gain admission. Over the next few weeks we were forced to turn away dozens of people, merely on suspicion. The place was immaculate, there was free travel home, soft drinks were available, and still we couldn't let them in. It was heart-rending to see their disappointed faces after travelling miles to see their favourite groups, but there was nothing we could do. Or was there?

After careful thought, I had an idea and went to see Mr Dixon. "Why don't we block off the top part of the ballroom where the bar is, and make the under 18s come in through the side door. They can then be admitted into the other two thirds of the ballroom where we'll set up a soft drinks counter. That way, we're not breaking any laws," I pointed out. Mr Dixon was sceptical, but after a few days of encouragement, he finally relented. It proved to be an immediate success, and soon we were able to start a fully fledged under 18s' night downstairs, while anyone over 18 could drink at the bar upstairs. Younger people now had access to the music, and it was gratifying to see them enjoying themselves. After the raid, the police never bothered us again, and indeed, the irony of it was that many of their sons and daughters became regular attendees, with their parents picking them up afterwards.

Although everything was running smoothly, there was no time for relaxation as it was a question of being ever vigilant, especially where rowdy or unruly elements were concerned. Inside, peace prevailed. Outside, heated arguments, disagreements and, in one case, a gangland vendetta ensued. It was certainly no place for the faint-hearted as Tommy Donnelly, John Tansey and myself steadfastly maintained order. Although fights and trouble at The Bay had now shrunk to a minimum, shortly after the police raid I was to experience a night of unprecedented violence which started on the late night transport.

As I was checking to see if there were any vacant seats, I felt a vicious punch from behind explode onto the side of my head. I turned to see a figure darting off the bus and heading flat out along the seafront. I was furious at this cowardly and unprovoked attack and immediately set off in pursuit. As I rounded the corner and straightened up for the long haul along the seafront, I could see he was really motoring.

What the guy didn't know was that when I'd been on loan to the Army Air Corps in Hildesheim, Germany, I'd won the half-mile on sports day, and when serving on board the *Ark Royal*, among 2,500 men on board I'd come second in the mile to a respected navy runner on a sports day in Singapore. Given a fair crack of the whip, I was confident I could catch him, even if it meant running all the way to town.

As we hared along, he had a substantial lead and I decided to pace it and reel him in steadily. In these situations, someone who has been drinking usually panics, puts in a big spurt over the first few hundred yards or so, and then begins to tire. Sure enough, after about half a mile, he had burnt himself out, and turned to face me.

"It wasn't me," he pleaded breathlessly. Not only was he sly, but he was a liar too.

"All right," I answered calmly. "Just tell me who it was?"

"I don't know," he replied fearfully.

Chapter 8

Having lulled him into a false sense of security, I suddenly unleashed a rapid combination of crunching blows.

"Stop, it wasn't me," he screamed as he lay in a confused heap on the ground.

"Every time you tell me lies, I'm going to give you more," I warned in a mad frenzy of retribution.

After grabbing his hair and bouncing his head off the kerb a few times as a permanent warning, I stepped back, looked at his prostrate body lying defenceless on the ground, and decided he'd had enough.

It was then I remembered the late transport was unable to leave until I'd paid the drivers, and set off at a fast lick to get the buses away. As I arrived, I noticed Tommy being attacked by two youths. I immediately spun one round and just as I was about to deal with him, a volley of blows started hitting me from behind. I turned to find four youths simultaneously raining punches on me from all angles and immediately knew I was in deep water, as I was out of breath from my run along the seafront.

By now, one of them had my neck in an arm lock, making it increasingly hard to breathe. "Get the c**t down," one of them said as I desperately tried to cover up, just as Dad had shown me at the boxing booths. Soon they had driven me up against the car park wall, with my shirt torn to shreds, leaving me bare from the waist upwards. The only thing keeping it attached to my body was one remaining sleeve, which obstinately refused to be parted from its restraining cufflink.

As they continued to rain blows on me, my back was covered in lacerations from scraping along the car park wall. My one overriding thought was to stay on my feet, because I knew if I went down, they would surely kick me unconscious. Meanwhile, instead of picking me off with controlled and decisive punches, they were swinging wildly in a mad frenzy of hatred, and seemed unable to finish me off, but I knew I couldn't hang on much longer. Why doesn't someone help me? I wondered.

Suddenly, I heard an almighty shout and as I looked up, I saw a huge giant of a man wearing a trilby, rushing fearlessly towards my attackers like an enraged bull. He appeared to be well over six feet, about sixteen stone, and dressed in a dark suit and tie, which gave him the appearance of being from the local CID. The blows stopped as my attackers took one look, before immediately turning and fleeing in a mad panic.

"Are you all right, son?" he asked anxiously. My body was in a state of shock and bent nearly double with blood oozing from my lacerations. He placed a strong arm underneath me and helped me into an upright position.

"Come on, I'll take you inside so you can get cleaned up."

"Thanks," I stuttered, although I had little strength left for conversation. My head was aching, and I could feel an assortment of swellings rapidly rising all over its surface. Once inside, the staff bathed my wounds and I was relieved to find no bones were broken. After a few minutes, I started to feel my muscles regaining strength and realised that fitness, good food, a young body, and a heroic rescuer had seen me through.

"Where has that chap gone?" I asked, on noticing my rescuer was missing.

"You mean the late transport driver? He left a few minutes ago," answered one of the bar staff.

"So that's who he was," I muttered disappointedly, as I had genuinely wanted to thank him from the bottom of my heart, but had been unable to do so.

After a while, it became clear what a lucky escape I'd had. It had been a fortuitous piece of luck that I'd changed to those luxury coaches, otherwise there's no telling what the outcome might have been. Sadly, I never saw that bus driver again, but he's forever in my thoughts.

As I sat recovering, big Tommy Trotter who had represented Durham County in the 400 metres, came rushing in with a triumphant look on his face. "We've got one of them outside, Geoff," he said, awaiting my reaction.

I stared at him momentarily, stood up, composed myself, put on my jacket, and went out to the car park. There, this chap was surrounded by the other waiters who had chased and caught him across some fields at the back of The Bay. As I stared at him, it was a bittersweet moment considering how quickly the roles had been reversed.

Chapter 8

While eyeing him up, I began wondering what possessed such an individual to take up a gang mentality. What went through their minds as they battered a defenceless person into a bloody pulp, especially one that had done them no harm? These were obviously sad individuals who needed help. Fortunately, I knew two social workers whose treatment in the past had had a remarkable success rate in difficult cases. Of course, social workers need astuteness and patience, and have to impress upon their fellow human beings how good always triumphs over evil. Unfortunately a faction remains who just aren't prepared to listen.

Looking at him, I decided it was time to introduce these social workers to him in a last desperate effort to teach him the error of his ways. However, these weren't social workers in the normally accepted sense. They were attached to my wrists, and never failed to obey my instructions. Now, as I was about to issue them with some fresh ones, I gave him one final warning in an effort to introduce some fairness into the forthcoming contest.

"I don't know who you are," I said, "but I'm going to do something you didn't do for me. I'm going to give you a fair chance, one onto one." He looked nervous, as though fearful of what the outcome would be. I then stepped forward and unleashed my two social workers in a savage and ferocious attack. There was little or no resistance and, within seconds, he was a helpless heap on the deck. In an effort to make him pay for his earlier indiscretions, I leant over his prostrate body, got hold of his head and for the second time that evening, smashed it off the kerb in an effort to give this brute a taste of his own medicine. As I did so the maintenance joiner leapt forward to restrain me.

"Stop, or you'll kill him," he screamed in a panic-stricken voice. I paused and took one final look at him before calmly walking away. It was time to go home. I'd had an extremely hard night and wanted the comfort of Dot's arms. Her voice was soothing and sympathetic while her face showed real concern. I just wanted to cuddle into her and feel the warmth of her body, but sex was the last thing on my mind. It was her kindness and compassion that I badly needed. She was already promising to buy me a new shirt, and here I was experiencing both sides of human nature in one night.

79

We climbed into my car for the journey home. I hadn't driven far when I spotted a gang of youths outside The Seaburn Hotel, situated about three quarters of a mile away on the seafront. I slowed down when I thought I recognised one of my attackers. As I looked out of the open window, one of them walked towards me.

"Are you all right, Geoff?" he asked sympathetically. "We heard what happened and wondered how you were."

"I'm okay," I grimly assured him.

From nowhere, a punch came through the window and struck me full on the mouth. My head jerked back and blood seeped from my lips. Fortunately, I'd left the engine running, and immediately dropped the clutch, before pushing the throttle hard against the floor. It was a 3.4 silver grey Jaguar and its powerful engine responded immediately. Directly in front was a major roundabout and I screamed round it, mounted the kerb and drove straight at the group.

There was a low wall along the front and, panic-stricken, they scattered before diving head first over it. God only knows what would have happened if they hadn't. After a quick appraisal of the situation, I decided to drive home. There were too many of them, I'd already taken a battering, and I realised the human body wasn't designed to take punishment of this nature.

This night changed my whole attitude to trouble. It was the second occasion it had happened and from there on in, I realised it was imperative to become less trusting, and faster on the trigger. If I didn't, I sensed I wasn't going to be around for much longer. Dad had always said you have to pay for your learning. Now I knew what he meant. It had been a hard and painful lesson, and one I wouldn't forget.

Chapter 9

With The Bay well established nationally, I was made an honorary member of The Speakeasy at 48 Margaret Street, situated just behind Oxford Circus in central London. This was a legendary club which all the known groups frequented, and on any given night The Beatles, Jimi Hendrix, Eric Clapton, Marc Bolan, John Peel, Rod Stewart, Roger Chapman, Keith Emerson, Free, or any visiting Americans groups could be present. Drugs, groupies and, on odd occasions, violence, were all part of its vibrant scene. One night, during one of my visits, a 'heavy' rushed up to a well-known lead vocalist and smashed him over the head with an iron bar. His crime? He was trying to switch managers, and this was his final warning not to go through with it.

In the days before courtrooms and lawyers, this is how disputes were often settled and word soon spread through the grapevine of who not to cross. With big money creeping into the scene, it inevitably attracted a fair share of villains, wheeler-dealers and opportunists, drawn into the rock world because of its lucrative pay days. Nevertheless, The Speakeasy was a great club and featured some wonderful bands, many of whom went on to become world famous.

The next big gig at The Bay, scheduled for 19 May, was another major American group – Steppenwolf. The previous year, their first album had gone gold, and the single, 'Born To Be Wild' had reached number two in the American *Billboard* charts. During the build-up to the gig, the single was never off the juke box and to be able to hear it live by the group who'd recorded it, was something which The Bay regulars eagerly anticpated. 'Born To Be Wild' – what a great title! It fitted into everyone's thinking perfectly, and I sensed it probably described the sort of night we could expect.

Two days before the gig, Debbie approached me in The Bis-Bar, wearing a pelmet for a mini skirt. As she sat down, her skirt rode higher, making it difficult to concentrate. Edging her face closer to mine, she thrust her ample bosom towards me, puckered her lips, and asked, "Will I get in all right to see the group?" As her warm breath cascaded across my face, I sensed Debbie could be mine, having realised the ensuing appearance of Steppenwolf had dramatically changed things. Inwardly however, I was already nursing a deep suspicion, and wondered if she really liked me, or was this just her way of using her feminine guile to make sure I introduced her to the group. Suddenly, I noticed a smear of lipstick on her cup, and this set me wondering. Where else had traces of it been left on previous occasions? It didn't take a vivid imagination to realise the obvious possibilities as I gathered my thoughts and answered the question. "Of course I'll make sure you get in," I replied.

Listening to her, I had come to recognise that a gig promoter was usually high on a groupie's agenda, because he had immediate power to grant them access to whoever they wished to meet. It was something I hadn't realised when I first set out, and some of them certainly weren't shy in offering themselves.

"No, I mean will you introduce me to the group as well?" she asked.

"Which one do you fancy?" I queried.

"I don't know till I meet them," she answered.

"What if they bring their own girlfriends?" I cautioned and a worried frown crossed her face at this unforeseen possibility.

By now, I knew a major rock group of this stature often had a retinue of girls following them around the country, and it was odds on that Steppenwolf would be no exception. Backstage, topless scenes were common, as were naked bodies, groping hands, and free love at parties afterwards. As Debbie stood there, I worried that she might come up against some real professionals, even though she was on home ground, and very attractive. Backstage rivalry can be bitchy, and she'd had a clear and unfettered run up till now. Despite my reservations about her way of life, I had developed a certain affection for Debbie, and was reluctant to see unnecessary hurt heaped upon her poor overworked body.

Chapter 9

"Don't worry, I'll make sure you get to meet them afterwards," I assured her. "What about Sarah, is she coming?"

"No, she's gone to live in London with a bass player in a band. He's cute and she's madly in love with him."

"I haven't seen you with Rob lately, are you still seeing him?"

"Afraid not, he was a bit too straight for me, and besides, he was a bit too clingy."

"You mean he wasn't in a band," I prompted.

"His dad didn't like me for a start, and his mother was a bit snooty. Anyway, who cares, just make sure I get in the dressing room, will you?" She slid off the chair as I ogled her long legs before taking in the rest of her. It seemed she was undeniably, born to be wild.

On the morning that Steppenwolf were due to play, I casually walked into the ballroom and was aghast to find the curtains missing from the huge floor-length windows, allowing bright daylight to pour in. Panic-stricken, I rushed to Mr Dixon's office.

"What's happened to the curtains?" I asked frantically

"I've sent them to the dry-cleaners," he answered, without batting an eyelid.

"Can't we get them back?" I pleaded.

"Not a chance. I have a dinner dance on Saturday and I want to make sure they're ready for that," he coolly replied. I began to sense an imminent disaster as hordes of people, unable to gain entry, were sent flying through the windows as they pushed against the glass while peering in at the group. Something urgently needed to be done, but what?

I had a brainwave. If I used blankets to black out the ballroom, it might just solve the problem. Within minutes, I drove home, and with renewed vigour, set about stapling my bed linen over the windows. Having completed the task, I looked around the darkened ballroom. It wasn't pretty, but it was effective, and had temporarily solved the problem.

Just then, I was interrupted by Mr Dixon's beckoning voice.

"Geoff, there's a telephone call for you in the office."

"Who is it?" I asked.

"I don't know," he replied. I sensed something was wrong and I hurried to answer it.

"Hello, Geoff Docherty here."

"Hi, Geoff, I'm the manager of Steppenwolf and I've got some bad news for you. I just thought I'd better let you know the group can't make it tonight because John Kay the lead singer has a sore throat."

"Oh, no," I gasped. "Isn't there any possibility of him making it, even if he just croaks?"

"Not a chance," replied their manager. "He's got a temperature and is under doctor's orders."

"What about another date?" I suggested hopefully.

"Impossible," he answered. "We're flying back to the States in a few days and we're fully committed."

Distraught, I finally accepted the inevitable and replaced the receiver. A major setback like this had already happened with Led Zeppelin. Trust my second booking disaster to involve a major American group that everyone was desperate to see.

Before long, there was a monstrous queue at the door. As I opened it, a huge surge of excited people raced towards the till. "Steppenwolf aren't playing tonight," I shouted above the din. Those at the front stopped and stared at me in disbelief.

"Did you say Steppenwolf aren't playing here tonight?" asked a disconsolate voice.

"That's right," I confirmed. A hushed silence descended over the queue as I felt hundreds of disappointed eyes boring into me.

"I'm very sorry but John Kay has a sore throat and can't make it," I explained.

"Who's on instead?" asked another voice.

"Breakthru, a band from Birmingham," I replied with all the conviction I could muster.

"Are you getting another date on them?" someone asked.

"Afraid not, they're going back to America soon."

As word rapidly spread, loud murmurings of discontent could be heard while people began dispersing with disappointment etched deep into their faces. Fortunately, Breakthru were excellent, and the night went off without a further hitch.

A few days later in London, I walked into The Speakeasy and there in the restaurant was John Kay and the rest of Steppenwolf eating a hearty meal accompanied by a retinue of pretty girls. I stopped and listened to him conversing. It seemed strange being so close, especially as he didn't know who I was, or the anguish he'd caused only a few nights previous. I caught his eye and looked him straight in the face without saying a word. He sure had made a spectacular recovery, but I didn't hold a grudge. To this day, whenever I hear 'Born To Be Wild', the memory comes back to haunt me. Nevertheless, it's still a great record.

After the Steppenwolf debacle, Debbie and Sarah approached me.

"Hi Geoff, have you got any more American bands booked?" Debbie asked hopefully.

"Yes, Three Dog Night are coming soon," I replied.

Her face lit up as she turned to Sarah and exclaimed, "I f★★king hope they turn up, otherwise we might have to go to London to see them!"

"I thought you were going out with a bass player and living in London," I asked Sarah.

"It didn't work out, so I've come back to live with my parents," she replied.

Groupies' lives intrigued me. Why were they prepared to go with anyone in a group, and what about their self-respect? Didn't they have any? In Debbie's case, what did these groups have that the local lads didn't? Obviously it was fame, power and money, but was life so dull that she needed to screw them to get her kicks? Maybe she was sex mad and rock stars appealed to that side of her. Whatever the reason, Debbie certainly made the most of the opportunities coming her way. I was to find that limousines, platinum albums, major gigs, drugs and music were a heady mixture. If a rock star also happens to be handsome, it's an intoxicating concoction which allows all other considerations to be conveniently ignored.

With Debbie it was sex all the way, and freely available. Not surprisingly, any vitriol or jealousy directed towards her from other girls seemed to roll off her back as easily as the rock stars did. Throughout all this, I remained at a discreet distance. After all, if she wanted to keep putting a smile on the groups' faces, what business was it of mine?

Having overcome the disappointments of Led Zeppelin and Steppenwolf, everything was back on an even keel when Three Dog Night, who went on to become one of the biggest Seventies groups in America, visited The Bay on June 9. Early that evening, Debbie and Sarah duly arrived with some friends, looking all set for another conquest. Unfortunately, the group member Debbie had her eye on seemed more interested in another girl.

"What's her name?" I asked by way of comfort.

"Caroline," she answered glumly.

"She does have a nice figure," I said, not realising how upset she was.

"It's not so nice when she takes her two hankies out!" replied Debbie bitchily. I was shocked as I wasn't used to seeing another more cutting side to her.

"Why don't you go for one of the others?" I asked innocently.

"They all have someone with them, and anyway, one of the girls has a big sister who has already threatened me."

"Threatened you? I don't like anyone issuing threats here, what's her name?" I asked.

"It's Melanie, but please don't say anything because I don't want any trouble with her in the future," Debbie pleaded.

"Of course not," I assured her, sensing her nervousness. "What does she look like?" I enquired.

"She's tall, with long black hair which has been back-combed and looks ridiculous. You can't miss her because she's wearing a bright red top and a blue mini skirt. The colours clash and she looks stupid. She's already been fined for being drunk and assaulting a bus conductor after he tried to eject her from the bus for swearing."

"Was he all right?" I asked.

"Well I suppose so, although he had a black eye," added Debbie.

My curiosity aroused, I wandered into the dressing room and began discreetly looking round. I spotted Melanie sitting alone in a corner as if she was the other girls' minder. Her chubby face was caked with excess make-up which looked as if it would need a chisel to remove it. There was also a ladder in her tights, while her back-combed hair somehow reminded me of Jimi Hendrix. As I glanced downwards I immediately noticed her two major assets protruding from a low cut top. Melanie wasn't beautiful by any stretch of the imagination, but like the rest of us, she was human and had feelings. Maybe she'd had to use a few threats to get what she wanted, but at least she'd made it to the dressing room. Not unnaturally, the group seemed too preoccupied to notice her, and intuition told me that one of the roadies would probably sort her out later. I sensed this wouldn't be the last time we'd meet, and I'd have to keep an eye on her.

As my eyes scanned the dressing room, every group member had a girl on his lap and it wasn't difficult to imagine the outcome. An American in town was something to be prized, and who knows, maybe a girl might end up marrying one. "Caroline," shouted one of the girls to her friend. I looked over and saw a very attractive girl with her arm draped around one of the band. A mini skirt, gorgeous legs, lovely face, and big brown almond eyes now confronted me as I smiled and she smiled back. I'd already noticed her on previous visits and I must confess, she wasn't just attractive, she possessed an earthy sexiness as well. Seeing me watching, she lowered her eyelids as if a guilt complex had suddenly overtaken her, but she needn't have worried. An American rock star in Sunderland was too good to miss. Three Dog Night had spotted her and wasted no time in capitalising on one of our finest young ladies, and who could blame them.

After the group had played an excellent set, we all retired to the bar. Eventually, I left Three Dog Night to the hordes who were keen to meet them and looked around. Melanie smiled and moved towards me.

"You're Geoff, aren't you?" she began. "I've heard a lot about you and how you often go down to London. I wouldn't mind a trip down there myself, especially if it's with you."

"Are you sure you're not just trying to use me to meet groups?" I asked bluntly.

A pained expression crossed her face. "Of course not, why would I want to do that?" she asked.

I shrugged my shoulders with an accompanying vacant expression. "I think I've already answered that question, haven't I?" came my reply.

She placed her arm around me and drew me in tight. "Oh Geoff, can't you see I like you. If it's just a free trip to London that you think I want you for, you're wrong. Why don't we go back to your place tonight, I'm sure we'll have a good time."

"I'm sorry, but I already have a girlfriend," I countered as things warmed up.

"Where is she then?" Melanie demanded.

"It's her night off and I'm going straight home," I explained. At that moment I glanced over at Three Dog Night who were surrounded by a bevy of attractive girls and realised that maybe I should have learnt to play a musical instrument after all, because it certainly hadn't done them any harm. It was unforeseeable how big Three Dog Night eventually became in later years, but that night they earned £250, and due to the poor attendance, I lost money on them. However, I didn't mind in the slightest. Everyone who was there, including myself, had thoroughly enjoyed them and an added bonus was that the seven piece group were all smashing guys.

Each week over the summer of 1969, I would wander into the newsagent's to buy the music press, which was not only informative but also gave critical insight into what was currently happening on the music scene. On the front page of an issue of *Melody Maker* was a strange looking man dressed in what appeared to be ragged stage clothes. I recognised him as Ian Anderson, the vocalist of Jethro Tull. The band took their unusual name from an eighteenth-century agriculturalist who had invented the seed drill, and this, together with the tramp-like way Anderson dressed, gave them a unique and distinct image.

After a show-stopping appearance at the Sunbury Jazz and Blues Festival in 1968 (forerunner of the present-day Reading Festival), everyone was talking about this group. Unfortunately, such had been the speed of their rise, they refused to accept any further dates and once again, America was beckoning. Could I get them to play at The Bay? It was a fascinating challenge.

After buying the music papers, I decided to have a tea and a quiet read in a small cafeteria just a few yards up from The Bis-Bar. On entering, a regular from The Bay happened to be seated there. Instinctively, he glanced at the *Melody Maker* lying on the table.

"What about Jethro Tull?" he said. "They're really making the news now, aren't they?"

My heart sank as I put down the *New Musical Express* I'd just started to read. "What about them?" I answered.

"Well, I'm just wondering if you're going to get them for The Bay?"

"I can't at the moment, they don't have any spare dates."

"Shame. I thought you might be able to pull a few strings because of your contacts in London," he enthused.

The *Melody Maker* front page caught my eye again. Ian Anderson was standing on one leg, playing a flute. It was his trademark stance, but it set me thinking. 'Can he be serious?' I wondered. As the waitress reached over to collect the empty cups, it dawned on me that people thought that all I had to do was click my fingers, and every group came running. As I politely explained the difficulties involved when groups like Jethro Tull were shifting monumental amounts of albums over in America, he seemed unconvinced.

"C'mon Geoff, you can get them, I know you can."

After countless telephone refusals, I felt obliged to make one last effort to secure a Jethro Tull appearance at The Bay, and set off for London. Once there, it was my intention to speak to either the group's manager Terry Ellis at Chrysalis, or their agent Kenny Bell. It was a long shot but I knew them both personally and I figured it was worth a try.

Kenny's words sounded ominous. "I'm sorry Geoff, there's no spare dates, and if there was one, you know I'd give it to you, but it's impossible, they've all gone."

The resigned look on his face had a discouraging finality about it, and I left his office in a sombre mood. Next day I rang and asked if there'd been any cancellations. There hadn't. "I'll ring you again tomorrow just to check," I added with more than a hint of desperation. After three days of wrangling, pleading and imploring, Kenny finally called me into his office.

"Listen Geoff, one final date has just become available because they've decided to leave a day later," he began. "You're very lucky, it's the last club gig they're ever doing because they're getting too big for them now. After that, it's City Halls and festivals only."

"Thanks Kenny," I told him excitedly. "I'll never ever forget this favour."

Late next day, I walked into The Bis–Bar and, somehow, everyone seemed to know they were coming. Dicky Robson, who was attending the London School of Economics, came over to speak to me.

"I hear Jethro Tull's coming."

"Yes, that's if they turn up," I confided.

"Why do you say that?" he asked.

"Well, they've already had two hit singles and a hit album in England, and now that their album *Stand Up* is selling like hot cakes in America, they've become absolutely massive."

"Oh, I see," he replied, as his girlfriend greeted us warmly.

"Hi Geoff, how are you?" she enquired in her cultured voice as the smell of expensive perfume wafted through the air. "Dicky and I are invited out to a friend's for dinner tomorrow night, should be super."

I looked down and noticed her finely manicured hands holding a cigarette holder that was so long, it could have been mistaken for a snooker cue.

"Have you heard about Dicky," she asked. "He's been accepted into university in London. Isn't that wonderful?"

"Yes I know, he's already told me, it's great news," I said, realising how proud his parents would be.

"We may pop along to The Bay later if we get time. We'll just have to see how it goes." Each word and mannerism was delivered with an unmistakable refinement and poise which I actually admired.

"Bye Geoff," she said upon leaving, and I sensed there was a huge chasm between her and most of us. It set me thinking. She was from a posh area, and had some posh friends. Maybe if I try to talk like her I might meet someone classy, and she might even invite me to dinner. Or perhaps I could learn to ride and play polo because there's a couple of sturdy pit ponies in the field at Castletown. The only problem is they're a bit short in the legs. Still, one of the girls from St Anthony's might lend me one of their hockey sticks. They might laugh at me but these pit ponies have big hearts and will still be running when their horses have tired. And what about if I score the winning goal. Can you imagine that? They'll all want to know me then.

But what about etiquette, it can be tricky. It's different to serviette, and I'll have to make sure I don't get the two mixed up! After all, I wouldn't want to embarrass the girl I was trying to impress, especially if her friends are watching. At home, we tilt the plate to get the last drop of soup from it. But if I do it in front of her, she might think I'm common and it could blow my chances.

I can't take her home though, because on the way in she might trip over the milk bottles and that'll set the dogs off barking and could be embarrassing if she finds out they're only mongrels. Still, I could lock them in the wash house and tell her they'd come straight from Crufts dog show. I won't say they won their best of breed, because she'll know I'm lying. But they were second, and we were robbed!

Thinking about this, there's a lot more than meets the eye. I'll have to ask Dicky. He's cleverer than me and will give me a few tips on what to do. Just then, I thought of "Dot", the little angel from The Bay, and realised none of this would be necessary. She possessed a kindness and humility which all the finishing schools in Switzerland couldn't possibly instil, together with a sincerity which could be matched against anyone. Besides, moving into the higher echelons of society might be fraught with problems and, in any case, I'm all right where I am.

Over in the far corner, I spotted Eddie. The Bis-Bar was all the richer for his presence. At an opportune moment, I went over to speak to him.

"How's things?" I asked. "Have you had any response from the record companies yet?"

"A couple of rejection letters saying it sounds interesting, but it's not what they're looking for at the moment," he answered despondently.

"Have you got a band together yet?"

"No I haven't. I usually get a couple of friends in to play keyboards or backing vocals if I need them on the demos. Who've you got coming next?"

"Jethro Tull and then The Nice three days later."

"Great! You'll be packed for Jethro Tull."

"Yes, but it could be difficult, I'm not sure I'll be able to get everyone in."

"You always seem to worry, don't you?"

"So would you if the place was full and the group didn't turn up," I reasoned.

With the Steppenwolf fiasco still fresh in my memory, I now knew I couldn't afford another non appearance, and decided that something had to be done to ensure they played as promised.

The night before they were due at The Bay, Jethro Tull were playing the Hull University Rag Ball. I decided to drive there with Dot and attempt to meet the group first-hand. On arriving, the university staff were most helpful, and quickly showed me to the dressing room.

With great trepidation, I knocked and entered, before presenting myself as the promoter of the gig the following evening. After explaining my anxieties about the group's scheduled appearance, overseer Wilf Wright (later to manage Robin Trower and UFO) confidently assured me they would be there.

I spoke to Ian Anderson who was just as positive, and as they both sounded sincere, I felt greatly relieved. I smiled as I noticed Anderson standing on two legs, looking perfectly balanced as he did so. After rejoining Dot I watched Jethro Tull deliver an exhilarating set, sensing the next night was to be another important milestone for The Bay.

A Sunderland café and one persistent music lover. Everyone needs motivation, and while I don't know who that guy was, I owe him a deep sense of gratitude. All he wanted was to see the band and there was no harm in that. Sure, he'd irritated me, with his lack of understanding of the machinations of the music business.

Nevertheless, he had planted a seed that germinated into Jethro Tull giving us a night we'd never forget. It smashed The Bay's attendance record wide open as hordes of people in never-ending numbers continually arrived. Ian Anderson and his flute certainly worked its Pied Piper magic as it seemed that every teenager in town had followed him. The Bay had never known anything like it, eventually closing its doors with over 1,470 packed inside, and hundreds locked out. It was then that I realised The Bay was too small for the groups which people wanted to see, and the situation was becoming intolerable.

To my great relief, Jethro Tull arrived and, as the clock ticked on, they finally emerged into the ballroom to begin their set, when the first unforeseen problem of the evening arose. The dressing room was at the opposite end of the ballroom to the stage, and the place was so tightly packed, it was impossible for the group to reach it without trampling over people sitting patiently on the floor. Everywhere I looked, people were hanging off curtains, and standing on window sills, tables and chairs. Outside the dressing room, the group were unable to move a solitary inch.

I was in a quandary, when I suddenly remembered there was a fire door just near the edge of the stage which could be approached from the outside car park. I'd used it many times to wheel empty beer crates into the storage yard and after dispatching a waiter to wade through the crowd to open it, I led the group out of a kitchen side door towards the exit. After waiting anxiously for what seemed an eternity there was still no sign of the door being opened.

By now, shocked local residents were peering out of their windows at Ian Anderson who, dressed in his stage gear, looked weird to say the least. He stared at me questioningly as I pondered the next move. I had the biggest draw in the country, but was in the unenviable position of being unable get them into the gig. It was a monumental cock-up. As I looked sheepishly at Anderson, he remained silent and unperturbed. Completely unprompted, little Pepé the tour manager, stepped forward and bravely punched the glass panel in, placing his lacerated hand through the jagged glass, and opened the fire door from inside. The stage was only a few feet away and within seconds the group stepped on to a riotous welcome.

Ian Anderson positively enthralled the audience as "The Pied Piper Of Rock". Songs such as 'Fat Man', 'Nothing Is Easy', 'Jeffrey Goes To Leicester Square', and 'Reason For Waiting' were just some of the original compositions played that night, with the group members Martin Barre (guitar), Glenn Cornick (bass), and Clive Bunker (drums) fitting in beautifully. As usual, I looked out at the crowd, who were dressed in all sorts of exotic and wonderful costumes which added a glorious assortment of colour to the occasion. Despite their discomfort in the stifling heat, the audience's behaviour was most admirable. It wasn't greed that made me let so many in, it was the imploring faces at the door, some who'd travelled long distances. Afterwards, the group finally made it back to the dressing room. Outside, the crowd desperately pleaded for an encore but as the group made a forlorn effort to reach the stage, it proved impossible. The largest attended gig at The Bay was over.

Afterwards, Ian Anderson asked me for a lift back to The Seaburn Hotel, which was the most upmarket in town. While driving there, he related a story about how the management had asked him if he would eat in his room instead of the restaurant, due to his mode of dress. This incident was a clear indication that freedom of expression which had now permeated into most sections of society, still hadn't reached some ears. We'll take your money, but you can't eat with us, seemed to be their attitude. Ironically, after their Bay appearance, Ian Anderson could probably have bought the hotel, such was their stunning worldwide success including 17 consecutive albums in the American charts over the next eighteen years. Two of them – *Thick As A Brick* and *A Passion Play* – reaching number one. I was to promote the group again in Sunderland, and the return visit was just as eagerly received.

A few days later a huge fight erupted in The Lighthouse Bar. As I dashed upstairs to try to quell it, I found it difficult to take in what was happening. Tables were being overturned, glasses were being thrown and two people were lying injured on the floor. One of them was bleeding heavily from an open face wound after being slashed with a knife, while a ferocious exchange of blows was still going on between two warring factions. Girls were screaming, and it seemed all hell had broken loose as I tried to assess the situation.

As I ran in among them, I quickly spotted who I thought was the main protagonist. On reaching him, I felt something being jabbed against my stomach and looked down to see the shiny blade of a knife glinting in the disco lights. "Get back," he ordered menacingly. I immediately stopped in my tracks, knowing that to show the slightest sign of fear, could be fatal. It was a heart-stopping moment as I defiantly stood my ground. As we continued to stare each other out, an eerie silence descended over the room, broken by the groaning coming from the wounded victim lying amidst a pool of blood on the floor.

As I continued staring at my aggressor, instinct told me to step backwards but I knew that the slightest movement might cause him to panic, and thrust the blade deep within me. Was he a psychopath who ruled by fear? What had upset him, and why was he so angry? I wondered. Suddenly, the juke box kicked in with another record. I took a deep breath and ordered him to leave with all the conviction my voice could muster. It was a tense moment and I sensed he'd become confused by his actions as his eyes turned to fear. My two colleagues John Tansey and Tommy Donnelly had arrived, and the odds were against him. "Get out now," I ordered. "If you don't, you'll get badly hurt." With that he turned and started walking towards the exit stairs, with me following cautiously behind.

On reaching the foyer, he began issuing ominous threats. "I'll be back next week to finish the job, and don't try to stop me, or you'll get hurt. Don't say I didn't warn you."

As he disappeared into the distance, I realised I'd have to take his threat seriously. There was a determined air about him which worried me. He'd already cut someone open and was liable to do something crazy. Suddenly, flashing blue lights appeared and an ambulance pulled into the car park. Within seconds a badly injured youth was lifted into it, with his face cut wide open extending from his ear right down to his cheek. It was a gruesome sight, and he had seventeen stitches inserted into the wound. Unfortunately, he still carries a prominent scar to this day.

After the attacker's threat, I had a serious problem bearing in mind the severity of what had happened, and I knew I'd have to be ready. I carefully formulated my plan, bearing in mind Mr Dixon had asked me not to involve the police because he was worried about his licence. Knowing this, I took a drive over to town and sought out the man who I knew to be the hardest in the area after a recent gangland scrap. I can only describe him as fearless, built like a tank, and possessing a punch that could fell an ox. He and his friends were notorious, and this was the factor I was banking on. With a bit of luck, my villainous friend and his heavies would act as a deterrent. On the other hand, if things went badly wrong, I knew I had excellent backing, and was confident we'd be able to handle it.

After outlining my plan, he agreed to come over.

"There's only one snag," I told him. "You'll have to wear a dickie bow and shirt, because it's important everyone recognises you are officially working there." Surprisingly, he agreed, and when the weekend finally came, I hid him and his team upstairs, issuing them with strict instructions not to do anything unless I gave the signal.

During the course of the following week, I instigated a rumour that the police were waiting to arrest the attacker, in the hope he would stay away. If he was willing to listen to reason, that was great. If not, someone could be seriously hurt, and I prayed it wouldn't come to that.

After an anxious wait, the weekend duly came, and about an hour after opening time, the knife-wielding thug duly arrived with six or seven unruly types. As I watched from inside the foyer, they sat outside on the car park wall, drinking bottles of beer, and I could feel the tension rising. As people entered, they began jeering and passing uncomplimentary remarks, especially toward the girls. I was incensed at such contemptible behaviour, and as the beer took effect, they became cockier with their insults, until finally my patience snapped. Now, there was nothing else for it, but to go out and confront them.

"Okay, it's time for you lot to move," I warned. "If you don't, there'll be trouble."

They remained impassively seated on the wall, and began sneering and laughing, as though it was all a joke. One of them spoke out defiantly. "We're not going anywhere. We like it here, so you just f**k off back inside and mind your own business."

Realising the situation was hopeless, I immediately summoned John Tansey and Tommy Donnelly plus the heavy squad to come

96

downstairs. I was now facing these louts with an impressive team behind me, and I felt a lot more confident as I approached them for the second time.

"Right, I want you off that wall now and out of the car park," I ordered. "If you don't, we'll make sure you do move." With that, the hardened villain I had brought in walked menacingly towards them.

"You heard what he said, now f**k off before you all get a good hiding."

Sensing they were fearful for their own safety, I stepped forward and pushed one off the wall. His friends turned and looked on helplessly as he struggled to his feet. My villainous friend laughed contemptuously and moved towards them in a threatening manner.

"You're just a bunch of wankers," he mocked.

"We didn't know you worked here!" one of them said, having recognised my dangerous accomplice.

"I don't want any fancy speeches, so just f**k off now," he demanded with more than a hint of menace. Realising my friend was in no mood for niceties, they turned and skulked away like frightened rats fleeing a flooded sewer. The plan had worked perfectly. Over the following few weeks, I continued to have my 'friends' call over, just as an insurance policy but, thankfully, nothing further happened.

"Geoff, when you had those hard cases come over," one of the waiters later told me, "the dance floor was always empty because nobody dared dance, especially the girls who were terrified."

"Well, they can now," I smiled. Such was life at The Bay.

Chapter 10

On June 16, The Nice played an excellent set with Keith Emerson on keyboards, Lee Jackson on bass and Blinky Davison on drums; David O'List, the guitarist, having only recently left. The attendance was dismal, and I lost money, although the group delivered a cracking perfomance. Songs from their recently released album, *Ars Longa Vita Brevis*, were the set's mainstay, with the crowd favourite 'Rondo' lifting the atmosphere to new heights.

At the end of the set, Keith Emerson, renowned for his showmanship, enveloped his Hammond organ with the American flag. Three of its stripes appeared to be dripping with blood, signifying their empathy with the assassinations of President JF Kennedy, Robert Kennedy and Martin Luther King. The group had first enacted this symbolic gesture and ingenious stunt at a charity gig for the Biafran situation, by making a paper template of the US flag, which was cut and sprayed with red paint giving the impression the flag was dripping with blood. Keith Emerson would then thrust a dagger into his Hammond organ and, at the finale, would wrap the flag around himself, usually to a standing ovation.

In 1969, The Nice were specially commissioned to write a song for the Newcastle Arts Festival called 'The Five Bridges Suite'. An album of the same name was released in 1970, but the group were under the mistaken impression that there were five bridges across the River Tyne, when in actual fact, there were seven! After The Nice split in March 1970, Keith Emerson's next venture, Emerson, Lake & Palmer went on to tremendous success in America, receiving no less than eight gold albums, and spending a total of 101 weeks in the American charts between 1970 to 1978. By a strange irony, I was due to promote the trio's first ever gig at Newcastle City Hall. Unfortunately, after organizing everything, they cancelled although in fairness, I was paid compensation by their management who, if memory serves me correctly, went on to manage T. Rex, Roxy Music, and Robbie Williams.

Tyrannosaurus Rex, consisting of Marc Bolan on guitar and vocals, and Steve Peregrine Took on percussion, held cult status on the underground scene, and had been receiving regular airplay from their staunchest fan, John Peel. They were also very discerning about where they played. Finally, after some good write-ups about The Bay from John Peel, they agreed to appear. Their fee was £350 pounds which was an awful lot of money for a duo. After careful consideration, I decided to take the gamble, by putting two differing acts on together. If it didn't work, it would be another lesson learnt, but somehow an inner force told me to go ahead. Who did I choose to pair them up with? The four piece who had impressed me six months earlier: the irrepressible Free.

On June 27, 1969, Free went on first and went down reasonably well. During the interval, while anxiously waiting for Tyrannosaurus Rex to arrive, I received a phone call from a distressed sounding June Childs, Marc's future wife.

"We've broken down at Sheffield, do you still want us to come?" she asked cautiously.

"Absolutely, the place is heaving here," I assured her.

"In that case we'll have to hire a taxi, will you pay for it?"

"How much will it cost?" I enquired warily.

"Seventeen pounds."

"Yes, I'll pay it," I answered in desperation. "But please hurry, the crowd here are getting restless."

"We'll do our best," replied June encouragingly.

I was in a quandary. The place was packed with everyone sitting on the floor patiently awaiting the headliners, but there was nobody to entertain them. Then I had the bright idea of asking Free to do another set.

"Yes we will," replied Andy Fraser. "But you'll have to pay us extra."

"Of course," I replied, and after agreeing a further £35, on they went. By now, The Bay was packed to capacity and the atmosphere was tense. When the group hit the stage again, they took one look at the huge crowd, and sensed this was their big chance to impress. Aged between seventeen and eighteen, but looking even younger, Free seemed as if they were hardly out of puberty, never mind adolescence. Nevertheless, although small in stature, they were about to prove the old adage that good stuff comes in small bundles, and The Bay never knew what hit it.

With an amazing voice, the strength and clarity of which never faltered, for someone so small in stature, Paul Rodgers was a revelation. He strutted, or should I say commanded the stage as if he was a young Elvis Presley. Paul Kossoff unleashed a series of exquisite solos from his trusty Les Paul guitar, while his dextrous fingers bent and sustained the notes with the intensity of a heart surgeon straining to save an endangered life. There was a majestic subtlety about his playing as the notes climbed and soared, while his face contorted into the agonised look of someone who had accidentally touched a high voltage cable. Andy Fraser, the bass player, seemed to take it all in his stride. Outwardly cool and unruffled, you sensed that underneath this calm exterior, his pulse raced with excitement. There at the back, his face dripping in sweat, was Simon Kirke, fiendishly determined not to miss a beat, hitting the drums with sledgehammer precision as he drove the group relentlessly on.

In the midst of all this excitement, some wit had plugged the jukebox back in and The Turtles' latest single came blasting out of the four huge speakers. For a few moments, bedlam ensued. I raced to disconnect it as Free hit full stride, flexing their musical muscles as they warmed to their task. Watching them that night was a wonderful experience and £70 for a group of this quality was an absolute steal. Such was their subsequent dramatic rise in popularity that I was soon having to pay them £1,500 a night.

When Free eventually left the stage to a tumultuous roar of appreciation, they were drenched in sweat and drained of every last ounce of energy. When someone gives their all like this, no matter what their occupation, it commands respect, and you get the impression that they'll never be out of work. From there on in, Free never were, and we couldn't get enough of them. This one gig had turned out to be phenomenal and, thanks to Mick Grabham, had inadvertently turned out to be a fantastic piece of luck for The Bay. Overnight, Free had become *our* superstars, and in some strange way we felt they belonged to us. The rest of the country weren't to latch on to them for several months, and The Bay had leapt ahead of the rest on this one.

As the evening wore on, and with time running out, there was still no sign of Tyrannosaurus Rex and I became frantic with worry as I was summoned to the phone again. It was June, seeking further reassurance.

"Do you still want us to come?" she asked, half expecting me to say it was too late and to head back to London.

"Definitely," I replied, panic-stricken.

"Are you sure?" she asked. "It'll be very late by the time we get there." "Where are you now?" I anxiously enquired.

"I don't know," she replied. "It's somewhere on the A1 near Scotch Corner."

"For heaven's sake, please hurry up," I urged. "The crowd here are getting frantic."

"Right, we're on our way, we'll be there as soon as possible," she said reassuringly, before replacing the receiver.

The minutes ticked away but after a nerve-wracking wait, Marc and Steve finally arrived and were ushered straight onstage to wild and rapturous applause. It was late and the crowd had been fantastically patient, but the night was far from over. Unknown to us all, we were about to witness what I regard as another of the top three gigs (with Country Joe and The Who) that I promoted at The Bay. As the duo walked on, they acknowledged the enthusiastic audience, before sitting cross-legged on cushions placed on the floor.

As they played, the mystique surrounding them began to unfold in an enthralling journey through their repertoire. 'Debora', 'Salamanda Palaganda', 'Eastern Spell' and many more were heard by an enraptured and attentive audience. On stage, they both looked so tiny and innocent, with Steve Peregrine Took giving the appearance of a fragile piece of porcelain, which if touched would shatter into a thousand pieces.

Meanwhile Marc immersed himself in the songs as if reaching for a spiritual and transcendental message from above. During all this, the audience remained transfixed, while seeming to attain the same level of tranquillity which united them as one with the group.

In between songs, I looked around and it was quite noticeable that Tyrannosaurus Rex had brought their own select band of dedicated followers wearing caftans and beads. The smell of lighted joss sticks began drifting above the heads of the audience, enabling everyone to inhale its pungent aroma. As I turned the lights down, the effect was both mystical and magical.

Backstage, the door leading to Marc Bolan's dressing room was jammed with female admirers who were desperate to meet him. Some were even crying with emotion. Others waited to meet their new young heroes in Free, especially Paul Rodgers. I'd never experienced female adulation of this intensity and found it impossible to empty The Bay that night. After checking with the group, I let a number of girls into Free's dressing room to collect their autographs, and it was obvious the group had now become sex symbols. Girls were flinging their arms around them in an unbridled show of affection, and as more continued to pile in, I found it impossible to control them. After coming off stage they had looked exhausted in the summer heat, but it soon became apparent they were eager to capitalise on their extremely good fortune.

For their part, the girls were only too eager to offer their own personal home comforts in whatever manner the group desired as they fought anxiously to be the chosen ones. When the group left The Bay, hordes of girls followed them out. I don't know how many ended up in the group's van, but there were a good few vacant seats on the late buses.

"Paul, Paul," cried one attractive girl who had been brushed aside in the rush as the van pulled away. I stepped hopefully forward to offer my services. She hesitated, looked at me and realised I was but a pale imitation of Marc or Paul. Then she put her arms around me, and kissed me. I was shocked, and decided to invite her back inside, but sensing her disappointment, I realised it was never going to work. It was Paul she wanted, and with her heart broken, she turned and left. Finally, after all the hysterics, I was alone.

To this day I'm often asked how much I was earning at the time. Firstly, I must reiterate that things began as more of a hobby and a way of being involved in the excitement of it all than being obsessed with the money to be made.

As successes like Family, Pink Floyd, The Who, Free, and Tyrannosaurus Rex came along, so did the financial pressures and careful budgeting was a must because a lot of the gigs lost money. Knowing this, it was essential not to live beyond my means because there were a lot of hidden costs, such as petrol for the drive to London, or rail fares, bed and breakfast while staying there, food, lengthy telephone calls, advertising posters, the hire of the hall, doormen and the support act to pay. There was also hospitality drinks for both groups, and things like 5% of gross ticket sales to record shops for selling them.

At The Bay, a typical breakdown was £20 for the hire of the hall; three doormen at £2 each; and painted day-glo posters at around £8. At first, there were no telephone costs because I used The Bay's. Generally speaking, it was usually pay at the door, so there were no ticket printing costs either. I always paid the bands in cash at the end of the night, settling up with the tour manager or, if they didn't have one, whoever from the group was delegated to deal with financial affairs. In the case of Free it was always Andy Fraser.

After all expenses, Jethro Tull made around £300, but three days later I lost £250 on The Nice.

The virtually unknown McMenna Mendleson Mainline from Canada also lost heavily, as did Three Dog Night and Yes. In order to survive, I worked on the door six nights a week, and had a day job at The Bay stocking the bars each morning. As a consequence, I was able to buy a second-hand 3.4 Jaguar on hire purchase which was my only luxury. A lot of the lesser names also lost money, mainly because only discerning people had heard of them, but it was all part of helping to establish the group and The Bay. Fortunately, as they didn't cost much, the losses weren't too disabling.

In 1970, when I opened The Locarno ('The Fillmore North') as a fully fledged professional promoter a whole new set of circumstances prevailed. The stakes had risen entailing a £100 guarantee for the hall and a 10p (2s) surcharge from everyone who attended. As the ballroom held 3,000 people it also meant a lot more trips to London as I needed to book much bigger names to fill it. By this time the rock scene had become much bigger and more commercialised, therefore groups who I'd booked at The Bay for £100, were now costing three of four times their original price. At The Fillmore, I lost money on a lot of acts. Ginger Baker's Airforce charged £1,500 but I lost £600 on them. Free charged the same amount but, in actual fact, they ended up costing me an extra £50. David Bowie, Christine Perfect, Traffic, Soft Machine, and the Bonzo Dog Doo–Dah Band were other losses.

In contrast, there were plenty of successes and packed houses at The Locarno, notably The Who, Pink Floyd, Family, Free, Ten Years After, Led Zeppelin, Tyrannosaurus Rex, and The Faces. I always paid in cash, no matter how big the loss, and word soon got back to London that I could be trusted, especially as around this time there were more and more cases of bounced cheques, or promoters disappearing with the money. As a result I was being offered major groups even before they decided to tour.

Moving to The Mayfair at Newcastle was a real eye opener. By then, the rock scene had become massive and attendances rocketed. I never once lost money there and, on one occasion, there was a surfeit of over £1,000. Unfortunately, as is explained later, disillusionment was setting in and it didn't take much for me to walk away. Nevertheless, despite this, it was a fantastic experience – most of the time.

Back at The Bay a group appeared who'd been getting some great reports whenever they played at The Marquee, but for some strange reason didn't seem to be making any great waves nationally. Yes turned out to be excellent, although the gig was poorly attended. Their line-up at the time was Jon Anderson (vocals), Chris Squire (bass), Bill Bruford (drums), Pete Banks (guitar) and Tony Kaye (organ).

Afterwards, Chris Squire asked me if I knew anyone who could put him up for the night. I immediately volunteered and, after arriving at my seafront flat, made him coffee and sandwiches. He seemed a pleasant sort as we sat and had a lengthy conversation about his band and various albums. In the morning, I made him breakfast and, after a further friendly chat, bade him farewell.

About six weeks later, I took a chance and re-booked them

Chapter 10

because they seemed to have so much potential. There was something different about their unique fusion of intricate arrangements and harmonies, topped by Jon Anderson's excellent voice. It seemed only a matter of time before they cracked it although in reality, it took longer than anyone envisaged.

After another great gig during which they played songs such as 'Endless Dreams', 'Walls', 'The Calling', 'Where Will You Be', and 'State of Play', the group left the dressing room to mingle with the crowd. This was the chance Debbie had been patiently waiting for and she immediately became friendly with one of the band. Within minutes, they had made their way out into the murky darkness of the car park.

Meanwhile, Melanie, Caroline and Sarah were hovering.

"The group were excellent," said Caroline. "We've been really looking forward to seeing them because we met them last time they were here."

Suddenly, all heads turned towards Caroline as she appeared to blush.

"Look, I promise you nothing happened, Geoff," she protested. A chorus of disapproval suddenly broke out.

"You liar," Melanie shouted. "You said he was a great shag!"

Caroline looked sheepish and stared disapprovingly at Melanie.

"What about you and the roadie from Three Dog Night?"

"I've never denied it, but you're pretending to be all prim and proper," countered Melanie. I left them to squabble among themselves. Perhaps the group were aptly named, as nobody appeared to say no.

Later, Chris Squire approached me and asked if I could put him up again. I was happy to oblige and, after reaching my place, we had another very interesting chat. My own observation was that he had a quiet, easy-going manner which made his conversation relaxed and interesting. In fact I could honestly say it was difficult not to like him. In the morning, I made him the usual breakfast and felt as though I'd made a real friend. I bade him goodbye, and told him I hoped the group did well.

Yes eventually had fantastic success, entering the American *Billboard* chart no less than 15 times between 1972 and 1994 with three platinum and nine gold albums, while selling out Madison Square Gardens more nights than anyone in its history. This seems particularly ironic in light of their two combined appearances at The Bay totalling less than 500. Despite losing money both times, it didn't colour my opinion of them because they were excellent.

Years later, I was to have a further encounter with Chris Squire, which led to one of my most embarrassing moments in rock. I'd gone down to London with two friends, Bill Elliot and Ray Hubbard to see The Eagles at Wembley Arena. Later, Ray and I decided to hire a taxi to see if we could somehow gatecrash our way into a reception being held for the group in a Mayfair nightclub. By a stroke of good fortune, a friend of mine, Nick Lloyd, the right-hand man for Richard Robinson who was head of Warner Bros. in England, was standing at the entrance when we arrived.

"Geoff, what are you doing here?" he asked upon seeing us.

"We're trying to get into the reception, but we haven't got an invite, can you do anything to fix it, Nick?"

"You and your friend just follow me," he confidently instructed us.

"Two VIP guests of Warner Brothers," he announced to the startled doorman.

"Good evening sir," came the reply as we followed Nick. Once inside, the whole of rock's cognoscenti seemed to be present, including Keith Moon who recognised me and waved. Everyone seemed to be in high spirits while bowls of tequila sunrise were being lavishly consumed in celebration of the name of one of The Eagles' tracks. Beautiful women were everywhere, and as the unlimited free booze was consumed, I was beginning to think the scene looked like The Fall of The Roman Empire, but instead of horse-drawn chariots, it was limos. As I looked around, girls were unashamedly draping themselves over their escorts, or latching on to anyone famous enough to warrant their attention. This was unbridled rock hedonism at its very height and I must admit the atmosphere fascinated me.

By now Yes were very big and in the revelry I spotted Chris Squire.

"Come on, I'll introduce you to Chris," I said to Ray as I walked over.

Chapter 10

"Hi, Chris, how are you?" I confidently began. "Glad to see the group's doing so well. I'd just like to introduce you to a friend of mine."

Chris Squire stared back at me with a blank expression on his face.

"I'm sorry, but I don't know you."

"It's me, Geoff, don't you remember? I promoted you twice in Sunderland and put you up at my flat?" I reminded him in an effort to jog his memory.

"I'm sorry, but I don't know you," he repeated, while shaking his head in bewilderment to the beautiful girl accompanying him.

I was shocked but decided to linger for a few seconds in the hope that it was all a dreadful mistake, and that recognition would soon follow. He then turned towards his girlfriend and, with a nonchalant shrug of his shoulders, began to walk away.

"I don't know him," I overheard him telling her as he disappeared into the throng. I was flabbergasted, and felt humiliated in front of Ray. It was one of my most embarrassing moments, or perhaps I'd got my just deserts for being a freeloader. Thankfully, vocalist Jon Anderson has a much better memory, and always greets me warmly on the rare occasions we do meet.

Chapter 11

One day at The Bay, I received a call from Lionel Conway, the ex-manager of Plastic Penny.

"Hi Geoff, I'm managing this singer-songwriter who's excellent. What about giving him a booking at your place?" he asked. "I know no one's ever heard of him but I'll let you have him for £50 because we're desperate for gigs."

My heart sank as it seemed an unworkable suggestion.

"I'm sorry Lionel," I answered, "but the last thing we want is an unknown singer-songwriter because it takes a band to go down well here. Besides, we've got plenty of singer-songwriters in this area who are desperate for gigs. I'm sorry, but if there's any other way I can help you, I will."

"Oh c'mon, Geoff, be reasonable, I'd really appreciate it if you would," he pleaded. It was an impassioned request, and I relented.

"Oh all right then, what's his name?" I asked.

"Elton John," he answered.

"£50 it is then Lionel, but he'd better be good!"

"Thanks Geoff, but you just wait and see, he's excellent, honestly, I'm telling you."

A few days later, an apologetic Lionel rang me. "Geoff, I'm sorry but Elton John can't make it. No one else wants to book him, and it seems pointless coming all the way up there just for £50."

"Oh that's all right, Lionel, don't worry about it," I said. "Besides, I don't think many people would have come to see him anyway."

After Jethro Tull's capacity gig, it was obvious The Bay had become far too small to accommodate groups whose fees had risen dramatically. If something wasn't done soon, we were in danger of being left behind by other venues with bigger capacities.

Chapter 11

Over the previous year, John Holton, the manager of a local Mecca hall which held around two and a half thousand, had approached me on numerous occasions to start putting bands on there. It was tempting, but I'd had no hesitation in deciding to stay where I was at The Bay. Besides, how could I leave all my friends and acquaintances who were part of the rich community spirit which bound us together. Each morning as I arrived for work, I felt it was my second home – and was the most rewarding and satisfying job I'd ever had. Knowing this, it was far too precious to give up lightly.

The problematic issue of aggression and fighting continued to rear its ugly head from time to time. It seemed that no matter how hard we tried, new and undesirable elements occasionally gained admission. One example of this occurred when a fight started in the ballroom. A big pit lad from nearby Whitburn village was laying into a victim who was patently unable to defend himself. Upon confronting the assailant, he immediately swung a vicious looking right hook in my direction, and followed this up with a fearsome left.

Fortunately, I was able to take rapid avoiding action and, in a split second, I retaliated with a swift left and right combination as he rushed at me in a determined effort to finish matters. While doing so, I sent out right and lefts with such rapidity, he was becoming flustered as they landed. However this guy was game, and kept coming at me with wild swings. I used my footwork to get inside and work him over, before back-pedalling in case he tried to grab me. We were now toe to toe, with no quarter given, and I sensed the speed of the punches he was absorbing was beginning to weaken him.

At The Bay, I always wore rubber-soled shoes, which gave me a much better grip on the highly polished floor. It was to pay a rich dividend as I spotted his leading foot was too far ahead of his body, rendering him unbalanced. Seizing the opportunity, I bent down, grabbed his leading ankle and, in a flash, flicked him into the air. His remaining leather shoe slid away from the waxed floor. I then disorientated him by instantly twisting him 180 degrees in mid-air. As he landed, I stepped over his prostrate body, and in one swift movement 'timpsoned' him heavily across the face in a half-volley as he bounced off the floor. For the uninitiated, this is done with the instep and not the toe, and has the effect of stunning a much bigger opponent without him incurring any serious damage. With him now unconscious, the final act was to drag his motionless body down the side passage and out into the car park where I left him to recover.

Afterwards, I felt uneasy, and had the distinct feeling this wouldn't be the end of the matter. Being from a mining community, I knew a pit lad has his pride, and doesn't like to be beaten. His friends would be baying for blood, and would rile him till he could take no more, so it was almost a certainty he'd be back.

Sure enough, about three weeks later, a burly figure strode towards me with a twisted look of hatred written across his face. I recognised him from the previous encounter, and wondered how he'd gained entry. I knew he was there to exact revenge and braced myself for the onslaught. As he closed in, I stepped forward and caught him by surprise with a full-blooded 'nut'. He reeled back in shock as I instantly followed this by a left, while a damaging right landed square on his jaw. To my astonishment, he went down and stayed down. His friends then helped him to his feet and walked him to the exit. Fortunately, he wasn't foolish enough to come back for a third dose and was barred for life.

Two days after this incident, I had a disagreement with Mr Dixon, which pushed me into making a fateful decision. On the morning in question, I was stocking the bars with bottles of Coca Cola for the under-age disco held each Wednesday. The previous week there had been lots of complaints about the drinks being warm so I resolved to remedy this by placing them on cooling trays. Mr Dixon appeared and ordered me to do some other trivial task.

Although I agreed to do it as soon as I was finished, he lost his cool. He berated me in a stern voice saying I thought more of the kids, and ordered me to leave it. I was hurt and brooded on his words. All the fights, the groups, the publicity, the mentions on John Peel's show, seemed to count for nothing as I evaluated all that had taken place over the previous months.

There were other things to consider. Fleetwood Mac's manager had rung twice for the group to play at The Bay, and on both occasions Mr Dixon hadn't passed the message on. Instead, they played at The Locarno and, of course, we were empty that night. I was already aware that The Who were due to play soon, and in all probability, hundreds of people would be locked out. Then there were the huge puddles that formed in the car park whenever it rained. People were forced to wade through them, and despite making huge profits, Bass Breweries seemed oblivious to our constant pleas to have the concrete resurfaced. I was also tired of the fighting, and having to constantly sort out other people's troubles.

Another incentive was that I'd finally be able to shed the title of bouncer, and become a fully fledged promoter. Dad would like that. He didn't like me being a bouncer, and wanted me in a safer job. He often reminded me that by repeatedly getting into tough situations, I was tempting fate, and next time I might not be so lucky. After being at The Bay for over five years, it was time to move on and, with great reluctance, I handed in my notice.

Over the following fortnight, Mr Dixon and I never spoke to each other. Pride is one of the seven deadly sins, and it seemed we were both suffering from an immense surfeit of it. As we wordlessly passed each other, I desperately wanted to break the impasse as he'd been so good to me, and I thought of all the wonderful times we'd had.

"Are you coming upstairs for a drink?" he would say to Tommy and I at the end of each night. "Yes, of course you can have Sunday night off to go to Redcar Jazz Club," also came to mind. Then there was the staff party where I'd drunkenly put a large bowl of trifle over a girl's head. There was the silver 3.4 Jaguar outside, which was something I'd thought I'd never own. I had a lot to be thankful for, but somehow changing my mind would surely lead to stagnation. The Bay had a living heart that was resilient, and had survived far greater setbacks than a mere employee leaving.

"Here's your money," said Tommy. I took the brown envelope with Mr Dixon's writing on it and its finality was total. I turned and walked into his office to say a last farewell knowing that pride no longer came into it. Manners had overridden every other consideration, and the values Dad had imbued in me were too valuable to be cast aside in a wanton show of stubbornness. Unfortunately he wasn't there. I took one last look at the empty office before making my way out. It was to be the last time I ever saw it.

As I drove away, it was one of the saddest moments of my life. If only I could take the waiters with me, together with John Tansey, Tommy Donnelly and Dot but that was out of the question. I was on my own now, and I wondered if I was doing the right thing. After driving a few hundred yards down the road, I had an uncontrollable urge to turn back, but realised this was impossible. I was committed, and fate had decreed that my journey into the unknown had to continue.

I reached The Locarno Ballroom where doubts were already beginning to surface. Would the Mecca staff respond, and understand the ethos of what I was trying to achieve? And how sympathetic would they be towards people who had vastly different ideas from their own? Only time would tell.

Chapter 12

A new word now began creeping into band negotiations with alarming regularity. That word was "business", which conveniently covered a multitude of sins. The merest hint of protest or indignation over an increased fee even though you had supported a particular group when they were unknown merely brought a shrug of the shoulders and a familiar catchphrase, "It's business, man."

The opportunists had arrived with money the sole motivating factor. A counter phrase, "selling out", became common among those who sensed a group or manager's actions were entirely mercenary. Principles and money are poor bedfellows. Put them alongside power and you have the recipe for many of today's musical ills. In later years, Nirvana's Kurt Cobain coined the phrase "radio friendly unit shifter" to describe the corporate key to success. Unfortunately, this has evolved into unscrupulous behind the scenes manipulators devising radio friendly unit shifters that are to say the least, mediocre, if not rubbish. "Oh! It doesn't matter as long as it sells. It's business, after all."

During the negotiations involved in moving to The Locarno, there were important hurdles to overcome. The first was the name. The Locarno was rooted in the past and hardly the kind of underground name to conjure up images of Pink Floyd or Jethro Tull. It was prudent to think of a name which people could accept, and readily identify with. After some deliberation, it came to me. Over in the States, promoter Bill Graham ran two highly respected venues on opposite coasts known as the Fillmore West and the Fillmore East. (Fillmore was actually the name of a street in San Francisco.) I unashamedly plagiarised the name by renaming Sunderland Locarno 'The Fillmore North' on the night I hired it. Whether I could persuade the best groups to appear was in the lap of the gods, but it was a start.

Secondly, it was crucial to book a group for the opening night which would have enough drawing power. Fortunately, I had such a group lined up. The third and most important requirement of all was to remove unnecessary dress restrictions, and allow people to come as they wished. If I couldn't get the restrictions lifted, underground music fans would simply stay away, making it pointless to open the venue up for rock in the first place.

After I had sorted out these three problems, everything was set for the opening night. Before making the decision to leave The Bay, I had carefully weighed up the pros and cons of the new venue. It could hold 3,000 people, had twin decks, which meant we could play albums as well as singles, and also boasted it's own crew of bouncers which would relieve me of the responsibility of security. With two separate dressing rooms, a huge car park, and an increased capacity, I now felt confident that I could take on the challenge of the big boys in London, and have a realistic chance of succeeding. Come what may, there would be no high ideals, just common sense, courtesy and fair play. These had been the very things which had got me this far, and while I knew I would have to adapt, I was determined not to change.

Meanwhile, there was only one group who possessed all the characteristics needed to open the new venture. It was of course The Who. *Tommy*, the rock opera, had been released to critical acclaim, and had reached No. 2 in the UK charts and number four in America. It proved to be a spectacular opening night, and surpassed all my hopes and expectations.

As I watched, The Who's faces were covered in sweat, while the explosive charge that had lain dormant in the dressing room was unleashed with unbridled ferocity. It was an awesome spectacle, as the four members played with passion, commitment, and most importantly, sheer enthusiasm. This transmitted itself to the audience who responded with such fervour, it was as if everybody was at one with each other.

Backstage, Roger Daltrey popped his head round the dressing room door and peeped out at the massed crowd. "Where are the birds?" he cheekily asked. "Don't worry," I assured him. "I know someone who'll take care of your every need, and the rest of the band's if necessary." Roger smiled and seemed relieved. If he wasn't now, he would be later, I chuckled to myself.

"Will I be able to get the group's autograph?" asked Debbie who was wearing a low cut top with a black mini skirt.

"I think you'll get more than that," I answered.

She smiled that knowing look.

"Where are they staying?" she asked.

I had to admire her, because she was smart, and always covered her options. If her mission failed backstage, she would know which hotel to go to, and more likely than not, which room each member occupied.

"I think it's The Roker," I said, "but you're bound to find out for yourself when you meet the group."

Behind The Fillmore's stage were two dressing rooms, one of which was besieged by autograph hunters. I noticed Roger was missing when people kept asking his whereabouts to complete their set of autographs. As I opened the door to the darkened dressing room, I heard groans and spotted a black skirt lying on the floor before quickly slamming it shut. A few minutes later, Roger calmly appeared among the melee of people.

"Everything all right?" I asked.

"Yeah, everything's fine," he smiled, as he signed another autograph.

After the opening night triumph, I soon noticed a disturbing trend among the bouncers. As harmless groups of people sat on the floor, innocently conversing or listening to the music, they were ordered to stand up for no apparent reason. If they were slow to respond, they were given a helping nudge by the bouncer's foot, who then arrogantly motioned upwards.

I was incensed, and immediately protested.

"I'm sorry but those are the rules, they must sit on the seats," I was emphatically told.

"Yes, but what if there aren't any, or they don't want to?" I argued.

"We've been instructed to make sure they don't sit on the floor, so that's what we're doing," I was informed curtly.

I stormed off furiously to speak to the manager, pointing out that in many other areas, such as festivals, parks, or even the school assembly hall, people often sat on the floor if they wished. After listening to my protestations, he promised to look into it with an unconvincing shrug of the shoulder. For the time being, I could only wait and watch.

On August 22, Family played to over two thousand people; providing undeniable proof that if attendance figures were any yardstick, leaving The Bay had been the right move. Liverpool Scene and The Soft Machine were next, and over the following weeks things clicked nicely into place.

On September 12, Free were supported by Island's new signing, Mott The Hoople. It was a big step up from The Bay's 800 capacity but just how well would Free do in a venue holding 3,000? Over the previous weeks 'The Hunter', a track from their first album *Tons Of Sobs*, brought everyone onto the dance floor. Now, it seemed, the whole town wanted to hear them play it live. As evening approached, I drove over the town bridge and was astonished to see hundreds of people making their way towards The Fillmore on foot. As I pulled up, there was already a huge queue snaking hundreds of yards away from the main entrance, and within an hour the gig was packed to capacity with 3,000 people inside and hundreds locked out. Nothing had prepared me for success on such a scale, and it was an amazing night. I walked into the dressing room and informed the group the gig was a sell out as the magnitude of the occasion hit me. Were Free going to be bigger than The Beatles? It seems a silly question now, but that night, far from being silly, it looked like a realistic possibility.

Mott The Hoople seemed staggered by the size and intensity of a North East audience. It was only the third gig they'd ever played, and to be thrown into a seething cauldron of mass adulation of this nature must have been an unnerving experience.

Free stepped on stage to a welcome that was unprecedented in Sunderland. Girls began fainting; having to be hoisted over people's heads to the safety of the stage. The atmosphere was electric, and I've never experienced anything like it since. As Paul Rodgers strutted and teased his lithe young body against the mike stand, his amazing voice delivered the songs with a wonderful strength and clarity.

Halfway through the set, the group announced 'The Hunter'. The hall erupted into a frenzy of excitement as more girls pretended to faint in a vain attempt to be lifted onto the stage to join their idols. When the band finally came off stage, I walked out into the ballroom, still in a daze. "When are they coming back?" was a question I must have been asked a thousand times.

Backstage, girls, sobbing with emotion, became desperate to provide the group with any home comforts they might desire. Such was their unifying power even the bouncers liked this group. From then on, apart from one gig, I was to promote every Free appearance in the Newcastle and Sunderland area until they eventually split. Life had changed dramatically, and suddenly I had found a new and exciting vocation as a full-time rock promoter.

Chapter 13

The following week I walked over to Roker Park football ground to watch Sunderland play. As I looked at the lush green turf, I thought of how exciting it would be hold a pop festival there. It had been on my mind for some time, and as I waited for kick-off, the thought of staging it was ever growing. Just then, two young men approached me.

"Somebody should do something about those bouncers at The Fillmore, Geoff. They seem to have an attitude problem."

"Why, what have they done to upset you?" I asked.

"Well, the other night, one of them pushed us away from the dressing room door when we were trying to get Chicken Shack's autographs."

"I wouldn't mind, but we weren't doing any harm," his friend chimed in.

"It's the way they shove you around, they think they're so tough," continued the first youth, "and another thing, do they ever smile? When you enter the place you'd think someone had committed a murder."

There was an expectant roar as the opening whistle blew. "See you on the seventeenth when Family are on," one shouted encouragingly as they departed. I stood and pondered the implications of what I'd just been told. The Fillmore had become my whole life, and as the game progressed my concentration began to wander. Until recently, I'd also been a bouncer, and I wondered what possessed people to become one? Maybe they just need the money but then again, it gives them power, and in the wrong hands, power can make people's lives a misery. What happens if you get a preponderance of the wrong types, all working at the same establishment, at the same time? I shuddered at the very thought. No, the manager's too nice a guy to let it happen. "Any

The author and older brothers Leo and Donald

On board HMS Ark Royal in Aden

The Bay Hotel

The author 2002
(Joyce Savage)

John and Sheila's wedding which I attended

RAK

Directors :
Peter Grant
Mickie Most
Lawrence Myers, A.C.A.

LOCARNO BALLROOM, Sunderland
FRIDAY 12th NOVEMBER

Led Zeppelin

7 - 12   Licensed Bar till 10.30 P.M.

TICKET   75p

LOCARNO, SUNDERLAND   Friday, 12th November

LED ZEPPELIN

7 p.m.—12 midnight   Licensed Bar
Tickets, 75p, on sale HMV Records

WARNER WEST END 2
THURSDAY
NOV. 4
8.30 for 9 p.m.
(Please be seated by 8.30 p.m.)
DRESS INFORMAL
PERFORMANCE ENDS 11.15 p.m.

ROW   SEAT
Q   28
TO BE RETAINED

LED-ZEPPELIN
THE-SONG-REMAINS-THE-SAME

FILLMORE Tonight!

RECORDING AN ALBUM "LIVE" WHILST ON STAGE

FREE

ALSO — A JOHN PEEL DISCOVERY

★ **GRIFFIN** ★

7 — 12   ADMISSION 10'-

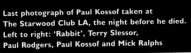

Last photograph of Paul Kossof taken at
The Starwood Club LA, the night before he died.
Left to right: 'Rabbit', Terry Slessor,
Paul Rodgers, Paul Kossof and Mick Ralphs

**Below and right:
Paul Kossof on stage**
(Lucy Piller)

Andy Fraser on stage at
The Fillmore North, Sunderland

SUNDERLAND
ASSOCIATION
FOOTBALL CLUB
LIMITED

OFFICES AND GROUND,
ROKER PARK GROUND, SUNDERLAND, SR6 9SW.

MANAGER: A. W. BROWN, TEL: 54308   SECRETARY: R. M. LINNEY, TELEPHONE NOS. 72277 & 58838
COMMERCIAL MANAGER: D. C. EATON, TEL: 72276   TELEGRAPHIC ADDRESS: 'FOOTBALL, SUNDERLAND.

18th April 1972.
(Tuesday)

Ref: RML/AB

G. Docherty, Esq:
53 Astral House,
Sunderland.

Dear Mr. Docherty,

Your letter of the 14th March was placed before my
Directors at their last Board Meeting.

I am instructed to inform you that your application
for the use of Roker Park Ground for the purpose of holding
a Pop Concert in August has been refused.

Yours sincerely,

Secretary.

SUNDERLAND TOP RANK SUITE
SUNDAY, 27th FEBRUARY, 1972
★ ★ ★
CHRYSALIS IN ASSOCIATION WITH FILLMORE NORTH
PRESENT

Jethro Tull
with Guests
Tir Na Nog

7.30 till 12   Ticket 60p

Nº 9989   **MAYFAIR**
FRIDAY, 20 OCTOBER
★ ★ ★
Fillmore North presents

Free
ALSO
BECKETT

8 - 1 a.m. Late Bars
Ticket £1   Nº 9989

TOP RANK SUITE · FRIDAY 7th MAY
(SUNDERLAND)

A FILLMORE NORTH PROMOTION

* * * * * * * * * * *

THE WHO

LATE BARS
8 - 1a.m.

LATE TRANSPORT
NO DRESS RESTRICTIONS

TICKETS 50p! YES ... ONLY 50p

On sale | BERGS | SAVILLE'S | DISQUE (Newcastle)

50P TICKETS **50**

THE WHO...AT NEWCASTLE

Next Thursday the Who (above) take the stage of the Mayfair Ballroom, Newcastle, for one of their rare appearances outside London. It should be a memorable night for their followers. But further interest lies in the appearance on the same bill of Curved Air, a group with a bright future. Watch out for their violinist Daryl Way and their girl singer Sonja Khristina, a former member of the "Hair" cast. On disc, the Who have a new Track single containing four numbers from their "Tommy" album, and Curved Air have their first L.P. out on Warner-Reprise.

To the Bay Hotel cool gig man

"Cool Gig Man" autographed photograph taken at The Bay Hotel
(L.F.I.)

Sunderland Echo

www.sunderlandecho.com

30p

FRIDAY, MAY 18, 2001

More fun on ▶ **Friday**

The man who made Sunderland a rock Mecca Page 33

Unsung heroes of Wearside
Pages 18 and 19

BIG MONEY BINGO
Coming on Monday!

MUSIC
Mummy's rotten, really

Life of an acting legend

PAGE 66

PAGE 66

PAGE 69

lunch

PAGE 66

With Entertainments Editor, Alistair Robinson
Tel: 01331 501 7250 e-mail: alistair.robinson@northeast-press.co.uk

The man who made Wearside a rock Mecca

★ PINK FLOYD ★
Buy Hotel this Monday

TOP RANK SUITE · FRIDAY 7th MAY
A FILLMORE NORTH PROMOTION

THE WHO

LATE BARS LATE TRANSPORT
8-1a.m. NO DRESS RESTRICTIONS
TICKETS 50!! YES ... ONLY 60p

Led Zeppelin

ROCK DOC: Geoff Docherty outside the Mecca, one of the homes of Fillmore North. Also pictured are poster and photo mementoes of the shows he put on.

CATCH THE FEVER!

THE ALEX JUNE DATES
THE ALEXANDRA, GRANGETOWN. TEL: 567 2774

Fri 8th THE FORCE £3

KERS £2
77
MOUTH £2
CE £3.50
PTON £3.50
ORT £3
TS £4
GO £2

IN years to come, if the rock heritage industry really takes off, there ought to be a plaque on the stairs at Sunderland's Astral House tower block.

It was here, in late 1974, that a wiry ex-boxer challenged one of the world's greatest guitarists to a race. The rock star reluctantly agreed, and after several stops for breath, and much puffing from his challenger, he eventually reached the flat on the 24th floor.

He may have finished second, but a big battle appeared to have been won. That night Paul Kossoff, the brilliant former member of the world-famous Free, slept without the aid of drugs for the first time in years.

SUNDERLAND's local band scene is thriving, but there was a time when the city also staged shows by the biggest names in rock. Entertainments Editor Alistair Robinson talks to Geoff Docherty, the man responsible for booking those bands, who has just written a book about his amazing experiences.

Kossoff has become one of the great dead heroes of rock, a wild-child musician who never did grow old. But he almost made it, and the man who briefly restored his health and his talent was a Sunderland bouncer turned rock promoter called Geoff Docherty.

Geoff, who had managed to serve in the Air Force, Royal Navy and Army, was a major figure in the rock business of the late 1960s and early 70s. It was a testament to his standing

that Kossoff, who had bucked at many a previous attempt to tame him, put up with his rigorous regime.

Geoff found Kossoff close to death, in a drug-induced stupor, at his house in London. With the permission of the star's father, actor David Kossoff, Geoff commandeered the bus belonging to North East group Beckett, who were in the capital for a gig, and brought Kossoff to Sunderland.
● Turn to Page 67

ALEXANDRA'S ROCK-TIME BANDS: Pub lines up summer season – Page 65

(The Sunderland Echo; used with perm

Music

Geoff's rock mecca

INCREDIBLE STORY: Above, Geoff Docherty looking through his book outside the old Mecca building in Sunderland. Below, Free, whom he helped on the road to stardom.

● From Page 33

Here, stocked up with supplies from Mrs Walker's health food store just off Fulwell's Sea Road, he forced Kossoff to do "cold turkey", keeping him prisoner for weeks at the Astral House flat so that he could not buy drugs.

Geoff squeezed oranges for him, and fed him fresh vegetables and wholemeal bread, and slowly the great man came back from death's door.

The night of the staircase race, the pair had been for a drink at Annabel's nightclub. Fans had been amazed to see Kossoff there. Only a handful of people had known that the rock star was in Sunderland. It would have been national news if it had leaked out.

After that Annabel's appearance, word did start to spread, but Kossoff was allowed to continue his recuperation in peace. The musician began to take pride in his appearance, and started to play guitar again. Geoff had the idea to team him with Beckett's singer, Terry Slesser.

Bryson Graham, former drummer from top band Spooky Tooth, was brought up from London and the group that was to become Back Street Crawler took shape, with rehearsals in the café at Sunderland Bowling Alley in the Newcastle Road – after midnight when the place was deserted and the muse was upon Kossoff.

This part of Geoff's story does not have a happy ending, however – for him or for the guitarist.

Kossoff contacted Free's former manager, Johnny Glover, who took the band off to London. The musicians secured a big-figure record deal, details of which were released to the music press.

Kossoff was back in the limelight, and prey once more to temptation. Geoff, meanwhile, was frozen out. In a little more than a year, Kossoff was dead.

Docherty's links with Kossoff, and the other members of Free, went back to 1969. If there is another suitable place for a rock heritage plaque, it would be on the wall of the new Bay Hotel at Whitburn.

It was at the old Bay, a 1930s building on the site of the present pub's car park, that Geoff, who had gained a reputation as a streetfighter after his return from the forces, had been employed as a bouncer.

In the 1960s, Geoff was already a fan of the emerging rock bands. When the Bay manager heard of this he asked him to book local acts. Geoff recruited the best he could get for the £50 on offer. Among them was The Gas Board, featuring a young Bryan Ferry.

Geoff quickly harboured ambitions of putting on some of the exciting new stars he was listening to on John Peel's Radio 1 show, but they would require a bigger fee. When the manager refused to pay it, Geoff offered to shoulder the risk by hiring the acts himself.

At this time he was earning £2 a week. He started saving. By January 1969 he had the £150 needed to book Family, one of the biggest "progressive" bands in the country. The pub's ballroom was packed. Geoff's gamble had paid off. With the £35 left over, he had enough to book the little-known Free. It was a flop – hardly anyone turned up. But Geoff could see they had potential.

Undaunted, he managed to book a band who were even bigger than Family – the legendary Pink Floyd. Further star acts followed.

From America came Three Dog Night and Woodstock Festival hits Country Joe And The Fish. British acts included Yes, Black Sabbath and Spooky Tooth. Imagine Oasis, Radiohead and Limp Bizkit coming to the

Barnes, and you will have an idea of the scale of Geoff's achievement.

Free returned, as a support act for Tyrannosaurus Rex, and it was there, at the Bay, that they made their national breakthrough, cementing their bond with Geoff in the process.

When the Tyrannosaurus hit car twice broke down on the way to Sunderland, Free played a second set.

They went down a storm, word got back to London and Free were on their way to fame.

News of Geoff and his amazing gigs began to make news in London. Radio 1's John Peel not only plugged the shows, but came to Sunderland, stayed with Geoff, and played his own records in the intervals at the Bay.

The pub's great days of rock culminated with a Jethro Tull concert that attracted fans from all over the North. Almost 1,500 packed the ballroom.

It was then that Geoff had to find a bigger venue. He switched to the Locarno ballroom, adjoining the bowling alley on

Newcastle Road.

The Who were the first of big names at the venue, which Geoff, cheekily but with some justification, dubbed Fillmore North, a reference to Fillmore East and West, the major rock venues run by promoter Bill Graham in New York and San Francisco.

Geoff pulled off ever-more amazing coups in booking such stars as Led Zeppelin, Pink Floyd again and Rod Stewart with The Faces, for a 1973 show that John Peel rates as his best ever.

After a disagreement with the Locarno management, Geoff switched to Newcastle Mayfair, where Eric Clapton's Derek And The Dominoes were among the big names he secured, and Newcastle City Hall.

At the City Hall, he gave Roxy Music (now reforming for an arena tour) their first "in concert" show, with the fans seated rather than standing.

In later years, Geoff progressed to band management. He brokered lucrative deals for Beckett and for 1980s outfits from the North East, The Showbiz Kids and Well, Well, Well, but each group just failed to get its big break.

Still in the Astral House flat where he tried to save Paul Kossoff, Geoff has spent the last six years writing the story of his remarkable life – and his rock years are only part of it.

The book, "Doc" Of The Bay, is now complete and he is looking for a publisher, but there is already talk of a television programme – a documentary or a drama – based on the work.

Geoff also has plans to return to the rock business, by opening a club for up-and-coming bands, but this time he might look to London rather than Sunderland. The kind of scene that the supported 30 years ago could never return, he says.

It is with some sadness that he looks back on those golden years. "It was a wonderful era, but the ideals of that time are gone," he concludes.

● The story of Free, and of Geoff's part in the rise of the band, are also told in Heavy Load, a definitive, hardback history of the band by David Clayton and Todd K Smith, which has just been released by Moonshine Publishing to coincide with the 25th anniversary of Paul Kossoff's death. It retails at £25, but can be ordered from Helter Skelter Books, London, for £3.1 to include postage and packing. Telephone 02078 361151.

● Terry Slesser is now running The Office, a pub rock venue in South Shields, where earlier this month he staged a Beckett reunion gig.

Cutting from NME: John Peel's favourite all time gig

BEST

THE FACES, SUNDERLAND, 1973

IT WAS the night Sunderland beat
Arsenal in the semi-final of the
Cup the year they went on to win
it. The Faces were always
wonderful live anyway and in
Sunderland on a night like that...
I mean, the entire place was in a
state of near-hysteria anyway an
The Faces were the perfect band
for that. I actually ended up
dancing onstage and I'm a man
who doesn't dance at all!

On their rider, they had about
crate of Blue Nun so we were
each issued with several bottles
and a riotous time was had by

And obviously The Faces cam
on hours late as they always di
and started kicking footballs in
the audience. The combination
football and music came togeth
in a unique conjunction that
night.

PICTURE: GARY MERRIN

Faces, Faces everywhere, at least they were in 1973 for John Peel problems, Geoff, just come and see me," were his reassuring words. Perhaps I was worrying about nothing. Maybe those chaps had been blocking the door, or had exaggerated what happened. Anyway, nobody got hurt, so what's all the fuss about?

I continued to ponder the bouncer dilemma. Why were they unable to grasp what we were trying to achieve? Didn't they have the foresight to realise that we were trying to create something worthwhile with the country's top groups coming to play for us? Looking at it rationally, it was bound to be a culture shock, but how long was it going to take them to adapt?

I was already aware of the excitement building up for the next big gig on October 24. It was to be Pink Floyd, with John Peel spinning the records, and once again everyone, including the media, was becoming excited about it.

Back at my seafront flat, the telephone rang.

"Geoff, is that you?" said a soft and gentle female voice.

"Yes, it is."

"It's Michelle here, can I come and see you?"

"When?" I asked cautiously.

"Straight away," she answered. "You do remember me, don't you?"

"Of course," I replied. How could I forget you after opening night at The Locarno?

"You haven't answered my question. Is it all right if I come round now?" she asked

"Of course you can," I replied eagerly.

"I'll be there shortly, bye."

Within a few minutes there was a knock at the door, and upon opening it, Michelle smiled seductively.

"Come on in, it's nice to see you," I said.

She stepped forward and embraced me as I felt her gorgeous figure pressing against me.

"Don't be shy Geoff, there are only the two of us here, aren't there?" she enquired.

"Yes, I'm just here on my own," I assured her.

"Haven't you got a girlfriend at the moment?"

"Not really," I replied. "I was taking a girl out from The Bay called Dot, but we seem to have drifted apart since I left."

119

"I didn't think you had," she said knowledgeably.

"Why, what makes you say that?"

"Well, I've often noticed you walking around The Fillmore, but you never seem to be with a girl. Is there any reason for this?"

"Actually, I'm very shy, and don't like discussing it," I replied.

She reeled back with a disdainful, if not, painful look on her face.

"Oh come off it. You don't expect me to believe that. You weren't shy the last time I was here."

"You're different," I replied.

"What do you mean, I'm different?" she quizzed.

"Well, I feel more relaxed with you and know you're not going to mess me about."

"Aren't I, Geoff? What makes you so sure?"

"Well, you haven't come here just to talk have you, especially after the way you hugged me when you first came in?"

"Why don't you try me?" she invited.

"Let's go into the bedroom, it's more comfortable in there," I replied. Within seconds she was naked as I stared incredulously at her stunning figure.

"What's the matter Geoff, don't you like what you see?" she smiled.

"What red blooded male wouldn't?" I answered, before pulling her under the sheets.

As we embraced, the warmth of her body was a wonderful contrast to the coldness of the deserted bed in previous weeks.

"Did you enjoy that?" asked Michelle afterwards.

"Couldn't you tell?" I replied.

An awkward silence descended over the room as she became pensive.

"Geoff, do you mind if I ask you a question?"

"Of course not."

"You know Pink Floyd are coming to The Fillmore soon?"

"Yes," I answered.

"I just want to make sure I get in that night in case it's full. You will make sure I do, won't you?"

A look of incredulity crossed my face. "So that's why you came round, you scheming little bitch. I should have suspected something, especially when you made it all too easy."

"Don't get me wrong, Geoff," she said defensively. "I still like you. It's just that I don't want to miss them."

"No, I bet you don't," I spat sarcastically. "Oh all right, I suppose one good turn deserves another. I'll leave your name on the door, but next time you ring, I'll check which group is coming!"

Afterwards, I realised I'd be a hypocrite to criticise groupies or those that slept with them, and if Michelle knocked on my door again, I'd be hard pushed to turn her away.

Chapter 14

"Do you get excited by the groups?" someone once asked me. I smiled knowingly because on nights like this, there were a multitude of things to co-ordinate: the groups' fees and expenses (paid in cash), the bouncers letting too many of their friends in, finding a moment to talk to the support band who were invariably excellent. Roadies and bands to be consulted about running times. Some souvenir hunters have nicked the posters advertising next week's band so I have to dash to the office and quickly replace them. During all this, people are pressuring me because they want to meet the groups and get their albums autographed. Michelle stops to say hello, and thanks me for putting her on the guest list. She's a good looker, and even though the other lads stop to admire her bodywork, she's coming home with me.

Meanwhile, the groups need a drink, but the bar's packed, and I don't seem to be able to find a waiter. One of the roadies is dragging a heavy speaker across the ballroom's highly polished dance floor. The manager won't like that, and will go ballistic if he sees him. I begin to lightly reprimand him, but he scowls, and complains he's tired and needs more help. An attractive girl approaches him and stops to talk. He's human, and I sense his hormones are starting to kick in as the scowl disappears. John Peel is at the bar and is fielding queries. Suddenly, I recall the chap's question. "Do you get excited by the groups?" Just then, Michelle was walking towards me, and it seemed there was only one answer. "Right now, I absolutely love it."

By a stroke of good fortune, *Atom Heart Mother*, Pink Floyd's latest album was released on the very day (October 24, 1969) they came to play in Sunderland. This greatly added to the excitement as well as media interest. John Peel duly arrived in his trusty Land Rover, and owing to the amount of records he brought with him, the police kindly allowed him to park it in the safety of the nearby police compound.

Inside I was approached by a beaming face.

"What's John Peel like?" the guy asked.

"He's quite a nice chap actually," I answered. With that, he pulled out a demo tape and thrust it into my hand.

"Will you pass this on to him for me? It's a band I'm in, and if it comes from you, he might listen to it."

"You're better off giving it to him yourself," I assured him. "You've got just as much chance because John's the sort of bloke you can't influence. If he likes it, he'll play it. If he doesn't, there's nothing I can do to change his mind. But don't be frightened to approach him, you'll find he's quite a friendly chap."

"It means a lot to us," he sighed. "One play from him could make all the difference."

"That's what every unknown band in the country is hoping for," I said before moving on, "but good luck anyway." Now I was beginning to understand the sort of pressure John was under, and how desperate bands were for some recognition. It seemed that every local group had brought a demo tape with them. Strangely, Eddie wasn't there, because his was one tape I would have encouraged John Peel to listen to.

Scotland's Stone The Crows, fronted by the white soul voice of Maggie Bell, with guitarists Les Harvey (Alex's brother, who was tragically electrocuted on stage in 1972), and little Jimmy McCulloch (later to join Paul McCartney's Wings), were the support group.

After they came off to rousing applause, John Peel stepped on stage to play his choice of records. Some wit asked if it was being broadcast. I smiled and walked upstairs to the bar to look down at the crowd. There were college lecturers, students, unemployed people, shipyard workers and nurses all intermingling with the sole purpose of enjoying themselves. Pink Floyd appearing anywhere is a big occasion. In Sunderland, it was an even bigger one, and I prayed there wouldn't be any untoward incidents, no matter how minor.

John was looking around The Fillmore and it made me nervous. He'd written some nice things about the venue, and I wanted it to continue.

"How's it been going?" he asked.

"Fine, up to now, especially when Free are here."

"Why did you leave The Bay? I thought you wanted to open your own club," he reminded me.

"I still do," I confidently replied.

He smiled and I was relieved my answer had met with his approval because John had liked The Bay. His relaxed disposition meant the Fillmore North had passed the audition, even though it was bigger, and potentially reeked of the very thing he disliked, commercialism.

At The Bay, Pink Floyd had promised to play another date, and it was most gratifying to see they were as good as their word now that their stature had increased immeasurably. Having given me initial cause for concern by arriving late, the group opened with 'Green Is The Colour', from the *More* album, followed by a succession of favourites such as 'Interstellar Overdrive', 'Point Me At The Sky', and newer material like 'Ibiza Bar', and 'The Nile Song'. Dave Gilmour recognised someone in the crowd and waved. I looked down to see it was the four 'freakers' who had first met the Floyd in The Bay car park. Dave hadn't forgotten them, and this one moment symbolised that The Fillmore was no longer a cavernous Mecca ballroom, but a personalised meeting place with its own beating heart.

Afterwards, I spotted Debbie surrounded by a gang of lads, and wondered who would be the lucky recipient of her favours. Would Nick Mason succumb to her feminine wiles once more? I wandered over and noticed a glazed look in her eyes. She was tripping, and in this state, I knew she could be anybody's. Not that this was unusual, but I sensed a possible gang-bang in the offing.

"Hi Geoff, I thought the groups were excellent," she said, wide-eyed.

"Thanks, but I'm worried about you."

"Don't worry about me, we're going to a party afterwards. Do you want to come?" she asked, after kissing one of her admirers. A familiar smudge of bright red lipstick appeared on his cheek, immediately reminding me of The Bis-Bar.

"Why don't you let me give you a lift home later?" I suggested.

"No thanks, I'm going with this lot," she indicated. A number of leering eyes settled on her as I reluctantly turned and walked away. Was I witnessing Debbie's descent into an even seamier side of life?

At The Bay and The Fillmore, I had a pretty good grapevine and was able to stop dealers or other undesirables from gaining entry. This vigilance, together with my own personal abhorrence of hard drugs, enabled the management to keep things under control, without falling foul of the law. Fortunately, it was never a major problem, and music remained the most important factor.

Cocaine was fast gaining a stronghold, but because of its scarcity and high price, only the more affluent could afford it. One record company executive usually carried it in his fountain pen top, and in The Speakeasy one night, I watched a major rock star pay £70 for a small amount, before it quickly disappeared up his nose.

Meanwhile, heroin was, and still is, a serious problem. I have had personal experience of this on many occasions, and after refusing to partake, was often accused of not being 'with it'. Sadly, it later transpired that some of these people weren't 'with it', or should I say 'with us', because they are now dead.

While walking around The Fillmore, I spotted a bouncer unceremoniously side-footing someone in the hips while they sat harmlessly on the floor. This was followed by the usual curt nod towards the ceiling and an order to stand up.

"Why do you need to do that with your foot?" I asked angrily.

"They know the rules. They aren't allowed to sit on the floor," came the surly, unsympathetic reply.

Up to now, everything had gone amazingly well despite the bouncers' behaviour and the last thing I'd wanted was a lack of understanding to spoil everything. I still hoped that everything could be peacefully resolved, while allowing things to settle into a harmonious, working relationship. Nevertheless, I sensed that sooner rather than later, I would be forced into an unwanted physical confrontation.

A couple of days later, I walked into The Bis-Bar, and spotted Debbie with her friends. Although her infectious smile was still as captivating as ever the youthful glow in her cheeks was noticeably absent.

"Enjoy yourself the other night?" I asked.

She blushed and shifted uneasily.

"I can't remember much about it," she stammered.

"I bet you can't even remember what the Floyd played?" I teased.

"It doesn't really matter what they played, it's the vibes they give off," she parried back.

"Was the party any good?" I queried.

"All I remember is meeting a really nice lad whose dad owns a garage. He lends him an MG sports car and we're going out to the lakes at the weekend," she enthused.

"That's good, it's about time you met someone sensible."

Suddenly, one of the glass doors swung open and in strode a policeman.

"Are you Geoff Docherty?" he asked.

"Yes," I answered.

"Do you mind coming down to the police station?"

"Whatever for?" I enquired.

"We've had a tip-off that you're selling drugs in here," he replied.

"Are you joking?" I spluttered. "I don't know what you're talking about. Besides, I'm a successful promoter and you don't think I'd be stupid enough to risk everything for the sake of a few drugs, do you?"

Ignoring my protestations, I was whisked away to the police station and taken to a small side room to be interrogated. After searching me and finding nothing, two detectives repeatedly asked the same questions over and over.

"It's probably someone I've barred from The Fillmore who made the call," I proffered by way of explanation.

After about two hours, they eventually seemed satisfied and allowed me to go. Nevertheless, the incident left a bitter aftertaste. I was arrested and taken away, in full view of everyone, on the word of some troublemaker. Naturally, you're never told the name of your informer, for obvious reasons, while an apology is non-forthcoming. Looking at it from their point of view, I realise the police rely on these methods to combat genuine criminal activity. However, the business of tip-offs is wide open to abuse. Fortunately, all's well that ends well, and I bore no grudges.

Chapter 15

Being a major rock promoter was a strange yet compelling experience. People with a shared interest in music often stopped me and suggested ways of improving things. Others had a fixation on a particular band, and never tired of urging me to book them again. Then of course, there were the troublemakers who had been barred. "It wasn't me," they would cry as they pleaded to be readmitted.

When dealing with someone who I'd barred, I sometimes felt like a probation officer. If they hadn't been the real cause of the trouble, and seemed to harbour genuine remorse for what had occurred, I would often reinstate them after a period of time. On doing this, their appreciation was most heart-warming.

One day, my friend little Tommy Clark who played amateur football for Bishop Auckland in the Northern League, and was now living with me, asked what it was like to be a promoter?

"It's difficult to describe," I answered.

"Yes, but you must feel really important, meeting all these famous people," he enthused.

"Not really, although I must admit, it does get a bit hectic at times."

"But what about all the parties with lots of girls and celebrities there? I bet you have the time of your life."

"Well, I can't deny that wherever there are celebrities, there are always girls hoping to meet them, especially in London," I replied.

On hearing this, his eyes lit up at the expectation of hearing some juicy bit of scandal. After all, it was only natural for someone not personally involved to be interested in what exactly went on.

Here, I must point out that Tommy was a special friend who didn't have a bad bone in his body. We'd gone to school together, and how he wasn't spotted by a professional football club remains one of life's great mysteries. An unassuming and discerning sort of person, you could trust him with your life.

Now he was intrigued about groupies, drugs, and other things which were part and parcel of the rock scene. Tommy was a bit like Eddie. If he asked you a question, it was because he was genuinely interested, and you felt obliged to answer. Anything less would have been discourteous, and besides, I really liked him.

"Geoff, you must have had some birds, after all, you're in the ideal position to meet them."

"Not as many as you think, Tommy. It's the stars they want to meet."

"Have you met Mick Jagger?" he asked.

"No, I haven't."

"What about Rod Stewart?"

"No, I haven't met him either, although he's sometimes in The Speakeasy when I'm there."

A disappointed look crossed his face as he changed tack.

"What about American girls, have you met any in London?"

"Yes I have, as a matter of fact, I often meet one in The Speakeasy."

"Is she nice?"

"I think she is."

"Have you slept with her?"

"Look Tommy," I replied uncomfortably. "This is getting a bit personal, but if you must know, the answer is yes."

"Well, that's one Rod Stewart missed, isn't it?"

"I wouldn't say that, Tommy. Girls are throwing themselves at him all the time. Anyway, I don't think I'd risk introducing her to him."

Tommy laughed. "Who else have you met?"

"Please don't keep asking me that," I pleaded. "When you're a promoter, you just say hello, and sometimes go on to a party, or back to someone's hotel for a few drinks. It's not the big deal that everyone thinks it is."

"Yes, but you had a stunning American girl in The Bis-Bar, who was she?"

"She was a go-go dancer and her sister is married to Carmine Appice, the drummer for Vanilla Fudge."

"What a figure, Geoff."

"Before you ask, nothing happened and I didn't sleep with her."

Tommy's face dropped. "You're joking aren't you?"

"No I'm not, but I must admit I would have loved to."

As Tommy continued questioning me, I began to feel like an apprehended shoplifter.

"Have you been to John Peel's place in London?" he asked.

"Yes I have. He lives in Upper Harley Street with a girl whom he calls 'The Pig', but her real name is Sheila."

"Why does he call her that?"

"I haven't the faintest idea because in actual fact, she's quite slim!"

"You know Geoff, when we used to play football in the school yard, who would have thought you'd be doing this, and driving a Jaguar. It takes some believing, doesn't it?"

"Well, it does, and it doesn't. It just sort of happened."

"Sort of happened! I wish something like that would sort of happen to me," he sighed wistfully.

"It's all relative, Tommy. Right now you might be happier on the football field than I am at The Fillmore," I said, thinking of my problems with the bouncers.

"What do you mean by that?" he asked.

"Oh, nothing" I replied.

Dicky and Chas, intent on forging their own way in life, had made their way down to London and, around this time, a bright energetic guy named Alan Ramshaw joined me in my efforts to make The Fillmore one of the country's leading venues. With major groups appearing on a regular basis, John Peel writing favourable things, and people from a huge catchment area regularly attending, The Fillmore was exceeding my wildest hopes in a musical sense.

In most clubs, DJs are obliged to play records non-stop. If the dance floor becomes empty, for no matter how short a time, they are deemed a failure and liable to be dismissed by the club's management. At The Fillmore, we were under no such constraints, and could play obscure but worthwhile music without the fear of any such reprisals.

We also recognised that playing two or three unfamiliar tracks had the added advantage of giving people an opportunity to hear new groups which they might otherwise have not been exposed to. Another bonus was that it was easier to make friends with the opposite sex, because a potential suitor could conveniently approach a dancer without having to walk into the middle of the floor. It may seem a small point, but definitely added to the enjoyment and relaxed atmosphere for all concerned.

After many successes, I was to promote my saddest ever gig. It all began a few weeks earlier when Christine Perfect, previously with Chicken Shack, was voted female singer of the year in a prestigious *Melody Maker* poll. With this boost, together with the resultant publicity from the hit, 'I'd Rather Go Blind', she decided to embark on a solo career and I was determined The Fillmore would be graced with her presence.

Her manager Harry Simmonds (brother of Kim Simmonds of Savoy Brown and also Chicken Shack's manager) was a friend of mine, and I immediately contacted him. As luck would have it, Harry decided to let The Fillmore have the opening date of Christine's British tour on November 14, 1969. I was ecstatic at such a major scoop, and eagerly set about promoting her appearance in the belief that I had one of the biggest draws in the country.

On the day of the gig, bouquets of flowers, congratulatory telegrams and telephone calls from all over the country were being received. Everything was ready for Christine's arrival, and when she finally walked in and saw the flowers, she was absolutely thrilled. On meeting her, my initial impression was that she was a lovely lady, whose manners, dignity and friendly nature were beyond reproach.

Here, I must explain that every week, The Fillmore never had less than a thousand people in, and for a place of its size, even that could look sparse. About an hour after opening, I casually looked out, and was visibly shaken to see that the place was still virtually empty. I quickly returned to the dressing room and put on a brave face.

This opening night was an important showcase for Christine, and now that she was well known, I was conscious of the pressure she must be feeling. Nevertheless, despite the empty ballroom, I had to appear resolute and calm. As the clock ticked on, I anxiously took one last look, just before she was due on stage, to assess the size of the crowd. On doing so, I froze as there were only about two dozen people standing in front of the stage. The attendance was a disaster, and there was nothing I could do.

"How many people are in?" asked Christine on my return. "I don't really know the exact figures yet," I replied, not wishing to destroy her enthusiasm. Her piercing eyes seemed to have sensed something was wrong. I squirmed uneasily as she walked from the dressing room to peep out into the ballroom. My heart sank as the shock immediately registered over her distraught face. She ran back to the dressing room, and began sobbing. It was the saddest sight I was ever to see at The Fillmore, especially after so many triumphs.

As an inconsolable Christine continued to sob, I was faced with an uncomfortable dilemma. Should I discreetly leave and allow her to compose herself in the privacy of her dressing room. Or should I stay and give her the moral support which she so richly deserved?

Instinctively, my better judgement told me to stay to try to help her through this frightful, professional crisis. I felt an overwhelming urge to put a comforting arm around her in the hope it would give her strength, but to do so seemed inappropriate and futile. The dressing room seemed like a morgue, and I'd never felt so helpless in my life.

Pulling herself together, Christine stood up, composed herself, and walked towards the dressing room door. As she did so, she glanced momentarily at me, the sadness in her reddened eyes clearly visible. It was in some strange way like Marie Antoinette walking towards the guillotine. By now, the flowers in the dressing room seemed to have wilted, while the congratulatory telegrams appeared to be meaningless bits of paper. With her face drained, and her pride shattered, she braced herself for the oncoming ordeal. On nearing the stage, her faltering steps took her nearer to what seemed an impending disaster.

As I looked on in reverential silence, Christine broke into her first song. The tension was unbearable, but to our amazement, she was magnificent. Upon hearing her sweet soulful voice, people from the upstairs balcony came down to listen, while others emerged from the shadowy corners of its vast empty spaces. Christine glanced at me as people gathered round to hear her. I smiled encouragingly from the side of the stage with admiration at her resolve and determination to succeed.

Then came her *pièce-de-résistance*, 'I'd Rather Go Blind'. As the final notes drifted above their heads, the audience responded with genuine, appreciative applause. After a well deserved encore, I returned to the dressing room to congratulate her on a brave and inspired performance. She smiled as the tension lifted, and the congratulatory bouquets of flowers seemed to have acquired a new and meaningful sparkle.

Later, we went upstairs to Tiffany's, a late-night club which adjoined the Locarno, for a congratulatory drink. I bought Christine a bottle of wine as we sat and conversed about all sorts of things. By now, she had totally relaxed and was marvellous company. Meeting Christine proved to be an enriching experience, and never once did she complain. From that day on, whenever the going got tough, her display of triumph over adversity was an example I always sought to follow.

The story has an even happier ending. Having married John McVie, Christine joined Fleetwood Mac in the early Seventies on vocals and keyboards, playing on ten albums, six of which went platinum in America. In 1977, their legendary *Rumours* album was released and has since sold over 25 million copies, making them one of the biggest live draws in America. So it really did happen for Christine in a way that was unimaginable on that desperately sad night in Sunderland.

Chapter 16

The following week I called into The Bis–Bar as usual, looking for a friendly face, when an unexpected voice piped up.

"They tell me it was a bit of a flop over there on Friday," said a stranger who seemed to know me. I winced inwardly as my injured pride reeled from his cruel reminder. It was hardly the sort of greeting I was hoping for, and it instantly put my back up.

"Did you lose much money?" he asked cheekily.

"Well, I've still got enough left for a coffee," I answered defiantly.

"One of my friends who was there said the atmosphere was abysmal," he continued. I looked him hard in the face as his barbed taunts struck home.

"Are you booking her back then?" he asked sarcastically.

"What does it matter to you whether I do or not," I replied.

"What do you mean by that?"

"Well even if I did, you wouldn't be there, would you?" I snapped with utmost distaste. "I'm not sure I like your attitude, it could get you into a lot of trouble."

"Why should it get me into trouble?" he asked. "I'm just telling you what a friend of mine said, that's all."

"Well next time I want something repeating, I'll go to a pet shop and buy a parrot!" I replied witheringly.

"Look, don't get heavy with me, it wasn't my fault Friday was a flop," he said with a smug expression. I could smell beer on his breath and decided to curtail the conversation, as my patience with him was wearing thin.

I turned and walked towards where Eddie was standing with a warm smile.

"I hear you've got Free on next week, should be packed for that."

Chapter 16

"I hope so, especially after Friday," I replied.

"Who's that guy over there, he seemed to be upsetting you?"

"Oh don't worry about him," I answered dismissively. "He's just had one too many."

"Dave's playing at the Londonderry on Thursday next week, Geoff. It's a folk night, why don't you come along? There should be some nice students from the Poly, they seem to like it there."

"Yes, I've heard good reports about it myself. It's probably because there's never any trouble. Anyway, what about a record contract, is there any sign of one yet?"

Eddie smiled resignedly. "You know the score, Geoff. I've got more rejection letters from record companies than I have for jobs." Just then, he glanced over to the far side of the café and nodded.

"That girl over there is lovely, I wonder who she is?" he queried.

"Her name's Val Smith," I replied. "Nice, isn't she?"

"I'd say she's more than nice, she's beautiful," drooled Eddie.

These last few minutes epitomised The Bis-Bar. Within a short space of time I'd gone from a disagreeable argument, to a friendly discussion about a beautiful girl.

"What about Dave Stewart, have you heard from him lately?" I asked.

"I think he's coming to see Free," Eddie answered.

"So he's back in Sunderland then?"

"At the moment he is, but half the time I don't know his whereabouts."

Just then, Val Smith waved over in our direction as my heart raced wondering if it was me she was waving to? Val was one girl in town that every boy fancied and secretly admired. There was an air of unfathomable mystery about her, yet she was friendly and approachable. In London, or anywhere else for that matter, you instinctively knew she would stand out, regardless of how beautiful the competition.

Her perfectly formed face, framed by short dark hair, together with her sweet smile and hourglass figure, was positively captivating. She was undoubtedly a stunner, and yet by a strange quirk of fate, was sometimes on her own. We often watched and admired, but none of us dare approach her; not that we didn't want to. It sounds silly, but we all thought she was too good for us. Maybe if one of the lads became successful, he would then have the courage to ask her out.

Yet that was highly improbable, because to make it, you have to go to London.

On the way out, I'll just smile as I walk past because it's terribly difficult not to stare, never mind trying to concentrate on what to say. Maybe if I buy a better car, she might notice me, which would at least be a step in the right direction. Later, I could offer to take her out for a meal to a posh restaurant in an effort to impress her. After all, in some ways I've made it. Even though I say so myself, I am putting on some of the world's top groups. Why doesn't she come over to The Fillmore? Doesn't she realise she wouldn't have to pay, and I'd get her a backstage pass.

A week later, on February 6, 1970, Free hysteria hit town, with 3,000 people in and hundreds locked out. Now, no clearer proof was needed that this group was happening in a really big way. The previous few days had seen me at a low ebb, and now I felt elated. Three hundred in the week before, now three thousand – what a contrast. The Fillmore was back, bigger and better than ever and the relief was incalculable.

It wasn't just money and numbers, it was something much more important than that. Seeing the joy and excitement on people's faces vindicated everything The Fillmore stood for. To think that four young lads could create this sort of impact, and it was Sunderland who'd discovered them, made it all the more satisfying.

Amazingly, while all this was taking place, Free were still being virtually ignored throughout the rest of the country; having to play support slots, or smaller club gigs. To have discovered an unknown group who were pulling in local crowds as big as for Zeppelin or The Who was sending shock waves down to Island Records in London. A few weeks later I walked into their office for the first time.

"I've come to see John Glover, the manager of Free. Is he in?" I asked.

"What's your name?" a secretary enquired.

"Geoff Docherty," I answered.

"Are you the Geoff Docherty who promotes Free in Sunderland?" she enquired with a look of surprised bewilderment. I sensed she had expected some high powered executive, and felt inadequate at not coming up to her expectations. She recovered, smiled, and pointed me in the direction of Johnny Glover's office.

I liked Island because it was small and felt homely. In fact it was so cosy I was half expecting to see owner Chris Blackwell's washing hanging out in the back garden, and some hens laying eggs for afternoon tea. I was a mini-celeb, and must admit I enjoyed the fuss they appeared to be making of me. On the wall was a massive poster of Traffic which reminded me of The Bay where their single, 'Hole In My Shoe', was a big favourite.

I was thrilled because Island was highly respected and had managed to retain its integrity in an increasingly commercial environment. This, allied to an uncanny eye for undiscovered talent, proved a highly successful formula with Millie, Traffic, Jethro Tull, Mott The Hoople, Free, Quintessence, Bob Marley, and U2 being just some of the label's major signings. Stevie Winwood's brother Muff, who had played bass in the Spencer Davis Group, also worked there as an A&R man.

Ironically, years later, I ended up playing for the Island football team alongside him, and once played for *Melody Maker* when they were a man short. While Muff has an undoubted track record for talent spotting, his football prowess hardly had First Division clubs waving their cheque books. However, it was great fun, especially as music publisher Lionel Conway was the team manager.

By now, music was becoming an all-consuming passion, with most of the latest albums from the record companies arriving at my flat on a regular basis. The telephone was constantly ringing, and I was being invited to many major record company functions. All this friendliness seemed a contradiction in terms because as a baby, nobody had wanted to take me in, and now, everyone was welcoming me with open arms.

This made me appreciate each kindness all the more, and while it was gratifying, I wondered if certain people were sincere. It seemed that on the bigger nights, everyone wanted a slice of the action, but once they had inveigled their way into the dressing room, they forgot about everyone else. Fortunately, regulars the four little 'freakers', who had witnessed Pink Floyd playing in The Bay Hotel car park, kept my values intact. Without them, I may have wavered, but fortunately, Pink Floyd turned out to be astute judges.

After the return of Family on January 23 to an attendance of over 2,000, seven days later we were hoping to welcome Ten Years After who were absolutely massive in America after playing the Woodstock Festival. TYA were far too big to do club gigs, so I was highly delighted to have booked them for a sold-out gig.

Unfortunately, two weeks before they were due to play, they abruptly pulled out. I was furious, and immediately took an over-night mail train to London. After arriving and freshening up at Kings Cross Station, I made my way to a coffee bar just opposite the Chrysalis office in Oxford Street. It was still early morning, and finally, after a three-hour wait fuelled by endless cups of tea, TYA's manager Chris Wright (QPR football chairman) disappeared through the front door. Within seconds, I was on my feet and hurried across the road into their offices, knowing the receptionist could hardly say he was out, which was all part of my strategy. A few minutes later, I found myself confronted by Chris, and his right-hand man, Doug D'arcy.

With the initial niceties over, I was determined that it wouldn't be a wasted trip and steamed into them.

"Sorry Geoff, we just can't do it, because we're behind on the album," Wright pointed out.

"But I have a signed contract," I protested strongly, "and all it means is one more day in the studio." I could sense the stench of dollars beginning to enter the equation. America was big bucks, and a gig in Sunderland seemed irrelevant in the grand scheme of things. As the meeting progressed, I realised that if I could only persuade them about the warm reception the group would receive, it would make a huge difference.

I pleaded and cajoled, but to no avail. "Sorry Geoff, we'd like to, but we can't. It's impossible," Doug D'arcy said in a rather forthright manner.

"Oh no, I'm not having that!" I interjected. "You signed a contract and agreed the date. I haven't come all this way to be brushed aside."

Having realised the cause looked lost, desperation took over.

"If you don't do this gig, I'll burn the studio down so they can't record anything at all!" The pair looked shocked at the seriousness of my threat.

"I mean it, we're not being treated like this. I've already advertised the gig, and your excuse just isn't good enough," I protested vehemently.

There was anger in my raised and uncompromising voice. On reflection, it was a last calculated throw of the dice, as I awaited their reaction. To my surprise the two of them began conferring while hurriedly checking the group's diary. After a quick consultation, they nodded and agreed to reinstate the date. I heaved a sigh of relief. They smiled as we shook hands, and everything was amicably settled. After ironing out a few contractual details, one of the biggest groups in the world was finally coming, and I was ecstatic.

It seemed everyone wanted to come along and witness what was more of an event than a gig. One thing was for sure. It had cemented The Fillmore at the very top of the area's music scene and for an hour and a half we could all imagine we were in that muddy field at Woodstock. Ten Years After hit top form immediately with 'Good Morning Little Schoolgirl', 'Two Time Mama', 'I Woke Up This Morning', and the crowd favourite, 'I'm Going Home', played at an exciting and frenetic pace by Alvin Lee (guitar), Chick Churchill (keyboards), Leo Lyons (bass), and Ric Lee (drums).

Alvin's speed and dexterity on guitar was amazing, and it was a truly memorable gig. Just ask the 3,000 there who refused to let them off stage. Encore after encore was demanded, and once back in the dressing room, the group looked shocked at the warmth of their reception. They were only too pleased to return and repeat the same performance at Newcastle Mayfair. The sheer enthusiasm and warmth of the North East crowd had seen to that.

A week later, on February 6, Free were back and had chosen to record a live album of their appearance. Chris Blackwell was also present to experience 'Freemania' for himself. When I arrived at The Fillmore, I was staggered to see a queue six or seven deep, stretching for hundreds of yards down to the Wheatsheaf, and into nearby Roker Avenue.

Police were on hand to control the traffic as people were in serious danger of being run over. I began to wonder, was there no end to the Free phenomenon?

I'd seen queues for football cup ties, but never anything like this. Inside, pandemonium scaled new heights when the group played an awe-inspiring set. Nearly two hours later, Chris Blackwell looked exhausted from the intensity of what he had just witnessed. When he first arrived, impeccably dressed, his manner had given him a sophisticated air of well-groomed authority. Now, his drained, sweaty appearance betrayed a smug satisfaction, and no wonder.

Originally his two A&R people (John Glover and Alec Leslie) had turned Free down, but Chris had insisted they sign them. Tonight was the vindication of someone prepared to stick his head above the parapet and back his own judgement.

In many ways, 1970 turned out to be a year of upheavals in rock music. Paul McCartney announced he was quitting The Beatles, riots broke out after four students were tragically shot dead by the National Guard at Kent State University, and both Jimi Hendrix and Janis Joplin died before they got old.

Jimi was innovative, spellbinding, and without equal. I once stood next to him in The Speakeasy, and was desperate to be introduced to him, but unfortunately, I never was. Years earlier, at the small Cellar Club in South Shields, I had gone to see him play. Tickets were 5/-, and his showmanship and playing was a revelation as he plunged his Stratocaster guitar shaft through the poly-styrene tiles of the low stage ceiling.

Ironically, he was discovered by Newcastle-born Chas Chandler, the bass player from The Animals who subsequently went on to manage him. Sadly, Chas too is now deceased, but by masterminding the building of Newcastle Arena, he has left a legacy that will never be forgotten, especially here in the North East.

On March 9, 1970, a virtually unknown group who I'd previously booked at The Bay, played support to The Third Ear Band at The Fillmore. Genesis were managed by Tony Smith (not to be confused with Tony Stratton Smith) who signed them to his Charisma Records label. Ironically, they had previously been with Decca who had turned The Beatles down, but had met with little success and were dropped.

Being a support group, Peter Gabriel (vocals, flute), Mike Rutherford (bass, vocals), John Mayhew (drums, vocals), Anthony Phillips (guitar, vocals), and Tony Banks (keyboard, guitar, vocals) set about trying to win over The Fillmore crowd.

With hindsight, it was a difficult task. A support slot can be most unrewarding when you are completely unknown and need an attentive audience to absorb and appreciate the finer points. Unfortunately, their best endeavours received relatively little audience feedback, and apart from a few hardy souls at the front, their impact was minimal. For my own part, I thought it wasn't a particularly inspiring set, giving no indication of just how huge they were to become.

Four years later, after various line-up changes, their achievements since appearing at The Fillmore were staggering. It seems strange to think their £50 fee that night would just about buy one of their tour sweatshirts now.

Four days later, David Bowie played with his newly formed backing band, The Hype, featuring Tony Visconti (bass), (later to become a major record producer), John Cambridge (drums), and Mick Ronson (guitar). I'd known about Bowie through Chrysalis booker Wilf Wright who told me he used to regularly pop in to Wilf's office and plead for work of any kind. It seems unbelievable now, but it's absolutely true.

David had experienced a long struggle and, unfortunately, the attendance at The Fillmore that night was disappointing despite

'Space Oddity' charting at number five in England the previous year, and there being three other bands on the bill. Bowie was dressed in blue and white, with a pair of wings strapped to his body. This was pre-*Ziggy Stardust* and appeared to be an early version of his courageous attempts to utilise the knowledge he had gained from working with mime artist Lindsay Kemp, and Natasha Kornilof, an avant-garde clothes designer.

Artistically, it was a brave move. Appearing in such an unusual costume proved to be a masterstroke because it stretched the audience's imagination, being so far removed from anything The Fillmore had previously seen. The night proved to be a magnetic marriage of rock and theatre, brilliantly executed to Bowie's own original compositions like 'The Man Who Sold The World', 'All The Madmen', 'Memory Of A Free Festival', and, of course, 'Space Oddity'. For those who were lucky enough to be there, it was certainly a gig to remember.

Afterwards, David shook me warmly by the hand and thanked me for having the courage to book him. I was touched by this act of courteousness and appreciation. Even though the gig had lost money, it was of little consequence as anyone with a modicum of perception could sense that success was inevitable for someone so talented.

Years later, backstage at the 1996 Phoenix Festival, Bowie walked past me after a tremendous gig and it was strange seeing someone so internationally acclaimed at close quarters after losing money on him 26 years before. At both shows he put in the same amount of energy, and maybe his secret is that he lives for his art. At Phoenix, 40,000 people certainly did.

Chapter 17

The unsettling situation with the beloved bouncers finally exploded one evening after The Fillmore had closed for the night. On checking everything was switched off, I signalled to John Irwin, a friend of mine who had been playing the records, that we were ready to leave. John was diminutive and quiet by nature and to my knowledge had never been involved in an argument or fight all his life. I noticed he was ashen faced, which seemed strange as it was unlike him, so I asked what was wrong, and why he was ignoring me?

"I can't leave the stage," he whispered. "That bouncer over there is waiting to get me."

"Why, what have you done?" I asked.

"He's accusing me of not playing a record he requested earlier," John replied anxiously.

"Well that's stupid, surely there must be some mistake. Come on down and I'll sort it out," I assured him.

"I'm not moving till he's gone," he trembled.

Sure enough, the bouncer in question appeared with an aggressive look on his face.

"What's this about you being upset at John?" I enquired.

"I'm just waiting till he comes off stage and then I'm going to have him," he snarled.

"But why, what has he done?"

"When I ask for a record to be played, I expect it to be played!" he threatened.

"Don't worry, we'll play it next week," I offered.

"I can't wait that long, I'm going to sort it out now," he said, glowering at John. I smelt trouble and instinctively knew there would be no other course of action but to bring my two social workers out of retirement. My late brother Donald's strongly imprinted words flashed in front of me. "Don't be frightened, if he gets cheeky, get stuck into him and I'm telling you, you'll win."

Without further ado, I stepped forward and nutted him. Unfortunately, at the moment of impact he tilted his head slightly back. As our heads met with an almighty crash, his front teeth pierced my scalp, and dark red blood began dripping down my face. As I prepared to follow up my attack, to my surprise, he staggered back, holding his face in a state of shock. It was a decisive moment as I only had a split second to play with. Finesse and guile are two very important factors, but so is aggression. I decided to hold off, half expecting him to rush me in a mad rage. If he did, speed, guile and fitness were required for the reception committee I had prepared for him.

Only a few minutes earlier the darkened ballroom had been alive with throbbing music and dancing teenagers. Now as we faced each other it was eerily quiet as I awaited his impending rush. Unexpectedly he stepped back and seemed unsure of what to do next. Blood was seeping from his nose while he held his mouth as if checking to see what damage it had sustained. In the silence of the ballroom it was a tense moment. If only he'd held his mouth earlier I thought to myself, there would have been no need for any of this aggro.

To my amazement, he turned and skulked away, the fight seemingly knocked out of him. For all his threats, he hadn't managed a single blow in anger. I looked up at John on stage and beckoned to him once again.

"C'mon, lets go."

"Are you all right?" he asked, worriedly. "I'm okay, but next time he wants a record played, let me know and I'll tell him we're not playing it." John nodded in agreement as we made our way out. Justice had prevailed, and a bully had been suppressed. Donald would have liked that.

Shortly afterwards, that particular bouncer left and, thankfully, I never saw him again. John went off to study at Nottingham University and became social secretary. He later booked Roxy Music and Captain Beefheart, and as a favour, a local band I was managing, Beckett, were support act on both occasions. It was great to see him and I like to think working at The Fillmore helped John broaden his musical horizons. He certainly helped broaden mine.

On March 26, I promoted my worst ever gig, and met an individual who gets my vote as the rudest man in rock. After his stint in the supergroups Cream and Blind Faith Ginger Baker was rated as one of the world's greatest drummers. His newly formed Airforce consisted of fourteen (!) all-star members headed by ex-Traffic/Blind Faith vocalist & keyboardist Steve Winwood, Rick Grech (ex-Family), Denny Laine (ex-Moody Blues), Graham Bond (Graham Bond Organisation), Trevor Burton (ex-Move), Alan White (ex-Plastic Ono Band), Phil Seaman, Bud Beadle, Harold McNair, Steve Gregory, Jeanette Jacobs, Eleanor Barooshian, and Remi Kebaka.

At the time, Ginger was managed by Robert Stigwood, while his agent was Roger Forrester, who later became Eric Clapton's manager for 28 years. On the phone, Roger's enthusiasm for Ginger's latest band knew no bounds, so I didn't hesitate in booking them. Their astronomical £1,500 fee (around £6,000 nowadays) was three times more than I'd paid for either The Who or Pink Floyd, and I needed a sell-out just to break even. Nevertheless, instinct told me that I had to book them if The Fillmore was to remain at the cutting edge. As far as I recall, they were playing only three dates in the whole of the country, which made the gig even more prestigious, and I was sure we had a real coup on our hands. Whatever happened, it promised to be a fascinating and unforgettable experience.

Unfortunately, in between booking them and the date they were due to play, Steve Winwood decided to leave the band. This was a huge disappointment and, unknown to me, became the first portent of disaster.

When the night of the gig finally arrived, I knocked confidently on the dressing room door to discuss what time the band wanted to be on stage. Ginger Baker opened it, took one look at me before promptly slamming it shut, without the slightest explanation or apology. I felt humiliated and was incensed at his rudeness, especially as the attendance was well below expectations and the gig was losing a fortune.

With the door only inches from my face, I turned and walked away, angered by his high-handed attitude which didn't augur well for the rest of the evening. Unknown to him, during the brief time the door was open, I'd managed a quick glance inside to see some serious drug taking in action. This was probably the reason for my unwelcome confrontation with Ginger.

After an interminably long wait, the group finally slumped on stage to commence their set. What a shambles it turned out to be. Phil Seaman was in a drug-induced torpor and had to be lifted onto his drum stool where he remained slumped in a fully unconscious state throughout the whole of the set.

Meanwhile, Graham Bond was obviously not in possession of his faculties and seemed to be leaning on his keyboards rather than playing them. While this was happening, many of the other members were also having trouble playing their instruments, and it looked for all the world as if a difficult and unrewarding chore had been thrust upon them. The instruments we did hear were, for the most part, a glutinous quagmire of tuneless jamming, which, considering the calibre and reputations of those on stage, was a disgrace. I stood and watched with a mixture of sadness and embarrassment, and can justifiably complain it was the most expensive jam I'd ever had the misfortune to see or hear.

When it was over, I approached Ginger backstage. He took one disdainful look at me before turning contemptuously and storming off. By now, I was very angry and was all for coming to blows with him but, fortunately, Wilf Wright was present and managed to calm me down. Having already met many rock stars with impeccable manners, I wasn't used to such rudeness. It certainly was a shock and I can only assume his behaviour was probably symptomatic of the drugs he was taking. Nevertheless, it tarnished my image of a great drummer.

At the end of it all, the night had been an unqualified disaster, and I knew that contractually and legally I would have been quite justified in refusing to pay them. However, this never crossed my mind as the good name of The Fillmore was at stake, and despite losing over £600 (£2,400 now) their full appearance fee awaited them in the office safe. After counting out the money, the tour manager's relief was obvious. He seemed utterly surprised at being paid the full amount because, apparently, at one gig in Stoke, they didn't get paid.

Thankfully, the group disbanded after five months, thus saving the British public's ears from any further musical damage. For this act of mercy, we are eternally grateful, and if that was the cutting edge of rock, I'd rather be at the blunt end. Most definitely a gig best forgotten.

Michelle continued to be a constant visitor to my flat in what seemed a symbiotic relationship. As the success of The Fillmore escalated, I got the feeling she was falling in love with the lifestyle, and not me. She was pretty and smart with it, in fact, cunning wouldn't be too strong a word, and it was difficult to resist her enticing charms. Voluptuous and leggy, she never failed to please, and when her sexy lingerie was deftly removed, the hormones un-failingly began to stir. It was nice to have someone like her around, and being young and carefree, the well of plenty seemed bottomless.

However, ridiculous as it may sound, life at times seemed less than satisfying, and had a vacuous feeling to it. Rock was now big business, and I was finding everything revolved around money, gross receipts, maximum capacities, and less about the music. The early ideals weren't just conveniently being pushed aside in a rush for a piece of the action, they were being trampled upon. I began contemplating everything I'd achieved. Success, money, car and girls were nice, but I was developing a guilt complex that was becoming difficult to live with.

In the early days of The Bay, I'd been one of those naïve souls who believed in the ideals of peace and love. Now, all we had railed against had become a part of my everyday life, and I feared I was beginning to 'sell out'. Ironically, everyone was telling me how wonderful The Fillmore was, and it became difficult to think in a rational manner. My doubts were compensated for by the sheer unbridled joy on people's faces when they were able to see and meet their favourite groups. This was something I always encouraged and witnessing it was undeniable proof of the pleasure being in the giving. At least this facet had stayed true.

Sadly, the whole scene now seems to have grown out of all proportion to what is actually taking place. 'The unacceptable face of capitalism' reigns supreme, while music fans have become simply 'punters', and this was, and still is, a word I strongly abhor. At huge gigs, people are ushered in and out to face stage barriers, robbing these events of any intimacy.

Music remains an art form to be enjoyed, and perhaps this is the secret of the annual Glastonbury Music Festival. The atmosphere is unique, and the people attending still retain much of those early ideals. If only those original Mecca bouncers could see these extremely friendly people sitting on the grass and soaking up the vibes, how educational it could have been. Until they've been, which is highly unlikely, they'll never know what I mean. Fortunately, hundreds of thousands do. And yes, John Peel was still a DJ there until 2001.

Chapter 18

In 1970, I arranged a deal with Mecca to promote bands at Newcastle's Mayfair Ballroom. Owing to its 3,000 capacity, The Mayfair had become the premier venue for rock groups in Newcastle. Before I took over the rock promotions were being run by Fraser-Suffield, a reserved partnership who were also holding down day jobs. Originally, we alternated on a weekly basis and I was happy with this arrangement as it gave me time to drive to London regularly in order to maintain contacts, and keep my ear to the ground.

By now, my amalgamation with Chrysalis meant I was also involved in other co-promotions at Newcastle City Hall which ensured I was kept busy, and was first on the scene if any dates were available. I opened up at the Mayfair on April 3 with Taste (featuring Rory Gallagher), and Black Sabbath on the same bill. It was an immediate success, and I now found myself promoting two gigs simultaneously. While I worked in Newcastle, my good friend Alan Ramshaw looked after The Fillmore, and did an excellent job.

Every Saturday morning I fly-posted as much of Newcastle as possible, and sometimes stuck posters on the corners of huge hoardings, taking care not to obscure their message. Unfortunately, these were owned by Mills & Allen, a well-known national advertising agency who had a monopoly on all the best sites in the centre of the city. Soon, they started sending me warning letters and threatened legal action unless I stopped immediately. It was a typical case of a major company attempting to crush a smaller individual, and I continued to ignore their threats.

After months of refusing to be intimidated, and pointing out their rates were far too expensive, they eventually agreed to display my posters on their official sites at a quarter of the normal price; the only proviso being that I didn't breathe a word to anyone. Needless to say, I didn't, not even to their staff who I often gave complimentary tickets to. Now I had the best sites in Newcastle and no longer needed to dodge the law. It was a significant step up in the standing of my promotions there, and I was no longer a 'pirate'.

As I walked around the city and saw the workmen putting my posters up, I would smile as we exchanged pleasantries, knowing they had no inkling I was the promoter of the gigs they were advertising.

The first major shock about the Mayfair turned out to be the startling difference in attendances. Whenever the same groups had performed in Sunderland, they attracted at least seven to eight hundred more people, and for the first time I was beginning to make some real money. Now that I was running the two venues with a total capacity of 6,000, it gave me tremendous bargaining power in London, and I became the North's leading promoter. As the excitement continued to intensify, more doors opened and everywhere I went backstage passes and invitations were constantly being thrown at me.

Meanwhile, sex, drugs and rock & roll continued to be a major part of young people's lives. Sadly, Debbie's relationship with her boyfriend John had fizzled out after he discovered her fascination with rock stars was more intimate than he imagined.

One day his red MG sports car pulled up outside The Bis-Bar, and he approached me.

"You know Debbie and I aren't going out together now, don't you Geoff?"

"Yes," I replied.

"Why didn't you tell me what was going on?"

"Well really, it was none of my business," I explained.

"None of your business?" he exclaimed. "You're the one who is putting these groups on and you knew all along she was making a fool of me."

I felt sorry for him as pangs of guilt pricked my conscience.

"She's taking drugs you know, and it's a lot worse than you realise. I tried to stop her but she resented it. Sarah is just as bad.

Chapter 18

Her parents are frantic with worry and think Debbie is a bad influence. Sarah goes down to London to meet a dealer."

I listened carefully, knowing I'd already warned Debbie and Sarah to keep their clandestine activities well away from The Fillmore.

"Listen, John, I'm sorry about what's happened, but please don't involve me. I'm sure you'll soon find someone else," I reassured him.

Just then, he looked down to the restaurant where he spotted Val Smith sitting with her friends. His eyes immediately lit up while his mood brightened at the thought of somehow becoming friendly with her.

"You're too late, she's going out with a Greek student called Pedros," I warned. "He's studying Naval Architecture at the Polytechnic."

"Hmmm, that's during the day, but I bet he studies her at night," he smirked.

To all outward appearances, The Fillmore seemed to be running smoothly. It was no longer just a question of me bringing the best and most interesting groups to the North East, the challenge was to keep everyone happy and to improve things.

One of the first of these improvements was for a professional light show to be employed. A young chap by the name of Rob Hutchinson had approached me, and after an impressive trial run, his light show became a permanent fixture. Since those early days at The Fillmore, he now owns a very successful company which supplies power for many rock festivals including Reading, Glasgow and Leeds. Another idea I instituted was for anyone over 18 who made a further payment of two shillings (10p), could, if they so desired, be admitted to Tiffany's club next door. This allowed them to drink and socialise after The Fillmore closed for the evening and meant we were able to compete with other night clubs which were beginning to open.

Unfortunately, soon after agreeing this concession, I began receiving a steady stream of complaints that some of The Fillmore's clientele were being refused admission due to their mode of dress. After heated protestations, a compromise was reached which meant jeans or T-shirts were acceptable, although people wearing trainers or with unduly long hair still couldn't enter. For the sake of keeping the peace, people reluctantly accepted it, although I felt it was an unnecessary violation of everything that had previously been agreed.

On April 24, 1970, Humble Pie arrived at The Fillmore in a blaze of publicity. Their line-up that night was Steve Marriott, Peter Frampton, Greg Ridley and Jerry Shirley. With two excellent vocalists in the group, it meant full houses wherever they played, and The Fillmore was to be no exception.

Watching Steve Marriott and Peter Frampton from out front, I began to wonder if this band was big enough for the two of them. It seemed as though Peter had been sculpted from the marble effigy of a winged angel, without a single blemish or imperfection. As the set progressed, there was no denying their rivalry and the inter-action generated excitement for the audience, but could it last, and for how long?

Backstage, I noticed it was Peter Frampton the girls were swooning over. His angelic features had previously been on the front of every *Jackie* magazine, sending adolescent girls into rapturous dreams.

By comparison, Marriott, despite his amazing voice, looked a pale shadow of his youthful self in The Small Faces. Drugs, fast living, late nights and constant touring had taken their toll. After a superb gig, I wandered into the other dressing room to find he was alone. He turned and looked at me when I asked if there was anything wrong. "The chicks prefer him to me," he said. I'd already noticed hordes of girls outside Frampton's dressing room, while not one solitary figure stood outside Steve's. Initially, I'd thought nothing of it, but now I realised how it was affecting him.

Eventually, he stood up and looked knowingly at me. Just having someone listen to him seemed to have improved his mood. I decided it was prudent to allow him to compose himself in his own time. He smiled and we shook hands. Out there on stage, Steve Marriott was a big star. Here in The Fillmore dressing room, he was a human being susceptible to life's foibles, just like the rest of us.

I was to meet Steve again in 1981 when I was managing a band called The Showbiz Kids who were headlining at The Marquee. Mick Grabham, now free of his Procol Harum shackles, had got a band together with Steve on vocals, Jimmy Leverton on bass, and a drummer who might have been Dave Hinds.

When he was unknown and living with me in Sunderland, Mick had gone to Newcastle City Hall in 1967 to see Jimi Hendrix play. There were two 'houses' but Mick had only enough money to see the first show. Undaunted, he stood outside in the freezing cold and listened to the whole of the second show, such was his admiration and respect.

Despite the group not yet having a name, Mick asked if his new band could play an unadvertised guest spot as a try-out to which I wholeheartedly agreed. It was a fantastic gig and as far as I know, the only one they ever did. Soon afterwards, they went over to America where Steve, whose voice was still amazing, had secured a potentially lucrative record deal with A&M. Unfortunately, it didn't work out because of Marriott's excessive and irresponsible behaviour. Another sad example of a lot of time and money being wasted on a most promising band.

My Humble Pie connection also extended to drummer Jerry Shirley, who wanted to sell me his Rolls. I really wanted it more for my father than myself, and to have pulled up outside his pit cottage in it would have given him immense satisfaction.

With a Rolls, the possibilities seemed endless as I imagined the two of us slowly driving past the colliery manager's mansion, and perhaps being invited in for tea. There was a certain snobbishness among these managers and their wives, but if you owned a Rolls, it could open doors. After we had had tea, dad could then walk into Castletown working men's club smoking a big cigar. That would get them talking!

Jerry and I started to negotiate for the Rolls, but it had a dent in the bodywork which put me off. Besides, the colliery manager would never allow us to visit him if the Rolls had a dent in it because he'd realise it was only second-hand. Still, it was a nice dream for a couple of days. Dad will just have to keep on doing the pools.

By now, I was making lots of new friends in Newcastle, and often popped into a coffee bar in a shopping precinct known as the Handyside Arcade. A lot of musicians hung out there, including Greg Burman, and The Junco Partners. Students and hippies also frequented it, while inside the atmosphere was a welcome contrast to the hustle and bustle elsewhere.

Greg, who had his own band, must have done hundreds of gigs with his colleague, John Chaytor. Greg and I tried unsuccessfully to reopen the Club-A-Go-Go on Percy Street in an effort to revitalise the music scene in Newcastle. Standing inside the legendary club I looked at the stage where The Animals, The Rolling Stones, The Who, Cream, Jimi Hendrix, Julie Driscoll and dozens of other greats had played.

In the end, it proved impossible because a kindly old lady living in the seaside resort of Whitley Bay refused to sign over her half of the lease. I pleaded, I begged, but, owing to a previous dispute, it was her husband's dying wish that she should never do so. I've not forgotten her wise words as I sat drinking coffee in her house. "I know you're disappointed son, but life is full of disappointments, and you have to learn to get over them."

Meanwhile in London, Dave Stewart had joined a band called Longdancer who were signed to Island music. They had blown their first advance on a huge slab of Moroccan hash, and Ian Matthews of Matthews Southern Comfort fame, who was producing their first album, walked out.

Chas and Dickie had made the break to London. Chas had a guest pass for Ronnie Scott's Jazz Club and it was great that he was able to see so many famous names. Thankfully, term breaks at University allowed Dickie lots of time at home and it was good to see him back up on stage. While they were away, The Fillmore had missed their innovative flair and I found it difficult to replace them.

In Sunderland, Eddie was still trying to make it, and Hoggy had opened a second shoe shop. The 'freakers' had become friends with

Dickie, and he was playing tracks for them off Pink Floyd, Roy Harper, Quintessence, Soft Machine, Fairport Convention and Incredible String Band albums. While everyone else waited for the more conventional tracks, they all danced in a seemingly mesmerised trance which was one of the most uplifting sights at The Fillmore.

Watching them in their long kaftan-type dresses, I felt as though a tiny part of Glastonbury had graced us because they were, in essence, among its founder members, having attended the very first festival there in 1971.

During this period, the attendances in Newcastle continued to climb and, at times, amazed me, while the bouncers and management co-operated really well, especially as I'd never expected success on this scale. Unknown to me however, I was about to see the end of The Fillmore dream which had begun with such high hopes and expectations. In theory, this should have been a sad farewell, but for some strange reason, it never felt like that.

On May 8, Traffic, who I'd been trying to get for some considerable time, were headlining. I looked out and noticed that Debbie, Michelle, Caroline, Eddie and dozens of local musicians were in the audience. Inevitably, the Sunderland groupies were hovering near the stage door and I wondered which one would get closest to Steve Winwood. I sensed they would find it extremely difficult because he seemed far too shy and retiring to even contemplate a liaison with some unknown, sexually rampant female. Nevertheless, these groupies had staying power and ingenuity. Underestimate them and they were in the hotel bedroom before the joints had been lit. I was confident Steve would go down well, and even if he didn't, I was sure Debbie would.

Halfway through Traffic's set, I heard a commotion. I turned and noticed a young chap being forcibly dragged down the stairs by the bouncers. I hurried over to see what was wrong but was too late to prevent them unceremoniously manhandling him through the exit doors. On reaching the foyer, I could see this forlorn and dejected figure standing outside and immediately asked the bouncers what grave misdemeanour he had committed to warrant such rough handling.

"He tried to steal one of our albums," one answered. I looked out and took a quick appraisal of the alleged thief. He was of small build, with smartly cut hair, clean blue jeans, and polished black shoes. He looked totally inoffensive and had a bewildered, if not frightened look on his face. Something didn't add up so I decided to go out and speak to him.

"Did you steal one of their albums?" I asked.

"No I didn't," he protested. "It was one of my own which I brought with me. You're the one who encourages us to bring them along so we can have a track played, but they wouldn't listen. They just threw me out," he explained tearfully.

A sixth sense told me he was telling the truth, although my assumption wasn't purely based on guesswork. For a start, I always brought a large selection of albums with me whenever I was the promoter, and if there were any on stage, they belonged to me. On nights like this, the Mecca's albums were safely locked in the office, to which this boy had no access. Besides, his meek demeanour made me warm to him. He had come to see Traffic, paid his money and, although seemingly innocent, had been thrown out in the most distressing of circumstances.

I walked back in to speak to the bouncers.

"I think you've made a mistake. He didn't steal that album, he brought it with him. Anyway, I've decided to let him back in."

They looked shocked at the very suggestion.

"No you're not. We've put him out, and he's staying out," blared one of them.

I looked into their hard, unyielding faces which showed not the slightest sign of sympathy or understanding, and knew I had a problem.

"Look, I've paid to hire this place. I'm paying your wages and I want him in," I politely but firmly pointed out.

They remained impassive and stood blocking the entrance.

"He isn't coming in, and if he steps over that doorway, we'll give him it," one of them threatened.

I could have just walked away and that would have been the end of it but to have done so would have been a contradiction of everything The Fillmore stood for. People in the town had been so kind

156

to me, supported me, and trusted me. These brutes didn't seem to have a single morsel of compassion in their bones, nor was there one shred of evidence to suggest this poor helpless figure had stolen the album.

I then spoke out with a conviction that seemed to take them by surprise.

"He's coming back in, and if anyone touches him, I'll get stuck into them," I warned.

They stared back contemptuously as if challenging me to make such an audacious move. The stakes had risen as I stepped forward and gestured to the hapless youth to accompany me. "Come on, no one's going to harm you," I urged.

He looked at me with a nervousness that bordered on abject fear and remained motionless as the bouncers glared at him menacingly. "Don't be frightened, they won't touch you," I assured him.

Finally, after more friendly coaxing, he began cautiously walking towards the entrance.

As he approached, one of the bouncers stepped forward and made a move to hit him. This was the signal I awaited. The talking was over, it was time for decisive action. Before the bouncer could reach him, I stepped in and sent a right hook deep into his midriff. In a split second, all hell broke loose. The three of them began raining blows on me and as I fought to protect myself, two of them grabbed an arm each, and began twisting them in opposite directions.

While I was in this defenceless position, the third was swinging wild punches towards my face in a frenzied effort to inflict damaging injuries. In those first few seconds, I recognised it was essential to keep a cool head and look for a way out. The punches were hurting, but not enough to knock the fight out of me and I was a long way from being beaten. With my arms twisted behind my back, I was almost bent double, and before the moment of impact from a clenched fist, I would shoot upright and absorb most of the blow. As the adrenalin flowed, I was fighting like a wounded animal. It was kill or be killed.

While this was happening, the other two thugs were finding me difficult to contain as I pushed and pulled them in all directions. Whenever my attacker tried to move in close, I kicked out, forcing him to throw his punches from long range which gave me vital time to take avoiding action. In a fight of this nature, everything is happening so fast, there's no time to think in the ordinary accepted manner of things. The brain automatically senses you don't like being hit, and you're depending on it to come up with the right answer. If it doesn't, it can be all over before you know what's happened.

As the fight raged on, a huge shout went up, and The Locarno's manager Mr Holton appeared. "Stop," he shouted. "Let him go." With my arms now free, I spun round and went berserk as all my frustration surfaced.

"You can stick this place wherever you like," I screamed. "I'm leaving and Procol Harum won't be on here next week."

He looked shocked as I raced up the stairs and leapt onto the stage in a mad rage while Traffic were still playing. As I threaded my way through their equipment, I reached up and, in a last defiant act, tore down a three-foot long poster advertising the following week's gig. Still seething, I screwed it up into a crumpled ball and threw it contemptuously to the side of the stage before storming off. I glanced at a confused Steve Winwood who continued to play on. I headed straight towards the manager's office; so angry, I'd have fought every bouncer in the place one by one.

My mind was made up. There were to be no more compromises. I was determined these bouncers had to go, if not, I'd walk. In the manager's office, all efforts to placate me were futile as I gave him my final ultimatum. Either I be allowed to have my own doormen, or the whole deal was off.

Mr Holton looked shaken as he listened, and said he would contact head office. I told him that no matter how long it took, I was in no mood to back down. Mentally, I felt strong and knew an important principle was at stake. Unless they agreed, it was definitely the end.

I then went into the dressing room to pay the band. Steve could see how upset I was and asked what had happened. After I'd explained and told him I wanted my own club, he said one of the nicest things ever said to me in all my years in rock. "When you do get your club, let me know, and I'll come and play for you," he said with a sincerity that was genuinely touching.

Finally, I'd met someone who understood, while his kind words spoke volumes about the man. I thanked him, left the dressing room and looked up at the empty stage in a confused state of mind. It all began to hit me when I realised that I might never stand on it again. Within minutes a handful of pig-headed intransigent brutes had undone all the good that had been achieved.

Over the following three weeks, negotiations took place as I continued to insist on having my own doormen on The Fillmore nights. The Mecca head office in London became involved, but after lengthy deliberations, they refused.

It seemed this was the end, but I was to return a year and half later under different management with my old friend from The Bay, Tommy Donnelly keeping an eye on the door. Incidentally I never again saw the young guy in question who was thrown out that night, and have been unable to trace him despite appeals in the local press. I really would like to meet him so he can substantiate my story and, out of interest's sake, remind me which album started the incident. When the fight began, I believe he nipped inside to see Traffic. At least the pain hadn't been in vain.

Chapter 19

Within days, the doom-laden clouds hanging over The Fillmore slowly began to lift. New and exciting challenges lay ahead which would amply compensate for any misgivings I felt. The first opportunity occurred in 1972 when Terry Ellis and Chris Wright of Chrysalis Records invited me to London and offered me a job booking and promoting groups at their recently acquired Rainbow Theatre in Finsbury Park.

It was a tempting offer, especially as it was a major venue where both The Who and Pink Floyd had played shortly after it's opening in November 1971. After looking around and meeting the Rainbow's manager, whose name I believe was Ted May, I reluctantly declined as I had an urge to open my own club. Nevertheless, I was still thrilled to be offered the opportunity and continued to promote Terry's and Chris's bands in the North East with the same unstinting enthusiasm.

Many years later, while I managed an indie rock band called Deadpan Joy, by a strange quirk of fate we all lived together in a flat on Seven Sisters Road, just a few yards from the Rainbow. It's now closed down but as I walked past, I often thought of what might have been. With its graffiti-laden walls and derelict entrance, it seems a travesty that this fine theatre now lies dormant.

I continued my efforts to find suitable premises to run my own club which proved to be more difficult than I had envisaged. What followed was a succession of unsuitable 'khazis' being offered to me by people who seemed to think that music lovers only attended damp and dirty premises with inadequate facilities.

"It's got atmosphere man, could be real groovy," was a stock phrase. It wasn't that I was overly fussy, but I knew it had to be right. Problems such as supporting pillars obstructing the view of the stage, small toilets, no fire escapes, poor loading facilities for equipment and, crucially, high rents were all encountered in most of the buildings. Finally, I did a deal to buy Annabel's nightclub, only for the Lloyds Bank manager to refuse to lend me the extra money to clinch the deal. This occurred twice and the unacceptable face of capitalism was rearing its ugly head once again.

In the meantime, I desperately needed somewhere to promote Procol Harum on May 15, and after a word with Mr Dixon, who was still the manager of The Bay Hotel, he agreed to me hiring the ballroom. Seeing him again was a wonderful experience, considering how we had parted, and I felt as if I was back on my home turf.

Wandering around, I couldn't help making my way into the ballroom and standing on the stage as the memories came flooding back. Country Joe, Pink Floyd, The Who, Tyrannosaurus Rex, Free, Yes, Jethro Tull and that smashed window. I looked over and thought of little Pepe on that fateful night. It had been replaced, but the memories hadn't as I walked out into the car park and continued to wallow in affectionate nostalgia. The late transport returning happy faces to their homes, the heroic bus driver rescuing me from a severe beating, and Steppenwolf not showing while disgruntled people walked away. Cannabis resin, groupies, the police raid and ballroom dancing.

It had been a truly amazing journey, and now it was about to continue with Procol Harum. 'A Whiter Shade Of Pale' had been on the juke box when I was first at The Bay, and now they were coming to play it in the flesh. I walked into the bar and noticed Dr Chipchase having his usual lunchtime drink. He smiled, and it seemed as if nothing had changed. His words of advice immediately came to mind. "You must exercise, Geoff, because it gets the blood coursing through the system. A slow-running stream has litter, old cans and unwanted rubbish at its side. But a fast-flowing one doesn't because it carries it all away."

"Hungry, Geoff?" asked Bill the chef. Even if you weren't, you always said yes because the food was so good. I glanced into the restaurant and thought of Mr Forrest and his wife. They always ate there, and because its windows overlooked the front entrance, they had seen me fight on far too many occasions. I thought back to the previous week's altercation at The Fillmore, and felt I had learned a (painful) lesson. Dad always said, "You have to pay for your learning son." There were still a few bruises and bumps, but now I realised what he meant.

I shook hands with a smiling Mr Dixon. I knew Tommy and I had judged him right. In fact, it seemed everyone was smiling and it felt good. Having climbed on stage and torn down the Procol Harum poster in full view of everyone, it was inevitable that questions would be asked.

"I heard about the three bouncers getting stuck into you," said Tommy Cooper, a friend of mine who worked at the local Royal Infirmary mortuary. In previous years, Tommy and I had lived in bedsits at 52 Otto Terrace, just outside the city centre. When times were hard, we'd share fishcakes and a loaf of bread, by knocking up a meal together in the communal kitchen. Tommy was someone who always held a morbid fascination for me because he once took me to the local mortuary and showed me the first dead body I'd ever seen. It was an old lady lying in a coffin waiting to be picked up by the undertaker. At first it was shocking, but then I moved closer. She was at peace, and her white face was almost angelic. It was as if she'd gone straight to heaven, and for some strange reason, it took the fear of death away from me.

Tommy spoke again. "Mind you, Geoff, you don't seem to be too bad, considering three bouncers worked you over." I smiled, because he'd seen me in a few scraps at The Bay and had great faith in me. Unknown to him I felt a deep hurt, but it wasn't physical, it was mental, and the scars would take time to heal. I felt like taking a team over there to finish what the bouncers had started. I was friendly with some dangerous people and kept telling myself it was no more than they deserved. However, after careful deliberation, I realised it would mean sinking to their abysmal level.

"What are you going to do now?" Tommy asked. I smiled wryly and informed him that I'd already done a deal to start promoting at Newcastle City Hall, as well as The Mayfair, on a regular basis. Tommy looked startled.

162

"Bloody hell, Geoff, you don't waste any time, do you? Now that you've got Procol Harum at The Bay, are you going to stay there?" he enquired. Tommy always kept his finger on the pulse and is still the same to this day.

"I don't think so. I can't have it every week because the manager has lots of functions already booked, but he's given me around eight dates."

"What about The Radha Krishna Temple. Where are you putting them on?"

"At The Barnes Hotel the week after Procol," I answered.

"Didn't George Harrison have something to do with them?"

"Yes, he saw them in Oxford Street and signed them to The Beatles' own Apple Records label. They've already had two hits, but it could be a strange sort of gig."

"What makes you say that?"

"Well, I don't know what kind of people will come to see them, but it could be very interesting."

"What made you book them?" he asked.

"I don't really know, they just seemed to have such good values about life, so I decided to take a chance."

"You're always taking chances, Geoff. If you're not careful, one of these days you'll be paying a more permanent visit to my little room at the hospital!" he laughed.

Tommy was that sort of chap. He could joke about death because he was used to seeing it on a daily basis and was inured to the shock of it.

As predicted, The Bay was packed for Procol Harum, but for some strange reason, the band went back to their early roots and played mostly old rock'n'roll numbers from their days as The Paramounts. When they introduced their worldwide hit, 'A Whiter Shade Of Pale', the place erupted.

Michelle, Debbie, Melanie, Caroline, Sarah, and a retinue of other females were all there. Welcome back girls. Michelle smiled and kissed me. She looked ravishing, but it seemed strange not seeing Dot there. Without her, The Bay didn't seem right. I asked what happened to Ritchie Wooler. "He's courting now, and I see you are," said one of his friends. I smiled as Michelle approached me again. Her pendulous breasts and mini skirt were easy on the eye, as I gave her an admiring look. She knew my weaknesses, and I knew her assets, as she wrapped her arms around me before kissing me warmly. It was a good start, and I was hungry for more. I looked over at two of the waiters who'd been watching and felt embarrassed. They knew I was shy and backed away.

"See you at the end of the night," she whispered. I nodded approvingly, knowing she'd certainly liven things up later.

"Bit of lipstick on your lips," said one of the waiters as he passed me a serviette. I blushed. The waiters were like that. They didn't miss a thing. Yes, I was back at The Bay.

The following week proved to be vastly different. The Radha Krishna Temple were certainly different to Procol Harum, and while The Barnes Hotel was smaller than The Bay, both groups were excellent. The remaining dates at The Bay were equally wonderful but, again, size was a limiting factor.

Quite soon, the chance of promoting Free in Sunderland came up, and I was delighted to remain a part of their set-up.

The Top Rank Suite (now a supermarket) in Park Lane, Sunderland, was a large ballroom, and I immediately arranged to hire it for June 26. The gig was a sell-out with 3,000 people in, and as at every Free gig, it was pandemonium. The support that night was Kevin Ayers and The Whole World, whose guitarist Mike Oldfield was then completely unknown.

A few weeks later, I accepted an offer from the Chrysalis Agency to co-promote their concerts at Newcastle City Hall in conjunction with Wilf Wright. It was a heaven-sent opportunity, and one that was to be most rewarding in terms of my involvement with major concerts there.

On July 31, 1970, Deep Purple appeared at The Mayfair. 'Black Night' had sent feet racing onto the dance floor while the excitement on young people's faces on hearing it was all too apparent. In the dressing room before the gig, I enthusiastically asked them if they intended playing the song during the course of the set. They looked surprised, and informed me that they no longer played it live. I was aghast and told them how popular 'Black Night' was at

The Mayfair. "If you don't play it, there'll be a riot," I warned. Realising I was serious, they agreed, and after a quick dressing room rehearsal, everything was set.

That night, The Mayfair was a complete sell-out with hundreds locked out. Outside, those unable to gain admission started to batter the doors down in frustration, with empty beer kegs. Eventually, under this tremendous onslaught, the doors gave way, and a huge tidal wave of surging humanity raced excitedly down the stairs. Fearful of being crushed, the bouncers jumped aside as hundreds poured in without paying. Once inside, they quickly merged into the joyous crowd without the slightest sign of trouble all evening.

Deep Purple were absolutely magnificent and totally tore the joint apart. A live appearance and a recorded album can be world's apart, and they were the only group that John Peel and I disagreed about. Fortunately, this in no way altered my opinion, or the fans who attended the gig that night. Ian Gillan, Ritchie Blackmore, Roger Glover, Jon Lord and Ian Paice certainly knew how to whip up a crowd's enthusiasm, playing until they virtually dropped from exhaustion. Two weeks later, 'Black Night' entered the British charts, and I'm convinced that over 3,000 people in Newcastle Mayfair that night helped put it there.

Chapter 20

One day I received a call from Roger Forrester, who worked for The Robert Stigwood Organisation. Our business connection hadn't got off to a great start with Ginger Baker's Airforce, but despite everything, I'd honoured the agreement. Fortunately, this was to stand me in good stead.

"Hi Geoff, how would you like to book Eric Clapton's new group?" he asked. I trembled with nervous excitement, not quite believing my ears. "I know you did your brains in with Ginger, but this is an exciting new group that Eric's put together," Roger enthused.

"What's he going to call it?" I enquired.

"Derek and The Dominoes," he replied, awaiting my reaction. "Mind you, there's a slight snag. Eric doesn't want to be advertised, because he just wants to be one of the group."

On hearing this, my heart sank.

"How the hell can I expect people to come if I can't advertise him?" I replied in exasperation. Alarm bells started ringing. My last deal with Roger had lost me £600, and now he wanted me to book a completely unknown band who hadn't played a gig yet. Furthermore, I wasn't allowed to advertise the major name who would pull people in.

Sensing my apprehension, Roger broke the silence.

'Don't worry Geoff, you won't lose your shirt on this one because I'm going to let you have them for half the price you paid for Ginger,' he assured me.

Don't worry are two words I'm always wary of hearing because it has the opposite effect, making me worry twice as much. However, having Eric Clapton on stage at The Mayfair was too enticing a prospect to ignore. Somehow, there just had to be a way round it.

"Can I advertise the members of the band underneath the name of the group?" I cautiously asked.

"I don't see why not. But his name mustn't be any bigger than the others. They must all get equal billing because Eric just wants to play some low-key gigs without any fuss," he warned.

Unknown to Roger, I'd already formulated a plan which, if it worked, I knew would produce a sure-fire sell-out.

"I'll take him," I replied. Roger seemed relieved and promised to dispatch a signed contract.

I was in a daze the rest of the day. I'd promoted some big names, but Eric Clapton . . . In 1966, he'd played with Cream at Newcastle's Club-A-Go-Go, and I was bitterly disappointed at being unable to go.

Now, the hand of fate decreed I was not only going to meet him but was promoting one of his first gigs with his new band. Even stranger, was the fact that the Club-A-Go-Go where he had first appeared was just a few hundred yards away. Any lingering doubts about my ability to bring the best groups to Newcastle had been quashed. I'd arrived, and it felt good.

Within days, the signed contract tumbled through my letterbox and I eagerly tore it open. There, in bold embossed lettering across the top, were the words, The Robert Stigwood Organisation. Within seconds, I began studying the expensive vellum paper and, sure enough, the one loophole they hadn't thought of was staring me in the face. I immediately dashed off to the printers and asked if Eric Clapton's name could be printed in a different colour, but remain the same size, as stipulated in the contract. The answer was an emphatic yes, and on receiving them a few days later, his name stuck out like a sore thumb.

It was then that I knew I had a sell-out, and sure enough all hell broke loose as people from Carlisle, Hexham, Sunderland, South Shields, Middlesbrough, York, Northallerton, Durham, The Lake District, and countless other outlying places, began ringing in the mad rush for tickets.

Word soon reached Debbie who approached me in The Rosedene pub and began quizzing me about Eric Clapton, but somehow I sensed she was out of her depth. I thought of Val Smith, and wondered if she would be there. She was one North East girl who could certainly compete with any of the models 'Slowhand' might meet in London. Come to think of it, why wasn't she one herself?

A couple of days later, I spotted her in The Bis-Bar. As usual, she was her immaculate and unperturbed self. I looked over and tried not to stare. Eric would like Val. Nobody had written a song about her, but that could soon change if they were to meet. Still, if she's there on the night, I might have the courage to send a glass of champagne over. You never know, it might work, 'local boy makes good' and all that!

In the meantime, I still have to consider Debbie. The bars will be packed and she may have trouble getting served. If I see her, I'll probably send half a lager over. Anything more and she might get ideas above her station. Mind you, knowing her ability to inveigle her way into dressing rooms, she might end up sending a glass of Eric's champagne over to me.

Time went by and the day of the gig (August 7, 1970) crept quietly up on us. The huge temporary stage built by outside scaffolders to accommodate the band's equipment looked most imposing, stamping the importance of the occasion on the night's proceedings. The girls had "glammed up", and it looked for all the world as if they were attending a first night gala. London and Hollywood may have had their premieres, but tonight we were about to have our own. The tension in the air was electric with anticipation. Eric Clapton's new group were in town, and while no one knew what to expect, everyone sensed it would be something special.

When Eric walked in with the band, I felt myself blushing as pangs of guilt overwhelmed me. Surely he must have spotted the posters everywhere, and he could hardly have failed to notice his name was in a different colour. As we shook hands, I sheepishly told him what I had done to ensure a sell-out.

"I'm sorry your name on the poster is a different colour, but if I hadn't done it that way, the attendance would have been well down," I explained apologetically.

He smiled as if he understood. "Oh, it's all right. I don't mind in the slightest," he replied.

Chapter 20

As we spoke, his handshake seemed to linger longer than usual, as if conveying the sincerity of his words. Fortunately, all my worries had proved groundless.

Watching The Dominoes – Carl Radle (bass), Bobby Whitlock (keyboards), and Jim Gordon (drums) – playing such tracks as 'Bell Bottom Blues', 'Let It Rain', 'Have You Ever Loved A Woman', 'Keep On Growing' and, of course, 'Layla' from their album *Layla And Other Assorted Love Songs* was another night to remember.

Eric was coaxing and bending notes in a succession of breathtaking and beautiful patterns. Watching his control and mastery, time seemed to stand still as the notes hovered in the air, before descending into the audience's appreciative ears. During the gig, everything was going better than I could possibly have imagined until, shortly before the end, I casually looked down from the balcony and was horrified to see a huge fight had broken out in the middle of the ballroom.

On closer inspection, I saw a young boy being savagely attacked, as he lay helpless on the floor. Instinctively, I dashed down in a frantic effort to rescue him, and after forcing my way through the packed crowd, attempted to drag him clear.

In an instant, his attackers realised what was happening, and began raining blows upon me. With my arms tucked under the boy's shoulders, I was defenceless, and found myself hopelessly outnumbered. Faced with a desperate situation, there was no alternative but to release my grip, and try to fight back. As I did so, I was being hit from every direction. Realising I needed help, I turned and sprinted for the door to alert the bouncers. Within seconds I was back with reinforcements but, unfortunately, the attackers and their victim had disappeared into the packed audience. During all this, Derek and The Dominoes continued playing, and after a series of encores, finally left the stage.

Back in the dressing room, Eric Clapton noticed my swollen lip and asked how I acquired it.

"While you were playing, a fight broke out just in front of you. Didn't you see it?" I asked in a surprised tone.

"Yes, I did actually, but I decided to keep playing," he replied.

Just then, Baz Ward, the legendary roadie cum tour manager walked in looking concerned.

"Are you all right, Geoff? I saw what happened from the mixing desk, but couldn't leave it," he explained apologetically.

"I'm okay," I answered, before pulling out a huge wad of notes from my back pocket and asking him to check that the group's fee was all there.

"Don't tell me you were fighting with all our money in your back pocket, were you?" he asked in amazement.

"Yes I was, where else do you think I can keep it?" I answered.

"Bloody hell, that's the first time I've ever known anything like that," he replied. For years afterwards, we always had a good laugh about it.

Outside the dressing-room door, hordes of fans were waiting to meet the group and obtain autographs. There were some beautiful girls among them and, suddenly, the full impact of Newcastle's stunning ladies hit me. A few weeks earlier, Roger had stressed Eric just wanted to be one of the boys, and didn't want any special attention. Now, it was all about to alter as everyone besieged him for his autograph.

I'd been through this procedure on many occasions with other bands, but this was noticeably different. They didn't get to speak to Eric Clapton every day and to see their faces light up as they did so is a memory I will always treasure. Posters, albums, bits of paper, beer mats, they were all thrust at him while he signed each one with a patience and willingness that seemed never-ending. If he reads this, I'd like him to know how much happiness he created in Newcastle that night, both on and off stage.

When this gig was first announced, it seemed that every unknown group in the country wanted the support slot, having recognised that playing in front of a packed audience, and supporting Eric Clapton, would almost certainly be a major boost to their careers. The Junco Partners had already appeared on many occasions, so there was only one other band who could possibly be considered.

They were Writing On The Wall, a Scottish group who were a great bunch of lads. Unfortunately, despite covering thousands of miles in their quest to make it, they never reached the status they deserved. Nevertheless, they knew how to rock, how to entertain, and how to play. An excellent group, together with a great performance, sealed their reputation in Newcastle that night.

While watching the band that night, Debbie tugged at my arm. "Thanks for putting me and my two friends on the guest list," she enthused.

I looked into her heavily made-up face and knew that, for her, the music was of secondary importance because it was Eric she wanted. Later, I noticed her at the side of the stage, talking to one of the roadies. It was an old ploy which often worked, because he might invite her back to the hotel, and possibly introduce her to the band.

On the other hand, the situation could rebound on her. These roadies were wily characters who knew the score and were no fools, especially when working with Baz. He looked after his men and made sure they got their share of the spoils, because you don't tour America as often as he did and not learn the ropes of sexual etiquette. Meanwhile, in the dressing room there was champagne and girls, but no Val.

Two months later, I saw the roadie in The Marquee. "How did Debbie get on that night, did she get to meet Eric?" I asked. He smiled, looked down, and pointed at his groin. "If that's what you want to call it, then I suppose she did," he gloated.

Chapter 21

Rock was now becoming a big and expensive 'business', making it increasingly difficult to break into. It wasn't just finance, it was also about personal contacts and dedication. Without them, a beginner might find it hard to compete against the big boys from London who were beginning to take control of its every facet. Everything was going fantastically well at Newcastle Mayfair, but inside there remained a deep urge to fill the musical void in Sunderland.

In an amazing piece of luck, I was approached by the manager of Sunderland's Top Rank Suite, which also had a 3,000 capacity. "Why not put the groups on here?" he suggested. It was a fantastic opportunity, and, having agreed there would be no dress restrictions, one which I eagerly grasped.

At The Fillmore, I'd opened with The Who, and it had been a spectacular success. I was looking for something equally special to open with. After careful consideration, I decided to stage an indoor Festival of Music. At first glance, the title may have sounded a little pompous, but it never felt like that – I just wanted to present the best at a reasonable price.

Free, of course, were a must and after hectic negotiations, Deep Purple also agreed to co-headline. Principal Edwards Magic Theatre, Cochise and local band Juice were added to the bill. The 'freakers' would like the fact I'd booked Principal Edwards Magic Theatre especially for them. The date was October 16, 1970, with admission being set at just £1, resulting in a mad scramble for tickets, and an immediate sell-out. The Fillmore North was now bigger and better than ever.

As I stood at the side of Berg's record shop counter, only two hundred yards from the venue, I watched as parents rushed in to buy tickets for their sons and daughters. With five groups of this calibre for £1, I knew that even the poorest of families could afford it, and this gave me great satisfaction. Occasionally, they would buy one of the group's albums, in the hope of having it autographed on the night. In London, major groups were appearing all the time, and people could unwittingly become blasé. But here in Sunderland, the excitement and anticipation was at fever pitch.

All over town, people were stopping me in the street, and all they wanted to talk about was the Festival of Music.

"I bet you know The Beatles. Do you think they will ever reform?" enquired one of them.

"No, I don't know them," I smiled, "and I couldn't tell you if they'll ever reform. But you know me, if they do, I'll try and get them."

He nodded approvingly. Some people delight in fantasising about things of this nature, and a small acknowledgement from me seemed helpful. But was it fantasy, or was there a chance? The Beatles to reform – in the light of events, it may have seemed beyond the realms of possibility, but in those days, I was riding high, and nothing seemed impossible.

As the day drew nearer, I realised that Mick Grabham (who had now formed Cochise) was coming home to play only yards from the public phone box where he would anxiously ring Lionel Conway at Dick James Music to see where Plastic Penny were in the charts, while Nigel Olsson was in London and there was talk of him joining Elton John's band.

Meanwhile, Dave Stewart struggled manfully on, determined to get the break he sorely needed, and Eddie was still in Sunderland, dreaming of owning his own studio. My hopes of romance were dashed as I discovered that the beautiful Val Smith's relationship with Greek student Pedros seemed to be an enduring one. In Sunderland, we could build men and ships of steel, but a broken heart was suffered in silence.

Caroline was pregnant, and didn't know who the father was, although everyone else seemed to know. In the local press, bouncers were in the news for being too aggressive, and one was charged with grievous bodily harm and sent to prison. On reading this, I smiled. It was a vindication of everything I had fought against, and now it was there for everyone to see.

This set me thinking. Were these bouncers social misfits, closet psychopaths, or inveterate bullies. I came to the conclusion that in many cases, they were all three. For some unknown reason, these types often go hand in hand with the kind of club they work at. Invest in them the power to refuse entry, and sadistic tendencies invariably begin to surface. On encountering this sort, no matter how frustrating it may be, it is prudent to let them exercise their authority and allow yourself to be programmed with a variety of unhelpful or predictable instructions. "Wait there. The club's full. There's no pass-outs. You'll have to take your coat off. Come on, get out, it's two o'clock," usually accompanied by an uninvited shove. Just then, you realise it's time to go home, even though you may not have got past the foyer. But don't despair. Someone, somewhere, wants your money. As you part with it, that false smile which belittles your intelligence is directed towards you. It's a relief to be inside, but it's not what you expected. There are no seats, and the drinks taste like they have been dispensed directly from a water main. Just then, a piercing noise hits your eardrums, and you realise you're standing directly under a speaker. The only way your partner can hear you is to shout above the din, but your throat soon starts to hurt, and eventually locks up. Unable to breathe, the combination of its stifling atmosphere, and the physical impairment you have just acquired, makes you realise that an emergency tracheotomy may be the only thing that will keep you alive. Undeterred, you feel an excruciating pain in your foot. You look down and realise one of the bouncers has stood on it. You grit your teeth and smile, knowing it's the only possible action you can take if you want to keep them intact. The manager approaches. "Having a nice evening?" Suddenly, there's more excruciating pain in the other foot. It's the bouncer again, and you come to the conclusion he must be blind and needs a guide dog that's trained to breathe through an oxygen mask.

A fight starts and the bouncer rushes in. This is his big moment. It's the one he's been hoping for all evening, and he means to make the most of it. Fists are flailing and someone appears to be seriously injured on the floor. The bouncer treads on him, or was it a kick? Either way you feel sorry for the recipient, and know how he feels. The condensation from the room drips onto your neck. It's icy cold and you use a tissue to wipe it. It's only two-ply, and quickly becomes a soggy mess as you desperately search for a receptacle to dispose of it. You spot one. It's the bouncer's mouth, and you're sorely tempted to risk life and limb just for the satisfaction it will give you.

It's time to go home. Outside, the hapless individual who was foolish enough to complain is being stretchered away in an ambulance. Your immediate instinct is to climb in, but you can't, as you don't have a dislocated jaw and fractured ribs. Next morning, with your feet in traction, you pick up a newspaper to find that someone in that vicinity has been shot. Your heart races as you hope he has finally got his just deserts. But no, you become crestfallen when you find it's not him. Still, not to worry. You won't be going there again for a while. That is, not until you've had a month's stay at a health farm to recover. Go on, ask me who is the worst bouncer I've ever encountered. It was unquestionably at The Powerhouse rock venue in Islington, London, somewhere around 1995. What an uncaring and bullying attitude he possessed. The only comparison I can draw is that he was so aggressive, he made Saddam Hussein seem like a peacekeeper from the UN.

Back at the Festival of Music, just when things seemed like they couldn't go wrong, I received an unexpected phone call from Tony Howard at NEMS explaining that, because Free were so popular in Sunderland, Deep Purple felt it was unfair competition and were pulling out. The gig was already sold out, and I began to wonder if I'd been too ambitious. Luckily, I'd become friendly with Deep Purple at The Mayfair and sensed that if I could only speak to them, I would be able to reassure them that their fears were groundless. They just had to be there on the night. If they weren't, it could ruin everything.

After my heartfelt pleas, to his eternal credit, Tony finally relented and gave me the group's home phone numbers. After explaining the situation, and with the warmth of their Newcastle reception still fresh in their minds, Deep Purple finally agreed to play. To my immense relief, I was back on track.

In tough situations, equally tough solutions are sometimes needed but I wanted sensible people on the door at the Festival of Music. John Tansey and Tommy Donnelly were both unavailable, but fortunately the head bouncer was a friend of mine, as the night turned out to be full of incident. It all started with Deep Purple failing to arrive on time, so Free kindly agreed to go on first.

A few minutes into their set, I received a message saying that Deep Purple's equipment was outside, but it was too late for them to appear.

"It weighs eleven tons, and there's no time to unload it now," said one of their roadies.

"Where are the group?" I frantically asked.

"They're at the Palatine Hotel, about a quarter of a mile away," he answered. I immediately became suspicious. It was all too low key, and there was not the slightest sign of regret or disappointment in his voice. It seemed obvious that they'd had second thoughts, and by turning up with their equipment, had theoretically fulfilled all their contractual obligations. Therefore, I would be unable to sue them.

With 3,000 paid-up patrons inside, I had to think fast as I wrestled with the problem. It was crushing to know Deep Purple were so close, and it would be tragic if they didn't play. Scores of people without tickets were outside, when I suddenly had the bright idea of asking the first twenty chaps if they would help carry the gear in if I let them in free, to which they eagerly agreed.

I then desperately rang the Palatine and pleaded with the group to come and play. "Your equipment is ready to go on stage," I told them. "Free have gone on first and there is absolutely nothing to worry about. There are 3,000 people here desperate to see you. Please come or it will ruin everything."

On hearing my plea, they eventually relented and within minutes had arrived at the stage door. Free had been excellent as usual, and Deep Purple took to the stage with a gigantic and appreciative roar in their ears.

Halfway through their set, a house fuse blew and the whole interior was thrown into total darkness. On stage it was pandemonium as clambering roadies desperately tried to find the fuse boxes. While drummer Ian Paice played resolutely on, the audience

176

incorrectly assumed it was all part of the act.

On stage, cigarette lighters were being lit in a desperate search for the elusive fuse boxes. After what seemed an interminable length of time, the power was finally restored, teaching me an invaluable lesson. From that day on, I always made a point of locating a venue's fuse boxes, and would tape two spare fuses to the outside of it, before the gig began.

Deep Purple were troopers and continued their show with the crowd demanding a string of encores. Afterwards, in the dressing room it was all smiles, as the band's fears of being upstaged proved groundless. Sunderland had fallen in love with them, and they eventually became another in a line of British groups destined to crack America in a big way.

On November 26, 1970, it was The Who's turn to play at Newcastle's Mayfair. This was the third occasion I'd promoted them, and knowing how electric the atmosphere was when they appeared, I eagerly looked forward to it.

When the night finally arrived, a huge stage had been built (as had happened for Derek and The Dominoes) while The Who's PA and lights were already in place. In the dressing room, Keith Moon, Pete Townshend and John Entwistle were all enjoying a pre-gig drink.

As Keith entertained us with his imaginative and witty repartee, the ballroom manager, accompanied by a police inspector, burst into the dressing room. Grim-faced, he beckoned me outside and thrust a telegram into my hand. "Read this, I'm afraid it's bad news," he warned. "Unable To Make Tonight's Gig. Am Fog Bound In Oxfordshire. Sorry – Roger Daltrey." On reading it, I felt stunned as I realised the implication of these few words.

It transpired that while the rest of the group had travelled up safely by train, Roger, in his wisdom, had decided to follow later in his Corvette Stingray. I was devastated. 3,000 people in and no Who. What was I to do?

After informing the rest of the group, Pete Townshend paced up and down in the dressing room. It was a tense situation as we frantically began trying to find a solution to the crisis. After a quick consultation with the group's production manager John Wolff, and

The Mayfair management regarding the hall's availability, it was agreed that The Who would return 17 days later to play the gig.

The next problem to resolve was the expectant 3,000 ticket holders still inside. There was no alternative but to face the crowd, and inform them of what had occurred. After asking Pete Townshend if he would accompany me to verify the explanation, he kindly agreed, and within minutes we were on the huge stage. The stunned audience remained silent as Pete stepped forward, apologised, and then promised The Who would return forthwith to play an even longer set. On hearing this from one of the band, the crowd accepted his explanation with graceful equanimity and, to my great relief, began applauding.

The tension was over as support group Curved Air took to the stage and turned an adverse situation to their advantage by becoming a huge draw in Newcastle as a result while at the same time rescuing me from a sticky situation. Only a handful of people, unable to be present on the rearranged date, asked for a refund, and sure enough, The Who came back on December 15 as agreed.

Thankfully, all four were present in the dressing room as Roger Daltrey came over to me and apologised. "Forget it," I replied. "I'm just glad that you're here."

The Who raced on stage as The Mayfair erupted into a cacophony of uproarious applause at the sight of them. It was a wonderful moment, and one I'll never forget. Roger began a blistering set by apologising for his previous non-appearance to the crowd. Did anyone care? Did anyone complain? Of course not. The Who were on stage, and that was all that mattered.

In early 1971, Free's manager, Johnny Glover, offered me a deal to sell their official posters on a UK tour. I jumped at the chance, not so much for the money, but to go on tour with Free was too exciting a prospect to miss. It was also the chance to have some fun and gain valuable touring experience, especially as I'd toyed with the idea of progressing on to band management at some stage.

Sure enough, it was fun all the way, and eventually the tour arrived in London for a prestigious date at The Royal Albert Hall.

Chapter 21

As it held over 4,000 people, I took hundreds of extra posters, anticipating a huge surge in sales.

When the doors finally opened, I was surprised to see that very few people showed any interest, and immediately hurried to their seats. I noticed that most of the beautiful girls spoke with cut-glass accents, while their escorts were well turned out in suits and ties. It was strange as it didn't fit the normal pattern of the rest of the tour.

When the same thing happened during the interval, it suddenly came to me. Seeing Free at the Albert Hall was an accepted part of the season. Ascot, Henley, Wimbledon and Hickstead all came to mind. Perhaps some of the Castletown Colliery manager's family might even be here. But if they were, would I have the time to acknowledge them? Now that I'm mixing with the cognoscenti of London society, I've certainly come up in the world, even if it is just for one night.

To polite clapping Free were on stage. To think the group I once booked for £35 were up there playing on one of the world's most prestigious stages, and I was there to savour the occasion. I hurried back to my position at the side of the stage and looked out. My mind started wandering as I fantasised about standing where all those famous names, including Bob Dylan and Cream, had played.

I was jolted back to my senses as the group broke into 'All Right Now'. How apt. It *is* alright now and I'm not worried about the posters any more. I'd only sold just over 30 but I didn't care in the slightest. It was that good.

Soon, hordes of people were up off their seats and grooving, while all pretensions of reserve or class were swept away by the excitement of it all. Free responded with magnificent and effortless playing, and were called back for five encores demanded by an ecstatic crowd. It was easily one of the best gigs I ever saw them play. As they passed me at the side of the stage, it was smiles all round. I didn't know whether to follow them to the dressing room, or remain and wallow in the fantastic atmosphere they'd created. As I entered the packed dressing room, which reminded me of The Bay, I shook my head in disbelief. Was there to be no end to this wonderful success story? I'd also learnt another valuable

179

rock'n'roll lesson. Never have any preconceived ideas about an audience.

Earlier in the tour, sales at Croydon's Fairfield Halls were alarmingly slow. I noticed that people were already clutching souvenir posters, so I stepped outside to see where they'd got them.

There, walking up and down the huge queue, were four white-coated guys bellowing, "Get your official posters here!" What a nerve, I thought to myself as I informed them that I held the exclusive rights, and they would have to stop. They refused, whereupon a heated argument ensued.

Suddenly, one of them produced a chain and threatened me with it.

"F★★k off now, before you get badly hurt," said one menacingly.

"Why should I?" was my indignant reply.

Just then, the chap brandishing the chain lifted his hand in the air as if he was about to strike me with it. People in the queue moved hurriedly aside as I rapidly took stock of the situation. Four of them and a chain. The odds were too great so I backed off. However, I knew we were due in Sunderland later in the tour, and I would be on home ground. Patience is a virtue, and I decided to bide my time.

On February 14, 1971, the tour duly arrived in my hometown. I was promoting this date as well as selling the posters and, sure enough, the pirate sellers were stationed outside. Each team has its own area and this lot were different from the Croydon mob, so they didn't recognise me.

"Why don't you come inside?" I suggested encouragingly to the one with the biggest amount of posters. "You'll sell a lot more in there."

"Will I be allowed to?" he asked in a surprised manner.

"Oh yes, nobody will say anything," I assured him. "The best spot is upstairs, I'll show you."

A broad grin crossed his face. "Thanks, mate," he eagerly replied.

On reaching the top, I pushed open a door and beckoned him through into the closed restaurant. Inside, it was cold and sparsely lit as I spun round and confronted him. "Give me those posters," I ordered. "You're not selling them here."

He looked shocked and afraid in the cold and unfamiliar surroundings in which he now found himself. Stepping forward, I wrenched the posters from his grasp. "Now get out of here," I snarled menacingly, "and if I catch you selling any more posters outside, there'll be trouble."

Within minutes he was back with a policeman.

"This man says you have stolen his posters, give them back to him," he ordered.

"But he doesn't have a street trader's licence," I countered. "He's ripping people off with inferior quality posters. You don't want that happening here in Sunderland, do you?"

The policeman thought for a moment. "All right, he can't sell them here, but when the concert's finished, you'll have to give them back to him."

Afterwards, the bootlegger returned to ask for his posters. "You can't have them, and if you don't get out of here, you'll regret you ever came," I warned before unceremoniously pushing him out into the street and bolting the doors.

A few days later at Hanley-on-Trent, near Stoke, two of the gang confronted me. "You're the guy who threatened us and took our posters away," said one. I braced myself for a scrap having realised there was no backing out as we stared menacingly at each other. The situation was tense, but they seemed to realise I meant business, and after a heated argument, the pair turned and left. Throughout the rest of the tour, I never heard from them or the police again, although the problem of merchandise piracy remains to this day.

Free continued to tour the world and do various gigs in the North East, which I promoted. Unfortunately, serious troubles within the band began to surface. It was an emotional time, and as things gathered pace, it soon became apparent that Paul Kossoff was hooked on hard drugs.

Gigs were continually having to be cancelled, while those that weren't were a farce. Often out of tune, and unable to play his guitar, the utter frustration on the rest of the group's faces was all too evident. One sold-out gig I promoted at The Mayfair in 1972 had to be cancelled at the last minute because Paul was rushed to Newcastle's RVI hospital; leaving me with the unenviable task of informing the sold-out audience that Free would be unable to perform.

Within seconds, a rumour spread that Paul had died. Outside, people lingered, desperately hoping for news, but there was nothing I could tell them.

"Is he alive?" asked a concerned voice. My heart sank and I felt unable to speak. If I said 'yes', it would give them hope. If I said 'no', it would send them into the depths of despair. I felt incapable of holding the responsibility.

"Is Paul all right?" asked someone else.

"I don't know, but I hope he is," I replied.

Later, at the hospital, I was told Paul was unconscious. No one was allowed to see him and the doctor seemed reluctant to commit himself as to the likely outcome.

Next day I was allowed a brief visit. "I think he'll pull through," the doctor said as I approached the side ward Paul was in. As I entered, he opened his eyes and looked at me. I forced a smile to communicate that no matter what happened, I would always be his friend. His eyes were dull, his skin pallid, while his body seemed lifeless. Every now and again he sighed, as if uncomfortable, or struggling for breath.

The doctor informed me that a young body, stricken like this, fights for the right to live. Unfortunately, if the person continues taking damaging substances in the amounts Paul was for any length of time, it becomes an unequal struggle. Listlessness, palpitations, and lack of appetite are early warning signs. Unconsciousness is the first serious sign of the body's inability to cope. If these warning signs are ignored, and the person continues in the same way, then the resultant consequences are almost always fatal.

Over the following weeks, I visited Paul each day and watched as he slowly improved. A few weeks later, he was well enough to play again. Unfortunately, each time he performed, it was obvious that something was seriously wrong. At Newcastle City Hall, a gig had to be rescheduled, while others were cut short due to his increasingly erratic playing.

The situation was becoming desperate and it seemed inevitable that, sooner or later, something had to give. Ironically I promoted what was to be Paul's last ever gig with Free at Newcastle Mayfair on October 20, 1972. Once on stage, it became distressingly apparent that the bright spark and ceaseless energy which had always epitomised his playing had now dissipated into a mere shadow of its former glories.

The crowd seemed to sense something was amiss and remained unusually quiet and subdued. Paul shuffled uneasily as the notes refused to soar, and the once biting solos were now blunted by unco-operative fingers. Watching him, I felt he was trying to coax one last performance from his trusty Les Paul, but it was not to be as a disillusioned Paul Rodgers glanced towards him with a fatherly and protective look on his face.

In the forces, I'd heard a Royal Marine bugler play the last post on hundreds of occasions. Hearing it was always poignant, and immediately made you think of the servicemen who had lost their lives. Paul's guitar playing had a similar effect that night.

Being the promoter I wanted to rush on and end it all there and then but the other three members may never have forgiven me if I'd done so. Mercifully, Paul Rodgers finally called a halt, and it was all over. Backstage, there was none of the usual celebrations, just an air of despondency as the group left for the hotel.

Why does he do it, and how can he stop it before its too late? These were my thoughts on that last night as Paul struggled onto the stage. Afterwards, I looked around at the empty Mayfair and noticed parts of the polished floor were wet with beer. If they had been pools of tears, I wouldn't have been surprised. Such was the feeling of hopelessness, I wasn't far from tears myself.

Shortly after the last-ever Free gig at Newcastle's Mayfair in October, the manager told me he was increasing the hire charges for the ballroom.

"I'm not paying it. You're making a fortune from the bar sales, and now you want more," I protested.

"If you don't pay it, others will," he countered.

"Well let them," I replied. "The success of The Fillmore is based on cheap admission prices. If this goes ahead, I'll have to increase them, and I'm not prepared to do that."

He gave me a nonchalant look, shrugged his shoulders and uttered the immortal phrase, "Well I'm sorry, but that's the way it is, it's business."

As the room fell silent, I'd already made my decision.

"Okay, count me out. I'm ready to do other things, including putting bands on at The City Hall."

The undercurrent of doubt which had festered for so long had surfaced in a manner I'd found impossible to ignore. The fun, the ideals, and the carefree spirit had dissipated and corporate opportunism had become its taskmaster. It was time to move on and look for a new challenge.

Chapter 22

Over the previous two years, while I had been promoting the major bands, every time I happened to be in London, I doggedly continued to call in to Peter Grant's office, but he was never there.

One cold morning, the telephone in my flat rang unexpectedly.

"Is that Geoff Docherty?" I recognised the voice immediately because of it being unmistakably high and unusually smooth, which I'd never forgotten.

"Yes it is," I replied.

"Do you still want Led Zeppelin?" asked Peter Grant calmly.

My pulse began racing with excitement and I couldn't believe my ears. I pulled myself together, and gushed out an emphatic, "Yes."

"Well you've got them. Can you be in my office at two o'clock tomorrow?"

"Yes, I certainly can," I answered.

"Okay, I'll see you then," he replied with friendly assurance before replacing the receiver.

I sat before the fire, my mind in a daze. Maybe I should ring Peter Grant and tell him I didn't want Led Zeppelin after all. They should have played when they had the chance. I'd got what I wanted and now it was time to tell him I didn't need his band. Everyone has feelings, and mine had been unnecessarily hurt. He'd caused me a lot of strife, and I wanted to let him see I wouldn't be messed about. Just because they're famous doesn't mean to say they can do what they like. It's about time somebody stood up to him and maybe it should be me. Anyway, who cares whether they come or not. Suddenly, I came to my senses. What was I thinking of? Cancel Led Zeppelin, was I mad?!

Early the next morning, I bought the music papers before boarding the train down to London. On reading them, Sunderland didn't rate a mention, and I realised if it wasn't for John Peel's column in *Disc & Music Echo*, people wouldn't know we existed.

A voice boomed over the intercom. "Buffet car now open." I stood up and made my way along the aisle. A queue had formed and I found myself standing next to two attractive girls, which put me in a good mood. They were easy on the eye as I gave them the once over, before discreetly looking away. I was too shy to speak, so I began wondering how I could break the ice. Maybe if I told them I was on my way to book Led Zeppelin, surely that would impress them, and they'd want to get to know me better.

I realised how pathetic using Led Zeppelin's name to meet a girl was, and anyway, they'd probably think I was some weirdo and move away with a disgusted look on their faces. In a flash of inspiration, another idea hit me. What if I invited them to the BBC to see John Peel broadcasting. Maybe that was a better approach as he's well known and a friend. Just then, York Station loomed and they prepared to disembark. I smiled but they ignored me. Never mind, I'd still got Led Zeppelin coming and there'd be lots of girls at the gig. With a bit of luck, I'd do better there.

Having finally arrived in London, the tube train pulled into Tottenham Court Road, and I emerged into Oxford Street. It was packed and everyone seemed too busy to notice anyone else as they hurried past. I wasn't used to this. In Sunderland, everyone was much more friendly and caring.

Before long, I was in Peter Grant's office. As I entered, one of the office girls approached.

"Don't tell me you've come to book Zeppelin," she asked in her usual sceptical manner.

"Actually, I have an appointment with Peter Grant, is he in?"

"Well yes he is, but there's nothing in the book about you seeing him," she said after flicking over a couple of pages.

"Please tell him Geoff Docherty from Sunderland is here to see him," I calmly requested. After disappearing into his office, she was soon back. "Please go through, he's waiting to see you."

Chapter 22

Stepping into his office to be warmly greeted, his size shocked me. I'd been told he was big, but this was ridiculous. He looked about 24 stone and 6ft 5ins, and now I realised why he could be so intimidating.

In his earlier days he'd been a doorman at the 2I's coffee bar in Soho, as well as tour manager for Gene Vincent and numerous other acts. For anyone to argue with him, they'd have to be mad, I thought as I eyed him across his desk.

As I stood there, a chap in the far corner was playing darts, and seemed completely unperturbed. It was Mickie Most, his partner in Rak Music, and the producer of dozens of hit records including The Animals 'The House Of The Rising Sun'. He turned and smiled before saying hello, which helped put me at ease as I wondered what the outcome would be.

Peter invited me to sit down, and after some initial small talk, I felt relaxed, and not in the slightest bit overawed.

"You never seem to be away from my office," he began. I smiled.

"It's the group I like, and if you let me have them, I'll like you as well," I cheekily replied.

With the small talk out of the way, he started firing questions at me from behind his big wooden desk, to suss out whether I could handle such a prestigious event. Fortunately, I felt confident as by now I knew every measurement inside the venue, its capacity, the price I hoped to charge, where the plug points were, and with indoor scaffolding, I could build a stage to suit any of Led Zeppelin's requirements.

"Where are you promoting now?"

"I've moved to Newcastle Mayfair," I answered.

"How many does it hold?"

"3,000."

"What's your normal ticket price?"

"75 pence."

He seemed happy and smiled. I was beginning to warm to him and from the way things were going, I sensed I was about to receive some startling news. Fortunately, I didn't have long to wait.

"Okay, you've got them. We'll give you ten per cent of the net profit after expenses. How does that suit you?" he asked.

"That's fine," I answered calmly, "but what about a date in Sunderland, everyone there is desperate to see them as well?"

He thought for a moment, looked up, and then stared at me. As he did so, for the first time I felt uncomfortable, realising I may have pushed too hard and end up with nothing.

"Okay, we'll give you a date in Sunderland later in the year. So that means you'll be promoting them twice. How do you feel about that?"

"Fantastic. By the way, you don't mind if I ask you a question, do you?" I cautiously asked.

"Of course not, what is it?"

"Why have you suddenly decided to give me a date after all this time?"

"It's because the group have decided to do some gigs at all the small clubs who booked them when they were unknown," he said. "You were one of them, so that's why I rang you. These clubs are the ones who deserve them."

I felt quite touched as I realised altruism was alive and kicking. He stood up and shook my hand in a vice-like grip that seemed determined to crush it into a powdery substance. It was a stark reminder that you didn't argue with him. Fortunately, I hadn't needed to. Just then a thought occurred to me.

"There's one other thing," I reminded him. "What about a signed contract?"

He smiled before answering.

"Listen, the last time I told you they weren't coming, and they didn't, did they? Well this time I'm telling you they are. So if I say they'll be there, they will be, you don't need a contract, just take my word for it."

With this confident reassurance, I turned to leave. The two office girls outside eyed me suspiciously and I couldn't contain myself any longer.

"I've got Led Zeppelin – they're coming to Newcastle and Sunderland, isn't that marvellous?" I asked enthusiastically.

Their faces turned ashen with disbelief.

"Led Zeppelin playing in Sunderland?!" one of them stammered.

Before she could finish, I interrupted her. ". . . and Newcastle as well." Just then, a feeling of elation overcame me as it meant I'd have to be taken seriously from then on. "Congratulations," she said after overcoming her initial shock.

"You do know where Sunderland is?" I asked jokingly, with a hint of sarcasm thrown in.

Why I said it I'll never know. Maybe it was all the frustration, together with the map of America on the wall which was full of coloured pins indicating where they'd been playing. New York, Seattle, Washington, Colorado, Philadelphia, Connecticut, Los Angeles, Boston, San Francisco, Miami, Missouri. Now it would need a British map with two more coloured pins for Newcastle and Sunderland.

I left the two stunned-looking secretaries before jubilantly making my way to King's Cross for the journey home. No tea, no champagne, but two unbelievable Led Zeppelin gigs in the bag. One thing was for sure. I'd be able to afford champagne on those nights.

Having promoted Led Zeppelin at Newcastle's Mayfair Ballroom on March 18, 1971, Peter Grant was as good as his word and the group were contracted to play Sunderland's Fillmore North on November 12. Unexpectedly, he contacted me and asked if I'd like to promote them a third time at Newcastle's City Hall the night before, on November 11. Led Zeppelin, three times in one year, and twice in two days. . . . I shook my head in disbelief.

Whenever you were in Peter's presence, he commanded respect, whether it was through fear, or the huge success he'd had. Now I began to sense that in some strange and reciprocal way, I had gained *his* respect. Peter was offering me 10 per cent net earnings from a gig that needed little promoting. A sole advert in the local press, and the gig was sold out within hours. The stage, security and tickets were all efficiently organised by Mr Brown, who was then the City Hall manager. From a purely impartial point of view, the gigs proved to be identical. By that, I don't mean the music, but the hysteria, police, telephone calls begging for tickets, and people queuing all night to obtain them.

I drove along to Bergs record shop in Blandford Street. It was cold and dark and, just as I expected, a queue had already formed to await the shop's morning opening. Personally, I've always hated queues, and I knew parents would be extremely worried about their kids being out all night in the cold. Upon approaching people at the front, I began offering to sell tickets at face value. At first, people refused, assuming they must be forged, but finally I managed to convince them they were genuine.

To my astonishment, as soon as they'd purchased their tickets, they immediately rejoined the queue which clearly illustrated the excitement that Led Zeppelin's visit was creating. At home, my telephone never stopped ringing, and I now had more potential girl friends than Robert Plant, with some of the calls being more than a little suggestive. It seemed ironic thinking back to those beautiful girls in Perth when the Ark Royal had docked there. I was on duty that night wearing a white belt and gaiters over my uniform, and as they walked towards the officers gangplank to attend a cocktail party, I was hardly afforded a second glance. Now things were different, but I was under no illusions. It wasn't me they wanted, but that all-important ticket.

"I need four tickets for my friends, Geoff," said Michelle as she slipped into my flat. I smiled knowingly as she thrust out those pendulous breasts, and kicked off her shoes. Her hips moved sensually as she turned to look in the mirror. I felt helpless as she picked up some spare tickets lying innocently on a table.

The phone interrupted the silence before she abruptly removed the receiver. "You don't want to be disturbed while I'm here, do you Geoff?" she cooed seductively. I looked at her alluring body and felt trapped with desires that could no longer be subdued. I moved closer and gently removed the tickets from her grasp. A look of alarm crossed her face but she needn't have worried. I'd had a few extra printed for special guests, and four of them were about to be consigned to the scheming possession of this sensual and irresistible siren.

"Why don't you ever ask me out Geoff?" she asked, while slowly unbuttoning my shirt.

"There's no bigger night out than seeing Led Zeppelin," I replied.

With that, she eased me onto the carpeted floor and ravished me. It was no contest. Two Led Zeppelin gigs, and a gorgeous girl. If this was burning the candle at both ends, tomorrow I'd buy another dozen. It certainly beat working in a factory.

A few days later, Debbie and Sarah approached me in the Rosedene pub. Debbie was angry and spitting venom.

"Who is this Michelle? She's been telling everyone you gave her four tickets for Led Zeppelin, and that she's your girlfriend. She's been with loads of guys, and if I was you, I'd stay clear of her."

I reeled back at her hypocrisy. It seemed inconceivable that Debbie of all people was complaining that someone had been with loads of guys. Sarah was quieter and more restrained, but her sunken eyes were betraying a lifestyle of men and drugs. Being a friend to Debbie, I understood how easily she may have fallen into this trap. They were young and craved excitement while the Rosedene was always a good starting point for a party.

"Where did you see Michelle?" I asked.

"At one of the Greek student's parties. She was naked in the bathroom with him," replied Debbie.

"I suppose you were a picture of innocence yourself?" I added mockingly.

"Listen Geoff, I don't pretend to be something I'm not, but she does."

Life seemed so unreal. All that worry, all those phone calls and cups of tea in Led Zeppelin's office. All those coloured pins on the map of America, and now the group were about to play in my hometown.

I thought of the dog wagging its tail on Whitburn cliffs the morning they had pulled out of playing at The Bay. Did it have psychic powers and know that it would all come good in the end? How would the local girls react to Robert Plant? He was a charismatic, multi-millionaire lead singer. By comparison, some of these girls worked at Jackson The Tailors and Brian Mills factories. Who could blame them for fancying an athletic six-foot rock god?

After finishing their shift in the shipyards, hordes of workmen hurried home in their sweat encrusted overalls, accompanied by young apprentices. They'd done a hard day's work, looking weary but proud. So was I. Led Zeppelin were about to hit town, and

I instinctively knew some of these lads would be there. Led Zeppelin, and who knows what else, all for 75p. Surely it doesn't get any better than that.

A week before the gig, I walked into Linx, Hoggy's small shoe shop in Derwent St. It was a little out of the way from the normal hub of things, and while it was never going to make him rich, it afforded him the luxury of being his own boss.

"Do you want to sell 50 tickets for the Led Zeppelin gig at the Fillmore?" I asked. He looked at me in amazement. I had to be joking. Led Zeppelin tickets on sale in a shoe shop. Had the rock world gone crazy? I thrust a bundle into his hand and watched as he flicked them through his fingers as cool as a Mississippi gambler. Without counting them, he placed them under the counter. I liked that. He trusted me, and I trusted him.

"Once word gets round that you've got tickets, there'll be long queues outside," I confidently assured him. It was a compelling moment. The lad who had once played cards with Tom Jones and Engelbert Humperdinck was no longer just a shoe salesman. He had now unwittingly become a co-promoter.

The day before the gig, I breezed in to see Hoggy. "How many tickets have you sold?" I asked.

"I've still got 20 left," he answered sheepishly. "Don't worry, I'll tell The Fillmore receptionist to let people know there's still some tickets here," I assured him. The following day I checked in, and to my surprise, he still had eleven unsold. After transferring them to The Fillmore, they were immediately snapped up.

Later, I spoke to the receptionist.

"Did you tell people there were tickets still left at Linx's shoe shop in Derwent St?" I asked.

"Yes," she replied. "But people just laughed at me and thought I was sending them on a fool's errand. I hope you don't intend to sell any more tickets in that shoe shop?"

I smiled and wondered what her reaction would be if I asked Tommy to sell the next ones at the mortuary. After all, if I ever promoted The Grateful Dead, it would certainly add an air of authenticity.

Chapter 22

Prior to their two Newcastle gigs, I picked up Peter Grant and Jimmy Page at Newcastle Airport. It was a wonderful moment, especially as the two gigs went like a dream. Later that year, on the night of their Fillmore appearance, there was an unexpected hitch when the bouncers failed to recognise the group and refused them admission. This resulted in a heated argument with their furious tour manager Richard Cole who, on eventually being admitted, hurled a stream of abuse about my lack of organisational abilities.

I was both stunned and furious at the door staff. After giving Richard and the group my heartfelt apologies, he calmed down, and within minutes the incident was forgotten. Thankfully, the gig was back on course as we set about making it a night to remember.

Jimmy Page seemed to thrive on the intimate atmosphere at The Fillmore. Just before going on stage, he wandered over to Chas McIver, and congratulated him on his choice of music. At the time, he was playing the original version of Albert King's 'The Hunter'. (This appeared on Free's first album, *Tons Of Sobs*.) Chas was quietly thrilled, and it clearly showed his time at Dobell's record shop in London hadn't been wasted. What a pity Jimmy didn't have more time to chat to him, because Chas was probably one of the few people present who could have named every player on the album.

Jimmy Page, John Bonham, John Paul Jones and Robert Plant hit the stage to a tumultuous roar, opening with 'Black Dog', then 'Dazed And Confused', 'The Immigrant Song' and 'Communication Breakdown', among others. The mood went from fever pitch to awestruck silence as the band sat on stools at the front of the stage to play three songs acoustically. These were 'Gallows Pole', 'Tangerine' and 'That's The Way'. Other songs in the set were 'You Shook Me', 'Good Times, Bad Times', 'I Can't Quit You', 'Rock & Roll' and 'The Lemon Song'.

Robert Plant was a living rock god with an excellent voice, which had a range, delivery and enunciation that was positively spellbinding. With a smile and personality to match, he was the perfect foil for Jimmy Page's exquisite guitar playing. This varied from being loud and aggressive, to mesmerising and sensitive, and whatever mood he deigned to play in, it was positively inspirational.

Behind these two were John Paul Jones on bass, and John Bonham, one of the finest rock drummers in the world. Meeting him in the dressing room was an experience in itself. He was friendly, raucous, inebriated, loud and down to earth. On making his way to the stage with those special heavy drumsticks, there was a determined and purposeful air about him. Every gig was a big one for a group of this stature, and if they were to rock, 'Bonzo' was the linchpin upon which their foundations were built.

Once on stage, he would go quiet, as if in deep concentration, and you wondered what he must be thinking. Somehow, you sensed he was already anticipating the first number, and couldn't wait to unleash the full power of his pent-up energy. Only Keith Moon of The Who could be placed alongside someone of his stature. How ironic that two of our greatest rock drummers were to die prematurely. Finally, there was John Paul Jones on bass, an ex-session musician who had played with Jimmy on many hits. Quiet, studious and sincere, the excitement of the occasion seemed to go over his head.

However, to think this would be an illusion, as once on stage, he slotted in perfectly to the thundering drum patterns being un-leashed in a never-ending ferocity behind him. Seeing the four of them locked in together like this, it soon became obvious why they had taken on the world and won. And to think I had first booked them at The Bay for £75.

After the gig was over, and the group had returned to the dressing room, I could hear a dog snarling in a vicious and seemingly uncontrolled manner. I couldn't believe my ears, and immediately raced out to investigate. What I saw horrified me.

Inside the ballroom was a uniformed security guard with a savagely snarling Alsatian straining at its lead, its teeth only inches away from young people's faces. Their look of terror remains deeply ingrained in my memory as this brute callously began order-ing completely harmless people to leave. To make matters worse, he seemed to be revelling in his task.

"Get that dog out of here," I screamed.

"I've been told by the manager to clear everyone out," he replied without the slightest concern.

As the dog continued to growl menacingly at people who had been slow to heed his orders, I grabbed the loose part of his jacket in desperation to restrain him. Suddenly, the huge imposing figure of Peter Grant arrived on the scene and towered over him.

"Get that f**king dog out of here," he screamed.

For the first time I saw the fear in the guard's eyes as he cowered behind the dog.

"These people have paid their money and aren't hurting anyone," Peter angrily pointed out.

Paul Mayo, one of the assistant managers who had also arrived on the scene, ordered the guard to make his way to the office to resolve the situation. On the way there, an argument broke out between Peter and the security guard who foolishly tried to justify his actions.

"How tough are you without the dog?" challenged an incensed Peter as he blocked his path. "Come on, come outside with me and let's find out."

Realising things were getting out of hand, I stepped forward. "You won't stand a chance against him," I warned. "He's an ex-professional wrestler and he'll kill you." (I'd already heard Peter had brandished a gun in Bowers, an all-night restaurant opposite Newcastle Central Station, in order to protect himself.)

"Come on," urged Peter. "You wanted the others outside, now try and put me out."

As Peter's uncontrollable anger was about to erupt into violence, the guard's face turned white with fear, before darting through the open office door and quickly slamming it shut behind him. I glanced at a chuckling Peter and nodded towards the dressing room. When Led Zeppelin came to town, this proved that anything was liable to happen.

Fortunately, this in no way affected my working relationship with Peter. On becoming manager of Bad Company, he asked me to promote their first ever gigs anywhere in the world – three consecutive sold-out nights at Newcastle City Hall in March 1974 where I was reunited with Paul Rodgers and Simon Kirke.

"What made you ask me?" I asked.

"You know the area, and we trust you," he replied.

In 1976, *The Song Remains The Same* premiered at a cinema in Leicester Square, and Peter Grant kindly sent me two complimentary tickets, and an invitation to an after show party at Covent Garden.

It seemed that anyone who was anyone was there. Paul McCartney, Bianca Jagger, Bryan Ferry and dozens of other celebrities entered and made their way to their seats. I arrived on foot with Edwina, a pretty girl who I'd invited, and as we struggled to make our way to the front, a policeman unceremoniously pushed me back into the crowd in the mistaken belief I was a gatecrasher. After a desperate struggle, I produced my two tickets to the disbelieving policeman who, after closely scrutinising them, waved us through.

As Led Zeppelin made their entrance, the house applauded in a respectful and reverential tone that acknowledged the group's superstar status. Afterwards, the party was a wonderful occasion to meet friends and wind down.

As I left, I remembered the words, "Peter Grant here, how would you like Led Zeppelin?" Whenever I see the figure of £75, I invariably think of him.

Sadly, Peter is no longer with us, but the memories certainly are.

Soon after the Led Zeppelin gigs, I received a call asking me to meet the directors of Mecca at their head office in London. On arriving, I was invited to sit at a highly polished table in their boardroom. After a quick exchange of pleasantries, they came straight to the point.

"How did you get Led Zeppelin to come and play at our Newcastle and Sunderland ballrooms?" they enquired.

"I'll tell you why we're asking," said one of them. "We'd like you to book them into all our establishments throughout the country."

With those words, a catalogue of disquieting thoughts went racing through my mind. The aggressive bouncers, the needless dress restrictions, the decision to clear The Fillmore with the aid of a vicious Alsatian, the ridiculous palm trees which some interior designer, in his wisdom, had placed in front of the balcony blocking the view of the stage, the irony of the very group they now wanted to book being unable to gain entry to their own gig.

My initial response was to burst out laughing, as it seemed such a preposterous suggestion. Did they really think you could just ring up and book the biggest band in the world for a nationwide tour of Mecca halls like some Sixties pop package? Hadn't they been told that things had changed dramatically since those days?

I wondered what these directors' reactions would be if Peter Grant or John Peel walked into their precious venues dressed in jeans, trainers and a T-shirt. They would have had been in fits of apoplexy. Come to think of it, the commissionaire on the door would have probably refused them entry.

Having kept myself in check, I gave a brief but polite explanation as to why this was impossible. A vacant look of disbelief descended over their faces. Inside I felt good. I'd finally reached the very top of the Mecca hierarchy and given them a taste of their own medicine. Considering the punishment I'd taken from three of their bouncers, I considered it a fair exchange.

Chapter 23

During my frequent trips to London, I often used to pop into the BBC Paris Studios in Lower Regent Street to see a live programme John Peel hosted. He would leave my name on the door, and it turned out to be a great way to see up-and-coming bands. "Have you had The Faces yet?" he asked, after one concert.

"No, they're a pop band aren't they?" I sceptically replied.

"Get them, they're excellent live," he urged. It set me thinking and knowing Rod Stewart's two solo albums were popular, I decided to heed John's advice and book them.

On the night of May 28, 1971, there were only about 1,700 in, but The Faces didn't let them down. After a fantastic show, Rod Stewart asked how many people were in?

"1,700," I replied.

"There'll be a lot more next time," he asserted confidently without the slightest trace of conceit. How right he was.

On August 27, they were back and with everyone in Newcastle desperate to see them, 3,000 people quickly snapped up the tickets. Once again, The Faces were tremendous with a rapturous audience refusing to let them leave the stage. Another John Peel tip had come good and he would soon be able to see why for himself.

Around this time, I decided to hold an outdoor rock festival at Sunderland's Roker Park football ground. The Faces agreed to headline, and I was invited to sit in the directors' box; two of them were most helpful, so I was optimistic that everything would come to fruition. Unfortunately, after a few weeks of groundwork, I received a short letter from the club secretary refusing my application to hold the concert.

On enquiring why, I was dealt with by a pompous official who dismissed my request for a reasonable explanation with what I can only describe as an ill-mannered brush-off. A few months later, I tried again with The Who, but this too was refused. I later applied to Gateshead council, some ten miles away, for the use of their athletics stadium, and was given the utmost help by everyone concerned. John Caine, who once represented England at running, did his level best to make it a reality, but unfortunately, at the time, there was no suitable headline act available.

Ironically, Gateshead Stadium now successfully hosts various major rock concerts, and thousands of people, including myself, have derived a tremendous amount of pleasure from attending them.

The Faces next appearance in the North East was to be at Sunderland's Top Rank Suite on March 5, 1972, with local support group Reuben James.

Chris Wright, from Chrysalis, was always pointing out how well the groups were looked after in America. Limousines, top hotels with fully stocked fridges, and every conceivable luxury were always laid on for them. Was he trying to tell me something? Well, a nod's as good as a wink . . . to a blind horse (as The Faces said), and not wishing to be outdone, I decided to lay on something special for The Faces after the gig.

On coming off stage, and relaxing in the dressing room which also had a private bar, I told them, "You've just made 3,000 people very happy, now it's your turn to be entertained."

With that, two hired sexy strippers appeared and began their slinky routine to a mobile disco I'd hired. The group looked on in amazement as one of the strippers edged her naked body towards young Rod. One of the biggest rock stars of the era was sitting right in front of her, and she wasn't about to miss her chance.

With thousands of girls lusting after him, here he was, only inches from her well-endowed figure. Her sensuality and gyrating hips were having a mesmerising effect on the rest of the group as they sat giggling like awestruck adolescents. Seconds later, she edged closer with her legs astride Rod who pretended to look cool but her breasts were in his face and you could sense his desire to caress them as she smiled, teased, and gyrated.

Suddenly, the other one was upon him, vying for his affections.

The Faces eagerly continued watching, while there was no telling where it would end. The girls finished their routine, and joined us for a drink. The group were delighted, and told me afterwards it was the first time anything like this had happened to them. The smiling barman had obviously enjoyed it too.

Later, I was to find our Northern hospitality was taken a stage further when Rod and one of the strippers vanished. Where to, I never found out, but one thing's for certain, the strippers didn't leave together, as the other one ended up at my place. Wait till I tell Chris Wright what happened. I bet Alvin Lee can't wait to come here and play again.

A year later, I promoted The Faces again at the original Sunderland Fillmore (then under new management). The scheduled date was March 24, 1973, but early that morning I received a telegram from their manager Billy Gaff informing me that the group were unable to appear due to illness (a telegram I have to this day).

After a succession of fruitless calls, the only option was to book a return flight to London. On reaching Billy Gaff's office, which was above The Marquee in Wardour Street, his receptionist calmly informed me that she was unaware of his whereabouts. Was she telling the truth?

As I sat and waited, certain doubts entered my head. There had been no mention of anyone in the group being ill, and everything seemed far too calm. As the clock ticked on, I felt the pressure building. My return flight was booked for late afternoon, and with 3,000 expectant people about to turn up, I knew how disappointed they would be.

Finally Billy Gaff arrived and I was quickly ushered into his office. He looked surprised to see me, and blurted out that one of the group was ill. Without a doctor's note, and no confirmation of the group member in question, I became highly sceptical.

"I'm not leaving here until I get a signed contract for another date, and a telegram sent on to Sunderland confirming it," I insisted.

On hearing this, Billy Gaff's face took on a pained expression as I continued to press the point home.

"If they aren't there on the date," I warned, "the police will arrest the both of us as conmen."

Chapter 23

With a signed contract and a duly dispatched telegram, I dashed to Heathrow and just made the return flight.

With the statutory blackboard announcing The Faces' non arrival in place, I went on stage to explain what had taken place.

"The group will be here on April 13," I assured the audience, "and everyone will be given a make-up ticket on the way out. Anyone who doesn't believe me can come up and have a look at this telegram confirming it."

Unconvinced, a young guy at the front immediately jumped up and after I handed it to him, he read it out to the crowd. The explanation was accepted with remarkable restraint, while the replacement local group seized their chance to play to their biggest-ever audience.

The replacement Faces date went on to become John Peel's all-time favourite gig, which he has continued to endorse over the airwaves and in print on numerous occasions.

The gig was made even more special because against all the odds, Sunderland's second division football team had reached the FA Cup Final, and were due to meet Leeds FC at Wembley Stadium. Having beaten Arsenal in the semi-final, the whole town was delirious with excitement, and every single team member had become a hero.

Backstage, John Peel, the man who had personally encouraged me to book The Faces in their early days, was accompanied by virtually the whole of the cup team, including Scottish winger Billy Hughes, and captain Bobby Kerr, known as the 'little general'. An occasion like this transcends any normal gig and becomes a spectacular event.

There was a real party atmosphere backstage as bottles of wine, champagne and lager were being consumed in copious quantities. Out front, a packed house was being entertained by new Warner Bros. signing, Beckett, a local group from nearby South Shields, who I was now managing.

When it was time for The Faces to go on, I asked John Peel if he would introduce them. Despite a long career in broadcasting, John is actually shy on occasions like this, and steadfastly refused. Being well under the influence of alcohol, the group and I began to good-naturedly push him out front, until suddenly he found himself under the glare of the stage lights in front of 3,000 ecstatic fans.

Entering into the spirit of the occasion, he duly announced The Faces to a roar of excitement. The Faces personified everything that is good about rock'n'roll; projecting a devil-may-care approach to the audience, showing that rock and roll is about enjoyment and, if mistakes occur, don't worry.

Precision becomes depressingly predictable. Fortunately, you could never accuse The Faces of this. Ronnie Lane, elfin bassist with a smile permanently etched on his cherubic features, sipping lager in between numbers, without a care in the world, was ably backed up by fellow ex-Small Faces and rhythm section compadre Kenny Jones. Ronnie Wood on guitar, cigarette clamped between lips, tottering unsteadily across the stage, playing bottleneck, with Ian McLagan coaxing rollicking rolls from his B3 Hammond.

Out front was the young Rod Stewart, twisting, pirouetting, and flinging his mike stand into the air as his rasping soulful voice provided the icing on the cake. Watching from the side of the stage, the Sunderland players were enthralled as Rod, the band and John Peel kicked a succession of footballs into the crowd. This wonderful gig seemed to last forever with The Faces looking as if they never wanted to come off.

The partying continued backstage as fans, initially intent on securing autographs, joined in the drunken revelry. To promote a gig of this stature, with 3,000 people watching and our local football team having the time of their lives, all I can say is that it was absolutely bloody marvellous. It may seem a long time ago, but to any of us present that night, time stood still. A wonderful memory and a wonderful gig. Just ask John Peel.

A few weeks later, another gigantic party erupted across the town when Sunderland beat Leeds 1–0, to bring the FA cup back home with them. The scorer was Ian Portefield and, without wishing to be obsequious, you couldn't wish to meet a more modest or nicer bloke. The FA Cup replaced The Faces as the partying started all over again at a celebratory 'meet and greet' held at The Fillmore.

Chapter 23

Following The Faces Sunderland appearance, Scotsman Billy Hughes and Rod Stewart struck up a friendship, resulting in Rod giving Billy a spare set of keys to his country mansion in Windsor. "You can stay there any time you're in London," Rod told Billy.

A few weeks later, I walked into The Speakeasy and bumped into Billy and John Harker, a local DJ. "I'm staying at Rod's house tonight," said Billy. "Why don't you come with us?" Later, we went on an eye-opening tour around Rod's sumptuous house that resembled a Hollywood film set. In comparison, it made the colliery manager's house in Castletown, pale into insignificance.

"If this is what a number one album brings," I thought to myself, "no wonder so many groups are trying to make it!" Finally, we reached Rod's bedroom. One of the wardrobe doors was open and I could see a fantastic collection of stage jackets and shoes. Tired and weary, I flopped into his bed. There were no blondes there, not that night anyway, but I'm sure there would have been if they'd known where I was sleeping.

Weeks later, I was tipped off that a 'sick' Rod had spent the night of his non-appearance in Sunderland at Elton John's birthday party on a Thames yacht. Whether it was true or not, I never found out, but Elton's birthday is on March 25, while the date of the scheduled appearance was March 24. Coincidence or not? Three weeks later in Sunderland, who cared? The Faces gave us a never to be forgotten night, and that's all that matters.

Chapter 24

In 1971, the North East rose again with the success of Lindisfarne's *Fog On The Tyne* album which went to number one in the UK album chart and stayed there for 56 weeks. Songs such as 'Meet Me On The Corner', 'Fog On The Tyne', and 'Lady Eleanor', had thousands singing along to them at their famous annual Christmas gigs at Newcastle City Hall. The original line-up was Alan Hull (vocals), Ray Laidlaw (drums), Simon Cowe (guitar), Rod Clement (bass & fiddle), and Ray Jackson (mandolin & harmonica). Their rapport with the audience was legendary, and to have promoted them twice (June 8, 1972 and July 20, 1973), while at the very height of their success, was most rewarding. Sadly, no North East band has made it as big since although individuals such as Sting, Mark Knopfler, Brian Johnson, Dave Stewart and Neil Tennant have become highly successful.

Late in 1971, during a visit to Annabel's nightclub, I spotted a local band named Beckett, and thought they were excellent. After agreeing to let me manage them, they were soon contracted to play 15 consecutive nights at The Top Ten Club in Hamburg, where The Beatles had played, in the notorious red light district of The Reeperbahn.

It turned out to be an amazing experience in more ways than one. Just before Beckett arrived, a man had been shot dead inside the club in a gangster feud. It was an unnerving introduction, but the club manager Ricky Barnes confidently assured us that providing you didn't look for trouble, everything would be fine.

On the Harwich to Hamburg cross-channel ferry, I'd arranged a deal for Beckett to play in the ship's disco in exchange for a free crossing, with food and accommodation thrown in. It turned out to be great fun as the group threw in some Chuck Berry numbers, alongside their own. In Hamburg, the hours were long and arduous. Each night, the group had to play eight half-hour spots, commencing at 8 pm, eventually finishing at four in the morning.

Another stipulation for the groups who played there was that they had to have a minimum of two vocalists, as one would be unable to last through the gruelling 15 day stint. Fortunately, this posed no problem for Beckett who had two very fine singers in Terry Wilson Slessor and Kenny Mountain.

The club was small and dingy, with the audience consisting mainly of tourists, strippers, and hookers from the St Pauli district. Sitting in the tiny curtained off dressing room where The Beatles had once sat was a strange feeling. Immediately outside was a small private counter where the waitresses collected their orders.

Inside the club, the beer was three marks a bottle, but the group were given a concessionary price of one mark, which in those days was a huge discount. While playing at The Top Ten, the band were accommodated in The Hotel Pacific, where strippers and hookers from the Reeperbahn lived on a permanent basis as it was cheap and within easy walking distance of St Pauli.

Outside the rooms, a small kitchen was available where people shared a small gas cooker to prepare their meals. Thankfully, everyone was friendly, and the group soon became friends with the girls who regularly took them on sightseeing tours of Hamburg. After fifteen gruelling nights in Hamburg, we played at a British service base in Holland, before returning to England.

A few months later, Beckett were booked back in Hamburg for a second stint of fifteen days. As usual, Ricky insisted on taking possession of the group's passports to prevent them leaving the country. He was small, bossy and ruled with an iron rod, and you soon learned not to mess with him. If you did, you were on your way home before you knew it.

After the statutory sound-check with Ricky controlling the volume, the group were warned about playing loud. "You don't want to deafen them, you want to entertain them," he warned. "That way, they won't leave and will come back for another night." On seeing our worried faces, an English speaking waitress spoke to the group. "Don't worry, everyone is told this," she explained. It was to prove invaluable advice, far sooner than any of us had imagined.

On the second day, I noticed an exceptionally attractive girl on the dance floor. Her hourglass figure, long dark hair, and sensual movements soon had me mesmerised. Before long she left, but the next night she was there again, and I couldn't take my eyes off her. Ever since seeing Marlene Dietrich in *The Blue Angel*, German girls had always held a certain fascination for me. As I watched her dance, I was too shy to approach her, which only served to increase my frustration.

At the end of each night, a retinue of girls would wait patiently for the group. A gorgeous dark haired Swedish girl caught Terry Slessor's eye and they quickly became friendly. She seemed to be besotted with him as she hugged and kissed him nightly to the envy of every other male in the club.

Terry was twenty years old and a great frontman whose athletic movements never failed to command the audience's attention. This girl was one of the most beautiful I'd ever seen, and it seemed they were made for each other. The true affection in her eyes ran deep as she watched Terry on stage and I can still picture her on the night he finally rejected her. It was a heart-rending moment as she became inconsolably upset.

Kenny Mountain later wrote an excellent song called 'Strangers', and two of its lines went, "I saw you cry for the first time today, didn't like it much, I had to look away." I often speak to Terry about that girl and wonder where she is now.

Sex in Hamburg was as readily available as the bratwurst sausages sold next door to The Top Ten. In the early hours of the morning, we would retire to an all-night club called Gibi's. The atmosphere was laid back, and I often wondered how the bouncers at The Fillmore would react if they could see couples happily reclining on the floor in the club's dark confines as they became better acquainted.

A few nights later, having watched Beckett do a seemingly never-ending amount of sets, I wandered outside to investigate the delights of the Reeperbahn. Walking around, it was an absolute revelation, with seedy bars, strip clubs, porn cinemas, sex shops, and a privately owned legal brothel known as The Eros Centre, just a short distance away.

Here, scantily clad girls leaned against poles in an enclosed courtyard which was conveniently surrounded by small rooms to facilitate their trade. After choosing which girl you liked, and on payment of a few marks, you were ushered inside. In the Fleet Air Arm, I'd been all over the world and seen some amazing sights, but nothing compared to this. Coming from Sunderland, where councillors and local people had railed with such fervour against condom machines in the toilets, it was a huge culture shock.

I shook my head in disbelief and continued my wanderings. After a few beers, I crossed the road and entered the famous street known as the Herbertstrasse. This was Hamburg's legal brothel district where sexily clad girls sat in windows, hoping to entice men in.

I began walking down when suddenly my eye caught this gorgeous looking girl. I recognised her immediately as she smiled and beckoned me over. It was the sensual dancer who had beguiled me in The Top Ten Club. Common sense told me to ignore her, and walk on, but a compulsive urge drew me closer. Her black lacy lingerie, heaving breasts, long legs, and friendly smile were irresistible as I found my willpower crumbling in a mad rush to be near her. It was a compelling moment and, within seconds, I found myself inside and couldn't believe my luck. We were alone together and as she stripped off her flimsy lingerie, the sight of her naked body sent me into a frenzy of excitement.

So this was Hamburg. It was certainly proving to be more exciting than The Park Inn, my local in Sunderland. After fulfilling my fantasy, I returned to The Top Ten where the group were playing their hearts out, unaware of where I'd been.

Next day, this girl was back at the club, seemingly unconcerned, and dancing in her usual sensual manner. After plucking up courage I asked her to dance and bought her a drink. Later, she invited me back to her flat at the end of the night. I was stricken with infatuation, and had visions of a long and lasting relationship culminating in me bringing her back to Sunderland.

With time running out, I asked her to give it all up, and come back with me. To my immense disappointment, she refused, saying the money was too good. That was the end of my holiday romance.

Hamburg certainly did Beckett an immense power of good. Within two weeks, they were playing The Marquee in London in front of Warner Brothers executives, Martin Wyatt and Ian Ralfini. After watching a flawless performance, the pair offered to sign Beckett to a new label subsidiary, Raft, that they were starting.

Within weeks of signing, Wyatt and Ralfini decided to leave Warners and, within a short while, Richard Robinson took over, which was absolutely fantastic for us. Nothing was too much trouble as he gave the group more attention than anyone could possibly expect. Disabled from a crippling disease which meant he permanently needed a wheelchair, his right hand man was the equally wonderful Nick Lloyd.

Tour support, badges, stickers, posters, a new Range Rover to travel in, booze, petrol, hotels and albums were all taken care of by Robbie and Nick. They believed in us and we loved them dearly. Any criticism I may have harboured at opportunists getting into the rock business were irrevocably crushed by their endearing kindness.

Whenever I was in London, Nick would let me sleep on his office couch at Warner Bros. offices in Broadwick Street to save money. Richard would let me shower in his luxurious offices on the top floor, and allow me the use of their telephones at any time. Despite the difficulties, with backing of this nature, life became highly enjoyable, and none of us will ever forget them.

Sometimes, Richard would come to see the group play at The Marquee, and I would sprint down Wardour Street pushing his wheelchair in front of me. He would laugh as I weaved in and out of traffic, enjoying the sheer exhilaration of it all. At times like this, he wasn't the all-powerful head of Warner's, but a schoolboy whose high office cares had been cast aside. Unfortunately, Richard is no longer with us, but every time I walk past the old Warner Bros. offices in Soho, the memories come flooding back.

Another character there was Dennis Goodman, the official chauffeur who used to pick up visiting dignitaries in the company's big Austin limousine. As a favour, he once picked Beckett up from their bed and breakfast in Sussex Gardens, and drove them to The Marquee where I had a photographer ready to take a picture of them alighting from it. Unfortunately, the photographer got pissed at the bar and didn't photograph the band on stage, but it was all part of the fun in which we revelled.

In the three years I managed them, Beckett did two John Peel *Top Gear* radio shows, 33 dates supporting The Sensational Alex Harvey Band, 19 dates supporting Captain Beefheart, 22 dates supporting Slade, five supporting Roy Wood's Wizzard, three supporting Ten Years After, the Reading Festival, and countless university and college gigs.

They also made an appearance on *The Old Grey Whistle Test*, and two weeks later, after watching them support Slade at the Hammersmith Odeon, Phil Carson, the boss of Atlantic Records in England, stepped in to sign them. Ahmet Ertegun, the American owner of Atlantic Records, had previously seen the group during one of their many appearances at The Marquee and recommended that Phil sign them, saying that Terry Wilson Slessor was a superstar in the making.

To be on the same label as The Rolling Stones, Led Zeppelin and Yes was a dream come true. With another sizeable advance, and two meaningful tours of America guaranteed, we were on our way.

Unbelievably, just as the deal was about to be signed, Bob Barton, the lead guitarist, decided to leave and form his own band. I was staggered that, after three years of hard work, travelling countless miles up and down the motorways of the UK, he would be crazy enough to jeopardise such a fantastic opportunity. Despite my implorings, Bob was adamant, and asked me to manage his new band. I refused and later learnt a personality clash with Terry Wilson Slessor was the reason for his departure.

On hearing of the uncertainty, Phil Carson immediately called the whole deal off, leaving everything in tatters. I'd spent thousands of pounds of my own money, had made countless phone calls in getting the group this far, and now it had all come to nothing.

I pleaded with Phil Carson to change his mind, saying we'd soon find another guitarist, but it was hopeless. The dream was over, and as I walked out of Atlantic Records offices near Oxford Street, I was in a desperate frame of mind. To be taken to a high like this, only to have it cruelly snatched away at the very last moment was heartbreaking. How could myself and the rest of the band ever forgive Bob?

Well, believe it or not, we have. Having spoken to him recently, Bob now realises the magnitude and foolishness of his actions. Regrets, he has a few, or should I say many. But he's still a great guitarist.

On one of my frequent trips to London in 1972, I received a call from Kenny Bell at Chrysalis.

"Hi Geoff. We've just signed a new group who haven't done any gigs yet, but they're going to be really big. They're rehearsing at Jubilee Studios in Covent Garden all this week," he continued. "I'd like you to go and see them and tell me what you think."

"I don't know if I'll have the time, Kenny," I replied.

"Oh, come on Geoff, if you like them, I want you to give them a booking."

"What's their name?" I enquired.

"Roxy Music," he replied. At that moment, I recalled how Kenny had done me a big favour by giving me Jethro Tull. It was a favour I hadn't forgotten.

"Okay Ken, I'll wander down there this evening and see what they're like," I agreed.

"That's good, I'll let them know you're coming."

That night I arrived at Jubilee Studios to meet the group.

"I'm sorry, but we can't play because the bass player hasn't turned up," one of them apologised.

"Oh, that's all right," I assured him. "I'll catch you another night."

I gave them my commiserations and thought no more about it.

To my amazement, 'Virginia Plain', the first single by that unknown group who I'd gone to watch not rehearse, had made the Top Five in September. I thought it was excellent, and with John Peel singing their praises, it seemed they could do no wrong. What made it all the more remarkable was that two of the group, Bryan Ferry and Paul Thompson were local lads and I'd previously promoted Bryan at The Bay when he was in The Gasboard.

"Kenny Bell here, Geoff," the voice said down the phone.

"Roxy Music want to get out of the clubs, and play their first ever major concert. Do you fancy putting them on at Newcastle City Hall, but we will have to have a guaranteed minimum fee?"

I thought long and hard. Roxy Music were undeniably becoming bigger by the day, but coming out of small clubs into a City Hall gig with 2,241 seats was a big step up. Could they do it? I decided to take the gamble, and after working hard on promotion, it eventually sold out on the night.

With a sense of elation, I walked into the dressing room for my second encounter. As I looked around, a stony silence greeted me, and I sensed something was wrong.

After introducing myself, with the honourable exception of Brian Eno, who was pleasant, I found them to be an unfriendly bunch, and felt uncomfortable.

Eventually, they became accustomed to my presence, as they began conversing among themselves. There was a superior air about them which I found disagreeable, and I decided that all the hype had got to them.

There had been no hard slog up and down the motorways of Britain for this group, and being the darlings of the media, they had rapidly been elevated to major stardom. But being there and being able to handle it are two separate issues. They appeared to be on intellectual overload, and while being intelligent is a wonderful asset, to look down on those less gifted is an injustice of most undignified proportions.

After checking they were ready, I left the dressing room before walking across the City Hall stage to announce them. It seemed a long way as it was the first time I'd ever introduced a group with over two thousand faces staring at me. After reaching the mike, I paused. "Ladies and Gentlemen, Roxy Music."

Eighty minutes later the audience were in raptures. Roxy Music's first major concert had gone down fantastically well, and out front, the atmosphere was unbelievable. Afterwards, I wandered into the dressing room to be met with the same air of indifference; Brian Eno again being the exception. He greeted me warmly which made me take an immediate liking to him as I remembered Dad's words. "It's nice to be nice," and Eno had certainly been that.

A few years later, I met Bryan Ferry at a party, and he was most friendly. Maybe the occasion of their first major concert had overwhelmed them and they'd been nervous, but I'm loath to make excuses for surly and unfriendly behaviour. Nevertheless, it was strange how fate worked. His father was a miner at Washington, where my dad had first worked before marrying and moving to Castletown. Now I'd promoted his first major concert. What other twists and turns would fate thrust upon us?

In Sunderland, I bumped into Debbie and her new boyfriend.

"Hi Geoff, this is Tony, he's a DJ, but during the day he works as a trainee draughtsman at Doxford's Engine Works."

I shook hands and Debbie seemed pleased with herself.

"He's playing some great music, maybe you can get him a job at The Fillmore," she suggested.

I winced inwardly knowing that that was impossible since I'd left but that was Debbie. She always had an angle and never missed an opportunity, especially where music was concerned.

"I saw you talking to a nice girl the other day, is she your girl-friend?" she asked.

"No, she isn't. Her name is Val Smith and she's going out with a Greek student who is studying Naval Architecture at the Polytechnic," I replied.

"Oh, I see. Have you heard about Melanie?"

"No, I haven't. Why do you ask?"

"She's dead, didn't you know? She died of cancer at the hospital last week. Caroline was at the funeral, and says it was awful. Her parents and sister were really upset."

"How old was she?"

"Twenty two. It seems unbelievable and I still can't take it in. She was trying to lose weight and wanted to join the army. Haven't you got a girlfriend then?"

"No, I haven't," I replied sheepishly.

She seemed lost for words as I shifted uneasily.

"Well don't forget, Geoff, if you need a DJ, Tony's your man."

I nodded in acknowledgement and walked away.

Relationships, how do they start and why? In the local papers, photos of happy couples were appearing all the time. Mick Grabham and Sandy were getting married in London, and Chas and I were invited. John Peel was marrying Sheila (aka 'the Pig') from Bradford, and I'd been invited to that, too.

John always used to fancy Vera Greenwell, a leggy blonde whom he'd met at The Bay, but that's out now. Anyway, Dicky likes her, but then again, he likes lots of girls. Chas is very shy. Can't see his photo in *The Echo*, not yet anyway. He'll just have to join me at the bar and watch the girls go by. Still it's nice to be among the flowers, even if you can't pick them.

There had been a few scraps around town, and some new names were starting to crop up. Cross them, and you might be seeing Tommy at the mortuary quicker than you'd hoped.

Dicky Laws and brother Jimmy still frequented Park Lane most days. With wooden gymnastic clubs in the back of their van, they'd been known to crack a few skulls. Being Vince Lander's heavies, they didn't mess about, and if they ever offered you a lift, you had to be wary because old habits die hard. Only they knew where the bodies were buried, so to speak, and one more wouldn't make a lot of difference.

I'm okay, because I'm one of their boys. They got me the job at The Bay and have seen me do well. A few tickets for the concerts keeps them sweet, and people leave me alone when they realise I know them. Protection racket? No, just a few tickets and some common sense go a long way in the town centre.

Trouble is, they're not there at night time when it can get a bit rough. Somebody got badly 'filled in' the other night and was taken to hospital. I'd better keep in training. The new kids in town might want to try me out, and if I'm not ready, I could soon be paying another visit there myself.

On November 22, Santana appeared at Newcastle City Hall. Mel Bush, a well-known promoter and manager, had rung and asked if I wanted to co-promote them. It entailed two concerts in one night, and I sensed his nervousness in the event of a non sell-out. Bearing in mind there had been a lot of concerts there lately, he obviously thought I would be able to help as both shows did sell out.

Carlos Santana. It rolled off the tongue, just like the notes from his guitar. I remembered we used to play *Abraxas* at The Fillmore as it was one of Dicky's favourites. The first snag was the length of the band's contract rider. They wanted everything but the kitchen sink. Having read it, they might as well have thrown that in too. Nuts, cheeses, bread, various bottles of wine, cans of lager, towels, orange juice, mineral water, cans of coke, plus a portable television. What the heck do they want one of them for? They're supposed to be entertaining us, not sitting back watching telly!

Unfortunately, none of my friends possessed one, and the shops wouldn't hire me one just for the day.

"That portable telly is important Geoff," Mel warned. "Muhammad Ali is fighting Bob Foster in Dublin that night, and the band don't want to miss it."

Ah, so that's it. Surely they can't watch a fight and play two concerts simultaneously, I thought.

Santana whooped with delight when they saw the portable TV, which I had finally managed to locate, resting on a table. After smoking a few joints, they went on stage to play their first concert to a rapturous audience. On returning to the dressing room, they began rolling more joints.

A policeman stood just outside and every time the dressing room door opened, the pungent odour of cannabis seeped into the corridor. At that time, smoking dope was classed as a serious offence, and people were being sent to borstal or prison for being in possession of even minuscule amounts.

The group smoked on, seemingly oblivious to the English law, and when the fight started they all eagerly gathered round to watch. By now the room was thick with smoke, while the policeman started to shift uneasily.

As the televised fight continued and I pleaded with the group to make their way on stage, a roadie emerged from the dressing room brazenly smoking a large joint. I was aghast, knowing that if the policeman decided to arrest the group, the inevitable repercussions wouldn't bear thinking about. The second concert would have to be cancelled, and the rest of the tour might even have to be scrapped. I looked at the policeman with pleading eyes. He smiled and said nothing. Somehow, I sensed he understood.

I wandered back into the dressing room to see the group happily enacting the fight blow by blow. Three minutes a round. It doesn't seem long, but when you're breaking the law and 2,241 people are waiting, it's an eternity. The fourth, fifth, sixth and seventh came and went as the tension mounted. Why doesn't Ali finish it? Maybe he can't, because he's fighting Bob Foster, one of the all time greats who's been world light heavyweight champion for years, and successfully defended the title on 14 consecutive occasions. For heaven's sake, won't somebody knock somebody out before the smoke in here gets any worse? If they don't, we'll all need oxygen masks to breathe.

In the eighth, Muhammad finally triumphed and I heaved a huge sigh of relief as the group headed stagewards. Next to me, our friendly policeman grooved away as Carlos unleashed one of his fast and intricate solos, while drummer Michael Shrieve steadfastly locked into the pulsating rhythms.

I glanced at the policeman. His face appeared to be a ghostly white. Is he stoned? The vapour drifting out across the stage over the last hour may have affected him. When the music finally finished, he turned and looked at me and I knew he'd enjoyed it. But there was still time for him to act. Both he and I knew that the law had been broken. One call on his radio and a posse of police officers could rush in and we'd all be taken away.

Instead he produced his notepad and asked me if I could get the group's autographs for his schoolboy son. If I'd have known that I'd have got the boy free tickets and let him meet the group. On second thoughts, that might not have been such a good idea. If the band offered to turn him on, the policeman would have to arrest his own son!

People often speak about the spirit of the law as opposed to the letter of it. I can only say that the policeman that night was very understanding, and personified what a little common sense can achieve.

In 1973, I promoted three interesting shows at Newcastle City Hall – Captain Beefheart & His Magic Band, John McLaughlin's Mahavishnu Orchestra, and Van Morrison & The Caledonian Soul Orchestra.

How can you describe Captain Beefheart & His Magic Band to someone who has never seen or heard of him? Strange, weird, unconventional, creative, charismatic, and yet so far removed from anything else, he and his band lived up to their magic name. After various personnel changes, Don Van Vliet (Beefheart's real name) eventually settled on what was classed as the definitive line-up.

In Newcastle on April 28, it consisted of Zoot Horn Rollo (Bill Harkleroad) on guitar, Rockette Morton (Mark Boston) guitar, Roy Estrada, bass, Mascara Snake on clarinet, and Dr Ed Marimba on drums. These tour dates were to promote Captain Beefheart's latest album *Clear Spot*, and at the beginning of the set, Rockette Morton would appear with a toaster on his head.

After maniacally strutting around, he would greet the audience by announcing, "I've just dropped in to give a little toast." What a band, what a maverick. To this day, Kenny Mountain, the rhythm guitarist from Beckett, who occasionally gigs, sometimes breaks into 'Big Eyed Beans From Venus'.

On June 19, John McLaughlin's Mahavishnu Orchestra introduced us to jazz-rock fusion. In many ways I regard this as being among the best concerts I promoted at the City Hall in terms of personal satisfaction. As I watched from the side of the stage, the band were about to take us on a new approach to rock music and it was an enthralling experience.

The Mahavishnu Orchestra also included Billy Cobham, one of the most respected jazz drummers in the world, and Jerry Goodman, a violinist who had previously been a member of It's A Beautiful Day. The band played a selection of tracks from three of their albums; each segueing into the next in a continuous stream of superb extemporisation. The sheer class of John McLaughlin's guitar playing, his fingers moving across the fretboard at lightning speed, demonstrated what a brilliant cohesive unit the band were.

Earlier in the evening, Billy Cobham related a story to me about what had happened when the group arrived by train the night before in Manchester. As they alighted onto the platform, a drug squad detective stepped forward, flashed his warrant, and told him he was about to search him for illegal substances. After Billy carefully scrutinised the card, he cuttingly remarked, "You look a lot younger on the photo."

On hearing this, the band burst into fits of hysterical laughter, while the officer became red faced with embarrassment. Fortunately, Billy was clean, but once again the incident emphasises just how strictly the drug laws were enforced in those days. This draconian approach was to be a constant worry for touring bands.

Many people believe that Van Morrison's 11-piece Caledonian Soul Orchestra, was his finest ever collaboration. A few days before the gig, I received a telephone call from his record company, Warner Brothers, warning me to tread warily as Van could get easily upset. At a previous show, it seemed someone had said something which had irritated him, and spoilt the atmosphere backstage. I told them not to worry and reassured them that everything would be alright.

On the night of the concert on July 27, I entered the dressing room with a certain amount of trepidation. Inside, Van was sitting with a small girl on his lap who I took to be his daughter. On seeing me, he smiled and said hello. I smiled back, sensing the ice was broken.

Just a few moments earlier, I'd walked the full length of the City Hall and had been struck by the tranquil atmosphere. I looked around to see if I could see the 'freakers' because they loved dancing to *Astral Weeks*. Unfortunately, there was no sign of them and I wondered why. Maybe they were at one of the many summer folk festivals dotted around the country. If they were I was happy for them, as distance wasn't a barrier in the gentle world which they inhabited.

In the other dressing room backstage, the refined and quietly spoken Caledonian Soul Orchestra, featuring John Platania on guitar, shared a bond of camaraderie that augured well for the wonderful setting awaiting them out front. To be allowed to mingle with such a gentle crowd was a privilege, as I'd never promoted a gig quite like this. Everything seemed positively uplifting, and when you are among such remarkable and appreciative people, the ambience is so overpowering, you never ever want it to end.

Minutes later, the band were on stage and that wonderfully expressive voice crept stealthily into our ears with 'Domino', 'Moondance', 'Gloria', 'Hard Nose The Highway', and 'Wild Children', among others. The atmosphere in the dressing room afterwards was one of total euphoria. Van was quiet and reflective, but the record company needn't have worried. Far from upsetting him, the North East people had given him a wholehearted and reverential welcome. Just then, he looked over at me. No words, just a smile which said everything.

A few days later, his record company, Warner Brothers, invited me to a plush reception at a riverside hotel in Chelsea. Mick Jagger, John Peel and numerous other celebrities were also there. Dicky accompanied me, and was overjoyed at seeing Mick. They'd both attended the London School of Economics, and now they were at the same reception.

Dicky and I looked at each other in amazement. The food was lavish, the women were beautiful, the free booze was unlimited, and we'd been officially invited. When I get back I can tell little Tommy Clark that I'd met Mick Jagger. Oh, all right then. I didn't actually meet him, but I was in the same room, and ate the same food. Honest.

Chapter 25

In 1974, I decided to visit Paul Kossoff at his house at 10 Goldbourne Mews, Ladbroke Grove, London. On entering, I was shocked to see him slumped unconscious in a chair. His girlfriend, Sandie Chard, told me she had been unable to rouse him from his drug-induced stupor. I sat and waited, not knowing what to do, when there was a knock at the door.

After answering it, Sandie shook Paul vigorously to tell him there was someone to see him. Somehow, he slowly forced himself out of the chair, before falling to the floor on all fours. Appalled, I watched as he crawled along before reaching up into a drawer, and pulling out a chequebook. Continuing on all fours, he made his laboured way to the door, scribbled out a cheque, and immediately swallowed a handful of substances. I'd seen him ill on stage, and in hospital, now I was witnessing at first hand a drug dealer callously shortening his life.

Sandie seemed helpless and I wondered how she could possibly allow something like this to happen. Paul was now unconscious as I sat for another two hours, hoping he would awaken and recognise me. Finally, in desperation, I left and immediately phoned his father David, the well-known broadcaster and writer. Informing him of the seriousness of the situation, I asked permission to take him up to Sunderland, away from the parasites and drug dealers.

"If you don't let me, I fear the worst," I warned him.

Without hesitation, he agreed and later that day, with help from my group Beckett, we lifted him into their Mercedes van for the long drive up to Sunderland.

Having already been given instructions about his prescribed medicine from Sandie, I was under no illusions about the serious task ahead. To be entrusted with someone's life which is in grave danger of ending prematurely is a daunting prospect. His father had already told me that he had paid for Paul to be treated in private hospitals on several occasions to no avail. It seemed he was doomed, unless drastic action was taken.

After a long journey, we arrived at my flat in Sunderland town centre where he immediately fell into a deep sleep. A few hours later, I heard a muffled shout.

"Where are my tablets?" Paul demanded.

I then gave him his prescribed tablets with some freshly squeezed orange juice. All next day he lay listless in bed, refusing to eat, saying he wasn't hungry. I continued to give him his tablets with the orange juice, and after two days, he cautiously clambered to his feet. It was an encouraging sign when he ate a small bowl of cereal at lunchtime, and had freshly grilled fish and vegetables for dinner. I sensed he was gaining in strength and soon the difference was remarkable compared to the condition I'd found him in, but I knew he still had a long way to go.

As Paul continued to get better, he became irritable and would demand to be let out of the locked flat.

"I'm in agony," he said in anger. "Can't you see I need to be back in London?" I felt an inner despair. Paul was usually quiet and gentle but now in the middle of cold turkey, he was becoming unbearable.

One night, he silently crept towards the kitchen where he suspected I kept his prescribed drugs. I jumped up and switched the light on and ordered him back to bed. He picked up the phone and threw it at me in a mad rage. As I ducked, it hit me on the shoulder. I lost my temper and warned him never to do it again.

"Paul, I'm your friend. Can't you see I'm trying to help?" I pleaded.

"The only way you can help me is to let me out of here. This is a prison and what you're doing is against the law," he angrily replied.

His outburst hurt me deeply but, despite everything, I knew I had to remain strong for the both of us. Meanwhile, his worried parents were ringing daily to enquire about their son who was three hundred miles away and seriously ill. I understood their deep concern, especially as I had no medical qualifications and they had entrusted him to my care.

Chapter 25

Slowly, everything changed. His appetite steadily improved and he was calm as we sat and talked for hours about his past, his parents, his love of music, and how he got that incredible sustain on the guitar.

"I used to practise with a Spanish twelve string my parents bought me, and that strengthened my fingers," he told me.

Occasionally, I took him for walks along the beach, and showed him the historic St Peter's Church, built in the seventh century which was the first in the country to have stained-glass windows.

Soon it was time to release Paul from the constraints which I'd placed upon him, and allow him to face the world again. His rehabilitation period had been tough, but now it was a joy to see him laughing and conversing, just like the old Paul I so fondly remembered.

One night, I took him out to Annabel's, a local nightclub, where he had his first social drink as I watched him eyeing up the girls. The sparkle was back in his eye, the hormones were flowing, and I could sense he loved his new-found freedom.

"Look, it's Paul Kossoff," I could hear people saying.

It certainly was, and that one remark gave me a tremendous amount of satisfaction. With no drug dealers, and no chequebook, he was among people who had a genuine affection for him.

Leaving the club we arrived home at Astral House, a block of town centre flats, where I still live at number 53 on the twelfth floor. I had already evolved a plan which would become an important step in the next stage of Paul's recovery.

I challenged him to ignore the lift and walk up the twenty four flights of steps instead. It was a daunting task, but I could sense his determination as he set off. At about the fourth flight, he stopped to catch his breath.

"C'mon, show me what you're made of," I urged.

He looked at me knowingly and set off again. After a few more flights, he stopped, and leaned against the wall.

"You're not there yet," I reminded him, as his tired and aching limbs began to show their unwillingness to co-operate.

Finally, after much prompting, he reached the twelfth floor. Entering the flat he headed straight for the bedroom where he collapsed into a weary and ungainly heap on the bed.

"Get me the sleeping tablets the doctor prescribed, will you?" he asked.

"Give me a chance, I've got to make your nightly cup of cocoa first," I protested.

An alarmed expression crossed his face. He wasn't used to being kept waiting, and I realised that since those first heady days of stardom, people had waited hand and foot on his every wish. For the first time that evening, he became angry.

"Where's my tablets, I want them now," he demanded.

"Just give me a couple of minutes, and I'll bring them," I replied in a calming manner.

After deliberately taking my time making his cocoa, I carried it into the bedroom to find him fast asleep. Just as I'd hoped, the climb up the stairs had totally exhausted him. As he slept, the first part of the plan was over and tomorrow was to be a big test for both of us. I'd now decided it was time to stop *all* drugs, whether prescribed or illegal, and shivered at the possible consequences of my actions. How would he react and would my resolve weaken? If it did, I had failed. If it didn't, and we got through tomorrow, he'd be cured, I thought as I fell into a deep sleep.

Next morning, a smiling Paul was up bright and early. His long flowing hair and bright eyes possessed a freshness from the invigorating North East sea air. I was nervous, but anxious not to show it, while Paul seemed unconcerned.

"Annabel's isn't a bad little club, is it?" he commented.

"It's the best one around here at the moment," I replied.

He picked up the morning newspapers, and stared at a picture of a gorgeous girl. It was a good sign, but then he asked, "Where's my tablets?"

A lump came to my throat as I answered.

"I've thrown them out. You don't need them any more. You slept like a log without them."

He stared at me in disbelief. "You've done what? You've thrown them out?!" he gasped in astonishment.

"Yes, and from now on, we'll only go out to have a quiet drink," I replied.

Paul remained silent. He knew and trusted me from those early days and realised I only wanted the best for him. I'd watched his meteoric rise to stardom, which had taken him onto a path of degradation and near death. Now he was back, and in full possession of his health and faculties. He smiled, paused, and turned away as the tension visibly eased.

Free had been a wonderful experience for me, and the whole of the North East. "Some people are all take and no give," Dad had often reminded us. Well, we'd all taken, but now we'd given a little back. It was a truly heart-warming moment, and I found it difficult to hold back the tears.

A few weeks later, Paul decided he wanted to form a band and play again.

"I want you to be my manager," he told me.

To deny him would have destroyed the one thing which inspired him, and so I began the next stage of his rehabilitation. Within days, I had arranged for his band to rehearse secretly at the local bowling alley.

Paul had already informed me he preferred to start around midnight as he said this was when he was at his most creative.

Each night, as the security guard admitted us through a fire door, the band slowly began to gel. It consisted of Bryson Graham (drums), Terry Wilson Slessor (vocals), Jimmy Wily (bass) and, of course, Paul on guitar. After a few weeks, I decided to ring Johnny Glover, the ex-manager of Free, to tell him the good news, and invite him into a management partnership.

On hearing that Paul was back to full health and playing with a band, John was thrilled. He began ringing regularly and, within days, invited Paul to stay with him at his sumptuous mansion, just outside Reading. It was a tempting offer, and as I drove Paul there, felt it would do him good to be among old friends.

Meanwhile, Paul's father David was delighted at his son's recovery and asked to meet me in London at a small pub in Broadwick Street, Soho, just around the corner from Cranks health food restaurant. After a quick chat, he pulled out his wallet and, to my surprise, asked how much he owed me?

"You don't owe me anything," I assured him.

"Then why are you doing this?" he asked bemusedly.

It seemed a strange question. It was simply a natural instinct to help a less fortunate human being, especially one who had been near death's door. As he listened I could sense he felt suspicious, as a loving father had every right to be. His son had been stripped of his dignity, together with huge amounts of cash from unscrupulous drug dealers. Why should I be any different? After convincing him I hadn't done it for money, he eventually replaced his wallet, and a new warmth crept back into the conversation.

"If I buy Paul a house near Reading," he asked me, "will you come and live with him and make sure he's all right?"

After quickly deliberating, I agreed. The major factor which led me to this fateful decision, was the affection I'd developed for Paul, while I feared he would once again lapse into the dreaded depths of drug abuse.

Saying our farewells, I made my way over to a rehearsal studio near Tower Bridge where Back Street Crawler (their new name) were rehearsing. John Glover beckoned me over.

"Geoff, I'd like to introduce you to a friend of mine, he's going to co-manage the band with us," he pointed out.

I was flabbergasted, and suddenly, I was a co-co-manager with someone I didn't know.

After all my selfless and unstinting efforts on Paul's behalf it was a sad and disillusioning moment, knowing the faint whiff of easy money had reared its ugly head. By now, John 'Rabbit' Bundrick (now keyboardist with The Who) had joined the band and during these formative stages, there were other line-up changes, as I watched from the sidelines. Later, as I walked over to the coffee machine, I heard a voice say, "just keep him alive for one album a year." I was appalled, and reeled back in shock as alarm bells started to ring.

Back in Sunderland, I wandered into the newsagents to buy the music papers. On the front page of one was a photo of Paul with a huge spread inside, while the others had major articles about Back Street Crawler.

I was furious. Unknown to me, John Glover had initiated a press conference at Island Records, and revealed a healthy Paul. Not only had I not been consulted, but I felt John should have been patient and waited until the group were about to commence their first tour. As an experienced promoter, I knew that to have this much press coverage on an emerging band would have almost certainly assured a sell-out wherever they played.

It was a perfect opportunity which had been thrown away in the mad rush for a major record deal, and the cash that comes with it. Unfortunately, I was 300 miles away, and while it seemed no one cared, I became increasingly concerned. Despite my protestations, a few days later, a record deal was signed, and Back Street Crawler received an advance of £200,000 (now equal to around £900,000) from Atlantic Records, which in 1975 was an awful lot of money.

A couple of weeks later, I moved into Paul's house in Reading. After an hour, I drove into London and rang John Glover.

"I'm leaving and going back to Sunderland."

"Why?" he asked.

"I'm not happy about the way things are going," I told him.

He remained calm and nonplussed as it meant he could now have an even bigger slice of the cake. Up till then I hadn't received a penny and wanted no further part of it, but was comforted by the thought that I'd acted without the taint of money being the main consideration. Once again, principles had been conveniently pushed into the background.

If anyone doubts me, just ask any member of Back Street Crawler. Starting their first national UK tour, the music press hardly provided any further coverage, and attendances were a disaster, while their album received lukewarm reviews. They were eventually evicted from their Earls Court flat due to unpaid rent, while Godfrey Davis Hire Cars which had squired them around during the tour, sent the bailiffs in. Everyone was asking what had happened to the money? Come to think of it, they still are to this day.

The next step was a tour of America, and on their second tour, Back Street Crawler played at The Starwood Club in Los Angeles. Bad Company happened to be in town, and two of the ex-members of Free, Paul Rodgers and Simon Kirke, together with Mick Ralphs (ex-Mott The Hoople) got up and jammed.

There were three members of Free on stage, and I know what a thrill it would have been for Paul, because his heart had never left them. Tragically, it was to be Koss's last ever gig. Next day, on the flight to New York, he died of a drug-induced heart attack, aged 26. It was a sad end to a wonderfully talented guitarist.

The scene was now changing with old faces fading fast. Backstage at Bad Company's three triumphant 1974 gigs in Newcastle City Hall which I was promoting, I saw Debbie. Her looks were fading, her waist was thickening, and the heavy make-up had failed to hide the years of abuse.

"Where's your boyfriend?" I asked. She looked downcast and embarrassed.

"He finished with me. Someone told him about my past, and the drugs I'd taken, but I think it was just an excuse. He's going out with someone else now but I don't care."

"What about Sarah," I asked.

"She has a lovely baby girl but her boyfriend is in Durham prison for burglary and assault at the moment."

"Well, that's nothing," I replied.

"Isn't it? Wait till he finds out who the father is," she said bitchily. "He's coming out soon, and there'll be trouble when he sees her with someone else's baby." She changed the subject. "Can you get me backstage, Geoff? I want to say hello to Paul."

"Not with Peter Grant around, he doesn't take too kindly to people pestering the group unless they've been personally invited," I replied.

"If Paul knew I was here, I'm sure he'd be pleased to see me."

"Things are different now, he's got a bit older, and so have you," I informed her.

"What do you mean by that?!"

"Look Debbie, please don't pressurise me. I've always done my best for you over the years but this isn't The Bay. You can't just wander into the dressing rooms anymore. This is a concert hall and he has friends of his own here."

"Are there any girls among them?" she probed.

"Debbie, please believe me. Paul has a girlfriend now, and she's here."

Tears began to well in her eyes. Nobody likes the brush-off, but that's what it was, and she knew it. Debbie's life as a top groupie was over. She reached out and held my hand. I pulled her towards me and hugged her. Our bodies pressed together, not in a sexual manner, but in a mutually comforting way. Having realised she was unable to see Paul, she broke off with tears running down her cheeks.

"How are you getting home?" I asked.

"There's a late train, and I'll walk from the station," she replied, before turning and walking away up the aisle.

As I watched, her stance was upright, just like those early days outside Maurice Velody's, and I couldn't help noticing her shapely legs seemed to have avoided the ravages of time. She turned and waved as I realised there was still an unwritten bond between us. Debbie had her pride, and though she'd spread it thinly at times, I still admired her. Another casualty would have to come to terms with the harsh realities of the rock & roll lifestyle.

Afterwards, Paul Rodgers and the rest of the group made their way to the stage door to be met by a whole new set of ready, willing and able young girls. As I left, I looked around but Debbie wasn't there. That's the way it was, and Bad Company's first ever concert anywhere in the world was over.

In 1976, Terry Wilson Slessor asked me to return to help manage Back Street Crawler. The considerable shoes of Paul Kossoff had been filled by Geoff Whitehorn, and I could detect a certain desperation had crept into the group.

A meeting at the London Hilton was fixed with Atlantic Records' Ahmet and Nesuhi Ertegun, Jerry Greenburg and Phil Carson to salvage something from the ashes. (I'd previously met the Ertegun Brothers when they had agreed to sign Beckett.) As I sat there with the band and manager Johnny Glover, I realised they were in dire financial straits.

Ahmet eventually agreed a further advance of £50,000 (around £150,000 nowadays) and shortly after, Back Street Crawler gigged at Surrey University with the Atlantic top brass present. When the time came for the support group to go on, they kept stalling, hoping for a better spot.

After numerous delays, I had to go into their dressing room and urge them to get on stage. The small guitarist named Angus held his head to one side, smiling, and I realised he had no intention of doing so. Finally, after much prompting, they went on.

After this gig, Atlantic Records signed AC/DC to a worldwide deal, and a few years later I shook my head in disbelief as I watched that same seemingly insignificant group headline a Donnington Festival in front of 80,000 people. That little guitarist on stage was still smiling, only this time he had a lot to smile about.

Having realised the hopelessness of the situation with Back Street Crawler, and once again not having been paid a penny, I left after a few weeks. I was mentally tired, and needed a rest. A mixture of fights, disagreements, pleasure and disillusionment had all taken their toll. Now, it was a relief just to sit back and enjoy it as an audience member without any of the worry or responsibility.

I had made it as a Sunderland promoter, and succeeded beyond my wildest dreams. I'd met stars, witnessed some great gigs, and watched as groups grew in stature into huge worldwide names. Fortunately, the people of the North East had been able to share most of these wonderful occasions with me, and this is particularly satisfying. Now, as I walk around, people still stop and eagerly talk about the groups. It was undoubtedly a golden period, and I'm really thankful to have been part of it.

In 1977, Punk Rock became fashionable and, while its principles were laudable, the reality was vastly different. Spitting, pogoing and a multitude of groups who hadn't the slightest semblance of talent began masquerading under its banner.

There were of course some good things about punk and a few groups did emerge that had real talent, Siouxsie And The Banshees being one that springs to mind. Ironically, John Peel had been one of punk's instigators in the belief that rock had grown away from its grass roots and had become too commercialised. It gave everyone a chance to play without having to have expensive equipment, or be a virtuoso. At the time, all of us were excited at the possibilities of this new surge of enthusiasm.

Another pleasing aspect was that young people could dress exactly as they pleased, especially after the confining restrictions which had been placed on them in the early years of my gig promoting. An amusing incident occurred when I walked into a punk club in Brighton dressed in a shirt and slacks. As I walked towards the bar, shocked heads swivelled towards me and I could sense they thought I looked oddly out of place. On sitting down they continued to stare, but I was unconcerned. The punks were dressed in bondage trousers, studded belts and Doc Martin boots, with a never-ending assortment of coloured hair. This was freedom of expression at its finest, and I was delighted to be part of it.

After a while I got talking to some of them who were startled by my mode of dress.

"Really, I'm the punk because you're all dressed the same as each other," I pointed out. "I'm the only one who's different here, which is the very thing you're all trying to be." This brought a look of bemusement to their faces, especially when I told them I was there because I liked the atmosphere. After a few more visits, I was accepted, and felt another prejudice had been broken.

At the start of '77, I was tipped off by *NME* writer Steve Clark about an unknown group called The Jam. The following night they were playing at the London School of Fashion and I accompanied him to take a look. Sure enough, he was right, and the excitement and passion I witnessed on stage stirred hidden memories of heady nights at The Bay, and I decided to promote them in Sunderland.

Three weeks later, they were on the front page of the *NME*, and The Seaburn Hall, the venue where I ended up promoting them, was a complete sell-out. The group came on and hit the stage at full throttle. Without warning a small section of mindless morons began throwing glasses at them.

I was ashamed because this was my home town and I was attempting to introduce it to the 'new wave'. To their everlasting credit, the group played on and were magnificent. I was appalled at the reception they'd received, and it was then I realised the dream was over.

After completing further contracted punk gigs with The Vibrators and The Saints, I settled back into being a member of the audience. My tour of duty as a rock promoter was virtually over.

Meanwhile, things were still progressing for Sunderland's musical talent. Dave Stewart rang to say he'd met a Scottish waitress called Annie Lennox in a coffee bar, saying she was a great singer and would I manage them.

The next time I was in London, I called into their rented flat in Crouch End, North London, and listened to a tape Dave had prepared. It was all electronic noises and reminded me of The Third Ear Band.

"What do you think?" he asked. I elected to be honest and told him it wasn't for me. He looked disappointed, but invited me to stay over as Annie walked in. Her smile and warm nature radiated throughout the room. I was impressed. I could hardly hear it on the tape and I realised Dave and Annie had the same problem as Eddie. No money and a poor quality demo tape, the two enemies of struggling musicians.

The flat was bare and in desperate need of redecorating. I felt sorry for Dave, but Annie continued to light up the room with her smile. Dave showed me to my sleeping quarters – a mattress on bare floorboards. The room was extremely damp so I slept with my shirt and socks on. Rising early in the morning to wash, I didn't bother cleaning my teeth because the constant cold water would have frozen them. I couldn't wait to get back to Sunderland to clean them and sleep in a warm bed.

Dave and Annie haven't got a chance in hell of making it, I thought. Talk about suffering for your art. They breed them tough in Sunderland but Dave must be crazy. I wished them both the best of luck and left. Ten years later, 'Sweet Dreams Are Made Of This' entered the charts. Dave now has a £2.5 million house in Covent Garden, London, his own record label and recording studios, as well as a half share in the new Marquee in Islington.

Although I haven't been involved at the sharp end of the music scene in recent years, I have kept in touch with many of the friends I made from those early days. These are lads who drank coffee with me in The Bis-Bar, or desperately pleaded for a gig before becoming members of successful bands. I still love music, and get to see as many gigs as I can. Some feelings never leave you, and when I see four or five 16-year-olds playing their first pub gig, I still get excited if I spot raw talent.

During my period of managing The Showbiz Kids, whenever we headlined The Marquee, a chap called Steve Dagger would ring and ask if his band Gentry could have the support slot. They were completely unknown and were desperate for work. In those days, you had to have your own PA, and as they didn't possess one, Steve asked if they could use ours, which I readily agreed to on each occasion.

On the night in question, the group were exceptionally quiet and subdued in the dressing room. When speaking to them, they would nod in acknowledgement but seemed to lack confidence. I sympathised with their nervousness because it was extremely difficult to get a gig at The Marquee, being the focal point for record companies and the music press.

After a workmanlike set they gathered their equipment together and left. Later, they changed their name to Spandau Ballet and, to my amazement, had a string of hits. I had never imagined that two of those quiet lads, Martin and Gary Kemp, sitting in that tiny dressing room, would go on to star in a film of The Krays, with Martin becoming a household name in the TV soap opera *EastEnders*.

Steve Dagger now handles Patsy Kensit's affairs and hasn't rung me since. Nevertheless, I'm delighted his band made it big and would like to think that, in some small way I helped them to gain confidence and some vital experience.

In the intervening years, I have had several rewarding and interesting jobs, including running a rock café on the Isle of Man for 18 months, and managing Brighton Palace Pier for two seasons. If you ever visit there, look out for the free deck chairs. It was one of my last contributions to the spirit of the peace and love era. In the Eighties, I managed bands and, in 1991, I worked in a nightclub in Dortmund, Germany, situated near the local university. German universities don't have 'freshers balls' for newcomers, so I decided to stage one for them. As I wandered around the large campus, I was eventually directed towards a lift. By an amazing piece of luck, inside I met an English professor who introduced me to The Asta (the equivalent of the entertainment's committee).

I managed to convince them I was genuine, and would stand any losses. The ball was a great success, with several groups and an alternative comedian called Fat Geoff. I wanted to hold more, but unfortunately I was called back to England. Nevertheless, I hope that I introduced a little of The Bay and Fillmore spirit into their hearts.

In the mid-Nineties, I lived in Chalk Farm, London, and managed an excellent Newcastle group called Deadpan Joy who spent two years playing the Camden club scene without being signed.

In 1996, I attended the annual Reading Festival, and afterwards, drove down to Aldershot to visit St Anthony's Convent, where my brothers and I had spent our early childhood years. I walked around the little yard where we used to play, and visited the new dormitories that have since been built and thought of Donald, John and Dad, who had all passed away.

I then made my way into the town centre and sat on the same bench where we had all waited for the cinema to open to see *Lassie Come Home*. As I wallowed in nostalgia, I wiped a tear from my eye and realised that Dad had taught us well. Without his indomitable spirit, none of this would have happened.

Shortly after, I bumped into an old Sunderland friend of mine, Rob Hutchinson, who started out by providing the lights at The Fillmore, and now has a flourishing business providing the power for many of the major festivals.

"You know Geoff, you should write a book about those times at The Bay and The Fillmore," he urged.

At the time I was between jobs, and the idea gripped me. Not being able to type, I enrolled for a year's part-time course in word processing at Bede College, Sunderland, and set out on the long mission to write it.

During the research involved, two things have been hugely rewarding. Firstly, delving into my own memory bank and reliving the enormous pleasure of those times. My brother Donald's help in the orphanage and the defeat of my first bully. Mr Dixon agreeing to hire out The Bay ballroom, allowing me to become a promoter in my own right. Booking Pink Floyd. Telling Dad I'd been onstage at the Albert Hall. Catching The Who on a proposed rest night and seeing the thrill on people's faces when they realised the group would be playing at The Bay. Meeting John Peel and Dot, and discovering Free. The move to Newcastle and the great nights there. Attending Led Zeppelin's film premiere in Leicester Square, London, and the after show party.

Along the way, there were a few fights, a few bruises, and a few disappointments, but these were a small price to pay for such an experience.

The other thing which has surprised me has been the obvious and sincere pleasure with which people recall those days. I have lost count of the number of times they approach and thank me for putting the bands on. It is all rather humbling, and I must admit that thousands of others would have done the same, given the opportunity. Here, I must express my grateful thanks to everyone who has helped me verify facts and assisted in jogging my memory. This has been a labour of love, and I hope you have enjoyed reading it. If so, it will have been even more worthwhile.

Where Are They Now?

All events depicted in this book are true, though the names of certain characters (in inverted commas below) have been changed to preserve their anonymity.

Alan Hogg is married with a son and recently closed his shoe shop due to the expiry of his lease. He still lives in Sunderland.

'*Debbie*' is now married and lives away from the North East.

'*Caroline*' has left Sunderland. Her present whereabouts are unknown.

'*Melanie*' is deceased.

Michelle is married and lives somewhere in Surrey.

Tommy Clark is a taxi driver and resides locally.

Dickie Robson is married, lives in Reading and is a computer expert.

Chas McIver is a social worker, and still resides in Sunderland with his son.

Tommy Cooper married a nurse and is now a taxi driver operating from outside Sunderland railway station.

'*Dot*' *Fisher* has two sons and lives in Devon.

Mr Forrest is alive and well and lives in Newark.

Tommy Donnelly still resides in Sunderland. For many years, he ran his own successful coal business, which he eventually sold.

John Tansey is married with a son. He is now head of security at Brogans, a newly opened bar, and also works at Privilege, a night-club above it in Sunderland city centre.

Val Smith is married to Bruce Shepherd, the brother of Freddie Shepherd, the chairman of Newcastle United. They live on the outskirts of Newcastle.

Eddie Fenwick still writes songs in Sunderland, still waiting for the break. He remains good friends with Dave Stewart, and everyone he comes into contact with.

The *Junco Partners* still play, while the drummer, John Woods, also owns a fashion boutique.

Lindisfarne still play gigs and *Ray Laidlaw*, their drummer, now works with *Geoff Wonfor* on independent films, documentaries and videos.

Of the four 'freakers' *Val Brown* (née Clark) is married with a son and daughter, and still lives in Sunderland where she works as a town planner. *Norma McAlpine* (née Clark), her sister, is married and lives in Hull, where she works in telecommunications. *Sandra Brown* moved to London, where she once worked for Marsha Hunt, and also The Simon Community for drug addicts and the homeless. *Hilary Stevens* (née Watson) is married with two children, and works at the Local Government Housing Office in Sunderland.

Ritchie Wooler is now married with children and is a successful property and garage owner, as well as a leading sunbed hire operator. He also played football for Island Records and points out that he'd rather be known for this, than his solo dancing.

Mickey Grabham is still married to Sandy and they have a daughter. He now lives in Cambridge and occasionally plays gigs with Rick Wills.

Nigel Olsson lives in America, and brought out a solo album. He has recently rejoined Elton John and is featured on his live album recorded at Madison Square Garden.

Terry Wilson Slessor still performs solo with backing tapes and has just recorded another Back St Crawler album.

Kenny Mountain has reformed Beckett, minus Terry, and handles lead vocals.

Dicky Laws still lives in Sunderland, and for many years ran his own successful tyre business. His brother Jimmy is deceased.

The Fillmore is now a nightclub called The Palace, and the Top Rank Suite is now a supermarket. The Bis–Bar is now named Chase and is owned by Ultimate Leisure.

The Bay Hotel was pulled down, and a modern pub without the ballroom was rebuilt on the same site, the loss of which brings me to tears.

Newcastle Mayfair has been purchased by a major London investment company, and is being pulled down to make way for a new development, despite strong protests from thousands of its former patrons. Ray Laidlaw and myself were interviewed on BBC Radio Newcastle in an attempt to prevent this sad fate, but it was to no avail.

Chronology Of Gigs Promoted By The Fillmore North (Geoff Docherty)

Fees paid to artists are correct to the best of the author's recollections. Where none is mentioned, the author cannot recall the fee paid.

1969

Date	Act	Price paid for act	Admission	Venue
6 Jan	Family	£150	6/–	Bay Hotel
13 Jan	Free	£35	4/–	Bay Hotel
20 Jan	Harmony Grass	£125		Bay Hotel
27 Jan	Keef Hartley	approx £125	5/–	Bay Hotel
3 Feb	Pretty Things	£150	7/6d	Bay Hotel
7 Feb	The Web	£50	5/–	Bay Hotel
10 Feb	Dr K's Blues Band	approx £75		Bay Hotel
17 Feb	Pink Floyd	£250	7/6d	Bay Hotel
21 Feb	Ferris Wheel	approx £75		Bay Hotel
22 Feb	Circus	£60	5/6d	Bay Hotel
24 Feb	Aynsley Dunbar Retaliation	£125	6/–	Bay Hotel
28 Feb	Writing On The Wall	£125	5/–	Bay Hotel
1 March	Episode Six	approx £100		Bay Hotel
3 March	John Peel, Van Der Graaf Generator & Black Sabbath	approx £75	6/6d	Bay Hotel
8 March	McKenna Mendelson Mainline from Canada	approx £175	5/–	Bay Hotel
10 March	John Peel, Spirit of John Morgan & The Music of Jan Dukes De Grey	£75 £60		Bay Hotel
17 March	Spooky Tooth	£150	7/–	Bay Hotel
22 March	Leviathan	approx £65		Bay Hotel
24 March	Country Joe & The Fish	£350	10/6d	Bay Hotel

Promoter's Tale

Date	Act	Price paid for act	Admission	Venue
28 March	Cliff Bennet & The Rebel Rousers			Bay Hotel
31 March	Idle Race (Jeff Lynne Pre Move & E.L.O. Days)	£75	5/-	Bay Hotel
3 April	Bakerloo Blues Line (Playing Upstairs)	£50	2/6d	Bay Hotel
7 April	Bakerloo Blues Line (Downstairs Ballroom)	£75	6/-	Bay Hotel
11 April	Plastic Penny	£150	5/-	Bay Hotel
14 April	Terry Reid's Fantasia	£125	5/-	Bay Hotel
19 April	Hard Meat	£50		Bay Hotel
21 April	John Peel, Liverpool Scene & Bridget St John			Bay Hotel
26 April	Eyes Of Blue	£50		Bay Hotel
28 April	The Who	£450	12/6d	Bay Hotel
5 May	The Keef Hartley Band & Mike Hart	£150 package	5/-	Bay Hotel
12 May	Chicken Shack	approx £150	7/6d	Bay Hotel
19 May	Steppenwolf (non arrival) Breakthru played		5/-	Bay Hotel
26 May	Savoy Brown & This Year's Girl	£180 package	6/-	Bay Hotel
6 June	Spirit of John Morgan	£60	6/-	Bay Hotel
9 June	Three Dog Night	£250	7/6d	Bay Hotel
13 June	Jethro Tull		12/6d	Bay Hotel
16 June	The Nice	approx £250	10/-	Bay Hotel
23 June	Aynsley Dunbar	£150	6/-	Bay Hotel
27 June	Tyrannosaurus Rex, Free & This Year's Girl	£350 £70 £20	12/6d	Bay Hotel
30 June	Yes	approx £60	6/-	Bay Hotel
7 July	Chicken Shack	£150	7/6d	Bay Hotel
11 July	Writing On The Wall	£75		Bay Hotel
14 July	John Hiseman's Colosseum	£150	10/-	Bay Hotel
18 July	Marsha Hunt with White Trash			Bay Hotel
21 July	Family	£150	10/6d	Bay Hotel
25 July	Third Ear Band			Bay Hotel
28 July	The Who	£450	12/6d	Locarno

Chronology Of Gigs

Date	Act	Price paid for act	Admission	Venue
13 Aug	Bonzo Dog Band, Eclection, King Crimson & This Year's Girl		12/6d	Locarno
22 Aug	Family, Grail & Bridget St John	£300	12/6d	Locarno
29 Aug	Liverpool Scene, Mooche & Junco Partners	£275		Locarno
5 Sept	Soft Machine	£250		Locarno
12 Sept	Free, Mott The Hoople		7/6d	Locarno
19 Sept	Atomic Rooster, Poet & The One Man Band	approx £200		Locarno
26 Sept	Chicken Shack & Principal Edwards Magic Theatre	£150 £100		Locarno
3 Oct	Keith Relf's Renaissance & Blossom Toes	approx £200	7/6d	Locarno
6 Oct	Pretty Things	£150		Locarno
10 Oct	Noel Reddings Fat Mattress & Big Fingers	approx £200	7/6d	Locarno
13 Oct	Pete Brown's Piblokto	£50	3/-	Locarno
17 Oct	Family & Man	£225	10/-	Locarno
20 Oct	Writing On The Wall	£125		Locarno
24 Oct	Pink Floyd, Stone The Crows & John Peel	approx £400	12/6d	Locarno
27 Oct	Roy Harper			Locarno
31 Oct	Savoy Brown & Barclay James Harvest	£225	7/6d	Locarno
3 Nov	Principal Edwards Magic Theatre	£100	3/-	Locarno
7 Nov	Edgar Broughton & Zoot Money			Locarno
14 Nov	Christine Perfect Band & Mighty Baby		10/-	Locarno
21 Nov	Free & Quintessence		10/-	Locarno
28 Nov	Tyrannosaurus Rex, John Peel & Spirit Of John Morgan	£475		Locarno
1 Dec	Hard Meat	£50		Locarno
8 Dec	Gypsy	£50	3/-	Locarno
15 Dec	Rare Bird	£50	2/-	Locarno
22 Dec	Gypsy	£50		Locarno

Date	Act	Price paid for act	Admission	Venue

1970

Date	Act	Price paid for act	Admission	Venue
1 Jan	Edgar Broughton, Principal Edwards Magic Theatre & This Year's Girl	approx £275		Locarno
9 Jan	Manfred Mann Chapter Three, Principal Edwards Magic Theatre & This Year's Girl		12/6d	Locarno
12 Jan	Jo-Anne Kelly with The John Dummer's Blues Band	approx £125	3/-	Locarno
16 Jan	Kinks, Quintessence (Kinks didn't play)		10/-	Locarno
19 Jan	Stone The Crows	£125	3/-	Locarno
23 Jan	Family + Emily & Muff		10/-	Locarno
30 Jan	Ten Years After & Junco Partners	approx £500	10/-	Locarno
6 Feb	Free & Griffin (recording live album)	£1,600	10/-	Locarno
9 Feb	The Music of Jan Dukes De Grey	approx £60	3/-	Locarno
13 Feb	Blodwyn Pig, Audience & John Peel	pkg approx £325	10/-	Locarno
20 Feb	John Hiseman's Colosseum & Jess Roden's Bronco	£225	10/-	Locarno
23 Feb	Siren	£50	3/-	Locarno
27 Feb	Chicken Shack & Quintessence		10/-	Locarno
6 March	Edgar Broughton & Juice		10/-	Locarno
9 March	Third Ear Band & Genesis	£100 £50	3/6d	Locarno
13 March	David Bowie & The Hype Principal Edwards, Circus & Man	approx £150	10/-	Locarno
16 March	Chicken Shack	approx £150	4/	Locarno
20 March	Blodwyn Pig & Writing On The Wall	pkg approx £225	10/-	Locarno
26 March	Ginger Baker's Airforce	£1,500	15/-	Locarno
30 March	Clouds	approx £60		Locarno
3 April	Rory Gallagher's Taste & Black Sabbath	£350 £75	12/6d	Mayfair
10 April	Edgar Broughton & Juice		10/-	Locarno
17 April	Groundhogs + Grisby & Dyke	approx £200	6/-	Locarno
24 April	Roy Harper & Humble Pie	£150 £250	10/-	Locarno

240

Chronology Of Gigs

Date	Act	Price paid for act	Admission	Venue
27 April	Steamhammer	£125		Locarno
1 May	Keef Hartley & Black Widow	approx £275	10/-	Locarno
7 May	Colosseum, Man & Raw Spirit	approx £425	12/6d	Mayfair
8 May	Traffic & If		10/-	Locarno
13 May	Ten Years After			City Hall
15 May	Procol Harum	£250		Bay Hotel
22 May	Radha Krishna Temple + Local Support		10/-	Barnes Hotel
25 May	Gypsy	£60	5/-	Bay Hotel
29 May	Tyrannosaurus Rex & Man	£475	10/-	Bay Hotel
5 June	Groundhogs	approx £150	6/-	Bay Hotel
12 June	Family	approx £150	10/6d	Bay Hotel
12 June	Edgar Broughton, Quintessence & Dogg		12/-	Mayfair
15 June	Quatermass	£75	3/-	Bay Hotel
19 June	Savoy Brown & Yellow	approx £200	10/-	Bay Hotel
22 June	Principal Edwards Magic Theatre	£100	2/-	Bay Hotel
26 June	Free Kevin Ayres & The Whole World Yellow & Juice	£1,500	12/6d	Top Rank Suite
26 June	Rare Bird & Hard Meat	approx £325	12/6d	Mayfair
10 July	Chicken Shack, Matthews Southern Comfort & Man		12/6d	Mayfair
23 July	Atomic Rooster, Van Der Graaf Generator & Yellow		12/6d	Mayfair
31 July	Deep Purple & Daddy Longlegs		12/6d	Mayfair
7 Aug	Derek And The Dominoes & Writing On The Wall	£750 approx £100	15/-	Mayfair
21 Aug	Quintessence, Mott The Hoople & Supertramp		12/6d	Mayfair
28 Aug	Tyrannosaurus Rex & Principal Edwards Magic Theatre	£350 approx £125	12/6d	Mayfair
11 Sept	Blodwyn Pig		15/-	Mayfair
27 Sept	Jethro Tull			City Hall

241

Date	Act	Price paid for act	Admission	Venue
16 Oct	Free, Deep Purple, Principal Edwards, Cochise & Yellow	£1,550 £500 £100 £60 £25	£1	Top Rank Suite (Indoor Festival of Music)
22 Oct	Keef Hartley, Strawbs & Pink Fairies		14/-	Mayfair
19 Nov	Chicken Shack, Yellow & Traction	pkg approx £350	14/-	Mayfair
26 Nov	The Who & Curved Air (The Who failed to play)	£125	17/6d	Mayfair
14 Dec	The Who (rescheduled date)	£500		Mayfair

1971

Date	Act	Price paid for act	Admission	Venue
1 Jan	Groundhogs, Quintessence & Medicine Head	approx £550		Mayfair
15 Jan	Chicken Shack, Third Ear Band & If	approx £500	12/6d	Mayfair
18 Jan	Black Sabbath, Curved Air & Freedom			City Hall
14 Feb	Free & Amazing Blondel	£1,600		Empire Theatre
18 Feb	Tyrannosaurus Rex & If	£350 £125	15/-	Mayfair
5 March	Fairport Convention & Stud	approx £475		Top Rank Suite
18 March	Led Zeppelin	(90% net receipts)	12/-	Mayfair
26 March	Mott The Hoople, Medicine Head & John Peel			Mayfair
2 April	Quintessence & Stray	approx £300	75p	Top Rank Suite
8 April	Skid Row, Hardin & York + Stray		85p	Mayfair
15 April	Groundhogs, Chicken Shack & Michael Chapman		50p	City Hall
30 April	Quintessence & Stone The Crows		80p	Mayfair
7 May	The Who	£250 (special half price gig)	50p	Top Rank Suite
14 May	Buddy Miles Express & Kevin Ayres & The Whole World		50p	Mayfair
21 May	Stud, Hardin & Yorke + Gin House	approx £300	75p	Mayfair

Chronology Of Gigs

Date	Act	Price paid for act	Admission	Venue
28 May	Rod Stewart & The Faces + Reuben James	£350	75p	Mayfair
18 June	Curved Air, Mick Abrahams Band & Mark Ellington Group	approx £475	75p	Mayfair
24 June	Deep Purple & Quiver	£500 £75		Mecca, Bullring
25 June	Deep Purple & Quiver	£500 £75	85p	Mayfair
Early July	Ten Years After?			Mayfair
9 July	Groundhogs, Heads, Hands & Feet	approx £350	75p	Mayfair
23 July	Colosseum & Osibisa		75p	Mayfair
30 July	Rory Gallagher & The James Gang	£500 £250	75p	Mayfair
6 Aug	Curved Air & Medicine Head		80p	Mayfair
13 Aug	Mott The Hoople & Gin House		75p	Mayfair
27 Aug	Rod Stewart & The Faces + Bell & Arc	£500 £125	85p	Mayfair
10 Sept	Cat Stevens, Mimi Farina & Tom Jans	(95% of net receipts)		City Hall
16 Sept	Ten Years After, Supertramp & Keith Christmas	(95% of net receipts)		City Hall
17 Sept	Curved Air	£500	80p	Mayfair
16 Oct	Yes & Jonathan Swift	(95% of net receipts)		City Hall
21 Oct	Steeleye Span & Andy Roberts	(95% of net receipts)		City Hall
22 Oct	Quintessence & East Of Eden?		80p	Mayfair
11 Nov	Led Zeppelin	(90% of net receipts)		City Hall
12 Nov	Led Zeppelin	approx £2,000	75p	Locarno
18 Nov	Edgar Broughton & Stray?		75p	Mayfair
1 Dec	Groundhogs, Egg & Quicksand?			City Hall

1972

7 Jan	Rory Gallagher & Nazareth	£500		Mayfair
21 Jan	Procol Harum & Amazing Blondell	(95% net receipts)	60p	City Hall
1 Feb	Free & Junkyard Angel	£1,500		City Hall

Promoter's Tale

Date	Act	Price paid for act	Admission	Venue
5 Feb	Black Sabbath & Wild Turkey	(95% net receipts)		City Hall
13 Feb	Free Vinegar Joe & Junkyard Angels	£1,500		Top Rank
20 Feb	Argent, Beggars Opera, Beckett & Brass Alley			Top Rank Suite
21 Feb	Free	£1,500		City Hall
21 Feb	Jethro Tull & Tir Na Nog			Top Rank Suite
5 March	Rod Stewart & The Faces + Byzantium	£1,500		Top Rank Suite
7 March	Jethro Tull & Tir Na Nog	(95% of net receipts)		City Hall
12 May	Heads Hands & Feet + Vinegar Joe			Mayfair
8 June	Lindisfarne Capability Brown & Beckett	£1,500 £125	75p	Top Rank Suite
22 June	Family & Audience			Mayfair
7 July	Stray & Third Ear Band			Mayfair
15 Sept	Free Smith, Perkins & Smith	£1,500	90p	Mayfair
25 Sept	UFO, Beckett & (*Melody Maker* winner) Lloyd Watson		Free	City Hall
11 Oct	Free (last ever Free gig in Sunderland) & Beckett	£1,500	65p	Locarno
20 Oct	Free (last ever Free gig before splitting) & Beckett?	£1,500	£1	Mayfair
26 Oct	Steeleye Span	(95% of net receipts)		City Hall
27 Oct	Beggars Opera			Top Rank Suite
10 Nov	Fairport Convention			Top Rank Suite
11 Nov	Roxy Music (first ever Roxy concert) & East Of Eden	£750 £125		City Hall
22 Nov	Santana	(two concerts in one evening for 95% net receipts)		City Hall

Chronology Of Gigs

Date	Act	Price paid for act	Admission	Venue

1973

Date	Act	Price paid for act	Admission	Venue
16 March	Procol Harum	(95% net receipts)		City Hall
13 April	Rod Stewart & The Faces John Peel & Beckett ?	£1,500	75p	Locarno
20 April	Geordie, Pans People & Medicine Head	approx £850		Locarno
27 April	Status Quo, Good Habit & John Peel			Locarno
28 April	Captain Beefheart & His Magic Band	£1,000		City Hall
1 June	Nazareth & Robin Trower		65p	Locarno
19 June	John McLaughlin's Mahavishnu Orchestra	£1,000		City Hall
20 July	Lindisfarne & UFO			Locarno
27 July	Van Morrison & The Caledonian Soul Orchestra	approx £1,250		City Hall

1974

Date	Act	Price paid for act	Admission	Venue
9 March	Bad Company			City Hall
10 March	Bad Company			City Hall
11 March	Bad Company	(90% of net receipts for all three concerts)		City Hall
21 April	Ten Years After	(95% net receipts)		City Hall

1977

Date	Act	Price paid for act	Admission	Venue
17 June	The Jam	approx £670	£1	Seaburn Hall
1 July	The Vibrators & Penetration		£1	Seaburn Hall
8 July	The Saints & Straw Dogs		£1	Seaburn Hall

1988

Further promotions undertaken:

Date	Act	Price paid for act	Admission	Venue
1988	Wishbone Ash			Newcastle Mayfair

Date	Act	Price paid for act	Admission	Venue
1988	Wishbone Ash			Roxy, Sheffield
1988	Wishbone Ash			MGM Nightclub, Nottingham

1991

Freshers ball promoted while working in Germany:

7 May	Still Got The Blues Fat Geoff, also The Pencil Sharpners		7 DM	Valentino's Nightclub, Dortmund, Germany

01/17 (46468)